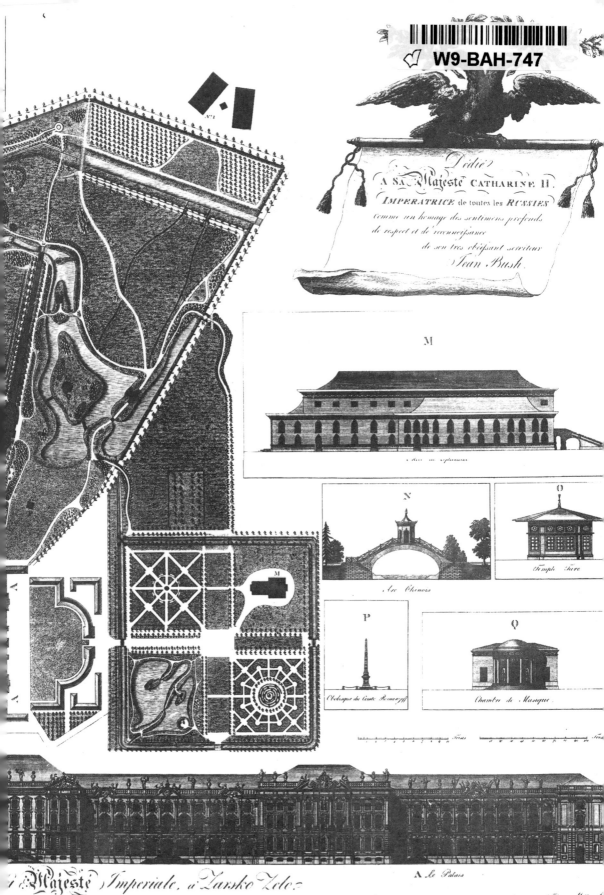

Dédié
A SA Majesté CATHARINE II.
IMPERATRICE de toutes les RUSSIES
comme un homage des sentimens profonds
de respect et de reconnoissance
de son tres obéïsant serviteur
Jean Bush.

M

N

Arc Chinois

O

Temple Chine

P

Obelisque du Comte Romanzoff.

Q

Chambre de Musique.

Toises

Toises

A le Palais.

Majesté Imperiale, à Zarsko Zelo.

Tobias Müller Sc.

GARDENS
OF THE TSARS

For my Parents

And come, I will tell you also the trees which you gave me in our well-ordered garden, and I, when I was only a child, was following you through the garden, and asking you for this and that. It was through those very trees that we passed, and you named them and told me of each one. Pear trees you gave me, thirteen, and ten apple trees, and forty fig trees. And rows of vine, too, you promised to give me, even as I say, fifty of them, which ripened one by one at seperate times — and upon them are clusters of all sorts — whenever the seasons of Zeus weighed them down. (Homer)

Margrethe Floryan

GARDENS OF THE TSARS

A Study of the Aesthetics,
Semantics and Uses of Late 18th Century
Russian Gardens

SAGAPRESS

Copyright: Aarhus University Press, 1996
Cover design by Inga Friis
Colour separation by Ploug Repro, Aarhus
Printed on permanent paper by Cambridge University Press, England
ISBN 089831 051 2

Published in the United States and Canada by
Sagapress Inc.
33 S.W. Second Ave.
Portland, OR 97204

Library of Congress Cataloging-in-Publication Data

Floryan, Margrethe.
    Gardens of the tsars: a study of the aesthetics, semantics, and uses of
    late 18th century Russian gardens/Margrethe Floryan.
        p.   cm.
    Includes bibliographical references (p.   ) and indexes.
    ISBN 0-89831-051-2
    1. Gardens--Russia (Federation)--History--18th century.
    2. Gardens--Symbolic   aspects--Russia   (Federation)--History--18th
century.
    I. Title
    SB466.R8F58 1996
    712´.0947´09034--dc20   96-18895
                                                                          CIP

Cover: Tsarskoe Selo, the Great Palace (front) and the Entrance Gate (back).
Endpaper: Tsarskoe Selo, plan by John Busch, late 1780s (detail).

Acknowledgements

It was the reality of a longstanding fascination with practical gardening, garden aesthetics and a five year stay in Russia which led me to write this book. Moscow's boulevards and gardens supplied many pleasurable and peaceful moments, and the flora and architectural motifs of the suburban sites further incited my preoccupation with the history of pleasure gardens and with their meaning to previous users as well as to today's large garden-loving audience.

I have dedicated this book to my parents. It was they who — primarily at our ancestral farm in Husby on Funen, the island in the heart of Denmark which is so often labelled as one luxuriant garden in itself — nourished and allowed for my practical and intellectual interest in gardening to develop. Russia entered the picture when my husband went there to work. He accompanied me to all of the gardens discussed below, and several more, and we were happy in sharing the experience of the imagery and enchantment of the tsarist and the Soviet gardens. Along with us came our three sons, as they were born in 1988, 1990 and 1991, and I think they too, came to enjoy the Russian pleasure grounds, whether our strolls and study tours took place on a glorious summer day or on a beastly cold winter day.

I took the outdoor photographs of this book during such visits. Many visits were repeated several times during our years in Russia (1988-93), and I have been back several times since. Anatoly Kovtun took Fig. 40 and Fig. 60, and he photographed the majority of the prints and other archival materials accompanying my text.

The individuals and institutions that I have consulted in the preparation of this book are many. In particular, I would like to express my thanks to Professor Dr. Lise Bek of the University of Aarhus for numerous enlightening discussions, guidance, attendance, and moral support. I received valuable comments on my manuscript from Professor Tom Simons, Dr. Lulu Salto Stephensen, art historian Kirsten Strømstad and art critic Gertrud Købke Sutton.

I am much indebted to the following Russian colleagues for having shared their knowledge about Russia's historical heritage with me and for having shown me the treasures in the collections of which they have responsibility for: Marta Gurenok of the Russian Department of the Museum of History, Moscov; Ludmila Kovshova of the Bogoroditske Palace Museum; Militsa Korshunova of the Drawings Department of the Hermitage, St Petersburg; Dr. Marina Maiskaya of the Graphics Department of the Pushkin Museum of

Fine Arts, Moscow; Tatiana Nikitina of the Museum of Architecture, Moscow; Galina Printseva of the Russian Department of the Hermitage, St Petersburg; Varvara Rakina of the Ostankino Palace Museum. I am also very grateful for the services that I have received from the staff of the Russian State Library, Moscow, not least those in the Department of Rare Books; the Saltykov-Schedrin Library, St Petersburg; the Russian Military Historical Archives, Moscow; The Royal Library, Copenhagen; the British Library, London; and the Bibliothèque Nationale, Paris. I also want to thank Berta Tamashina for translating the summary of this book and Natasha Bubenova for her editing of the summary.

Financial support for the publishing of the book was generously furnished by the Danish National Research Council for the Humanities and by the New Carlsberg Foundation.

It is finally a great pleasure to thank Dr. Tønnes Bekker-Nielsen, head of Aarhus University Press, Inga Friis and Kirsten Poulsen for nursing the book through the press.

Margrethe Floryan
Charlottenlund, 1996

Contents

INTRODUCTION

Rediscovering the Gardens of the Past

Serious ecological problems have drawn the world's attention to the Russian nature and environment in the past few years. But the landscape as it presents itself today, also has a fascinating story to tell about garden aesthetics. It is a story which goes back to the 10th and 11th centuries. Various written and pictorial sources complement — at least on some points — what time, devastation, new developments, and many other factors have erased from the grounds.

This book proposes a history and an analysis of the aesthetics, semantics and uses of pleasure gardens of the second half of the 18th century. Under Catherine the Great (1762-96), the Russian Empire experienced its days of glory, and the dialogue with the West was as intense as never before — or after, for that matter. Both these circumstances had an immediate effect on the arts and culture. Next to the Imperial Court, the nobility and the gentry manifested themselves as patrons of major importance, and pleasure gardens in new Western-inspired manners were laid out near St Petersburg as well as around Moscow and out in the provinces.

The analysis has three parts: "Patrons and Programs", "Styles and Semantics", "Uses and Users". Within this framework, a series of closely interrelated topics and cases will be discussed in view of creating an imaginary 18th century garden scenario, including the main types of patrons, and which geographically reaches from the Northern capital St Petersburg to the Crimean peninsula.

Very few Western narratives on garden history have as yet paid much attention to the Russian contribution. Reference has very often been limited to Peterhof, Peter the Great's summer residence which was patterned after some of the great French and Italian gardens, and which was very demonstratively placed in the westernmost corner of Russia. Although a few more Imperial pleasure gardens are usually mentioned in the international garden dictionaries, Russia's historical garden heritage at large is far from well published outside the borders of the former Eastern bloc. In fact, C.C.L. Hirschfeld's 18th century *Theorie der Gartenkunst* (1779-85) holds more data on the Russian gardens than most general garden studies of the present century. Yet even Hirschfeld complained about his difficulties in getting information about the Russian material.

Numerous historians and intellectuals have since discussed the physical as well as psychological distance between East and West. To many a Westerner the Russian language has also been an obstacle to overcome. In the Soviet period, the problems took on a different character. Unless the regime was able to take advantage of a specific research project, obstacles such as visa and travel restrictions were put in the way, effectively damping many a Western researcher's ardour. It should be added that few European and American resources represented any serious alternative to the Russian ones, as far as art and historical research is concerned.

Today however, Russia is another country. Following the disintegration of the Soviet Union, a strong interest in communicating with the West has become evident in numerous fields. New dialogues between professionals and people are being initiated across the borders, and Western historians are now generously allowed to consult the archives, libraries and other collections. This change of circumstances and attitude has been of great importance in carrying through the research leading up to this book. Without a long-term stay in Russia, without numerous visits to the gardens still in existence and without having been granted access to a number of source texts, plans and other visual resources belonging to museums as well as archives, I could not possibly have carried this project through. It should be noted that a fair number of source texts presented and discussed in the following have previously only been accessible in Russian, whereas some visual material is published here for the first time.

Another relevant circumstance to the collecting and developing of material for this book has to do with the new orientation towards the tsarist past, which in recent years has come to the fore in the Russian arts and humanities. It is a trend which benefits directly from the reborn Russian state's future being in the melting pot, and the vacuum this situation still gives rise to. Many a creation of the tsarist period is now being studied with new intensity. The historical gardens form one such domain. Besides, families who for generations lived in the suburban residences but were forced to leave their homes and often their country too, after the Bolshevik coup, now strive to recreate traits and traditions of life in tsarist Russia. Not surprisingly, several of the many recently published monographic studies hold a certain nostalgic element. The initiatives of the newly revived Society

1. Peterhof. View from the Upper Garden of Peter the Great's suburban residence. The Neptune figure in the central basin faces towards the palace.

for the Study of Russian Country Houses should also be emphasized. Russian specialists are very much in the process of revising data concerning the genesis of individual gardens, and questions of restoration, attribution and dating are also very much the order of the day. The recent opening of several newly restored palaces, country houses and gardens proved equally stimulating to me from the very beginning of my Russian field studies right up to producing photographs for this book.

On some major points, though, I have applied a methodology somewhat different from that of most Russian and Soviet garden studies.[1] Firstly, my scope is not monographic, and I do not intend to cover the entire empirical field defined by the gardens of the Catherine period. This book has grown from a desire to look upon Russian 18th century gardens as a hermeneutical complex. The application of the three analytical categories — aesthetics, semantics and uses — means the introduction of some angles, viewpoints and facts that allow for a synthesizing approach to the subject. One of my primary concerns is to focus more on garden semantics than has usually been done in Russian garden studies. With the use of a broad range of historical sources, this analysis proposes to illustrate how allusive the late 18th century Russian gardens actually were. Pastoral, political, mythological, literary and several other aspects will be touched upon.

Secondly, the inclusion of comparative Western materials, such as garden treatises and concrete examples of gardens, and the discussion of a number of foreign artists' work in Russia will help to throw in relief the indebtedness of Russian gardens to Western paradigms. This very dependance seems manifested regarding the gardens' genesis as in the targeted perception of the garden landscape. Dutch and Italian influence was important from the Petrine age and onwards, but it was the French formal tradition and the British landscape garden that fascinated the Russian garden patrons of the Catherine period most. However, my analysis shows that there is also a great need to stress the role of some German sources.

Thirdly, it seems timely to draw more attention to the interplay between the art genres as another characteristic feature of the palace and country house culture of the period. Garden history has usually been considered a sub-branch of architecture, and focus has traditionally been on the patrons and the architects. But it took the users to explore the gardens, once they had been created. The painters and the poets constituted a particularly devoted group of garden visitors and interpreters towards the end of the 18th century, and in this book, special attention is therefore devoted to the works of some painters and poets. Besides, the genesis of landscape painting and nature poetry was much nourished by the new attitude to nature, as embodied in the contemporary landscape gardens.

It is my hope that the arguments and visual resources accompanying the analyses below will give a positive answer as to whether a hermeneutically oriented approach is profitable in the case of the tsarist gardens. And if, for all the lacunae and misunderstandings this book may contain, it may ultimately help to set in relief the Russian contribution to garden history, another intention will have been met. Long before cultural exchange was made a slogan in bilateral agreements between the East and West, people of the arts, crafts and sciences learnt from each other. The Russian pleasure grounds testify to this in a most convincing and charming way. Therefore, when today's Western visitor moves from Moscow's turmoil into suburban Kuskovo or Sukhanovo, he or she is actually making a journey back home. This is where our hermeneutical path will now lead us.

PATRONS AND PROGRAMS

You have understood the aim of life; you are a happy man
You lived for life's sake. During your long and serene life,
You were wise from your very youth
And diversified the monotony of life,
You sought for the possible, were moderate in your pranks,
Entertainments and ranks followed in turns.

You remain the same. Stepping over your threshold,
I am suddenly carried away to the days of Catherine II.
The library with books, and idols and pictures
And formal gardens show me that you favour muses in peace,
That you breathe with them in noble idleness. (Pushkin, 1830)

The patron of the arts whom Pushkin addresses in the eulogy "K velmozhe" (To the Master) is Prince Yusupov, and the pleasure palace and garden he refers to is Arkhangelskoe on the outskirts of Moscow. The faultless humanistic climate evoked by the poet makes it obvious to compare Arkhangelskoe to the Roman Villa Albani. The extensive garden though, had been laid out in imitation of a wide spectrum of aesthetical patterns, of which the Italian Renaissance only represents one model.

As in so many other countries, the indebtedness to foreign sources and concepts had already long been a key element in the development of gardens in Russia. At one stage, focus was on Byzantium. Greek gardeners were asked to demonstrate their skills in the convent gardens of Old Rus. Another outcome of this fashion was the hanging garden at the Moscow Kremlin. Some of the tsars of Old Muscovy were, on the other hand, very much drawn towards contemporary Italian culture, and several features of the Izmaylovo garden were inspired by the Boboli gardens in Florence, which a travelled nobleman had told Tsar Aleksey Mikhailovich about.

But it was Peter the Great who initiated a systematic import of ideas and technologies from the West, and garden art was immediately affected. Consequently, a thorough Westernization of Russia's princely gardens took place from the early 18th century. In the Catherine period, this process was further intensified and the garden patrons' fascination with the formal tradition of the Netherlands and

2. A shady alley in Peter the Great's Summer Garden. The palace, now a museum, was built in 1710-12.

France was now supplemented with a highly informed interest in the British landscape garden tradition. Catherine the Great played as important a role in this change of tastes as Peter had done half a century earlier. It therefore seems appropriate to discuss the Imperial garden heritage taking the Petrine as well as the Catherine period into consideration. Peter's Summer Garden and Catherine's Tsarskoe Selo are the main cases to be dealt with.

As St Petersburg was the seat of the Imperial Court and of all major administrative and commercial organs since the days of Peter, the changing fashions in garden design were most visible in the developments on the outskirts of the Northern capital. But Moscow's position as the old capital of tsarist Russia should not be underestimated. After all, nobles and merchants, among others, had moved north under Peter only with considerable compulsion, and many such families never gave up their homes in and around Moscow. So, along with the Court, Russia's big noble families, the officials and the richest merchants manifested themselves as diligent and imaginative garden patrons in the St Petersburg region as well as in Moscow, and so it remained all through the 18th and 19th century.

Two of the most impressive noble estates situated on the then outskirts of Moscow will be discussed in the third chapter on patronage and the patterning of pleasure gardens on Western sources. Kuskovo and Arkhangelskoe not only owed Western architects and gardeners their layout, but also those in the Russian serfdom. However, both gardens came to represent a grand-scale compilation of Western traits that were no longer new and unexplored in Russia. The aesthetical and perceptional characteristics had all been thoroughly experimented with in the St Petersburg gardens of the élite in the preceding decades.

Although the scale and level of ambition was different, a considerable number of big and fashionable gardens of the Catherine period were also laid out adjacent to country houses out in the provinces. In particular, the projects carried out by Andrei Timofeevich Bolotov reveal of the popularity of Western-inspired gardens several hundred kilometres away from the main cultural centres, whether it be St Petersburg or Moscow. Besides, Bolotov was one of Russia's first horticulturists and the most productive garden publicist in this country ever. His oeuvre is hardly known outside Russia, and this is yet another argument for going into detail with his prime garden projects and his theoretical writings.

Peter's Western Patterns

The garden of the Imperial summer residence in St. Petersburg, situated on the wide Neva river, is the first garden which Peter the Great, in 1714, had develop in his favourite Dutch taste. (Hirschfeld, 1785)

When the curtain goes up at the Bolshoi Theatre, and the golden ears of corn and other Soviet symbols of prosperity no longer dominate the view, one may find oneself among nannies airing babies and dogs in the shady alleys of the Summer Garden in central St Petersburg. It means that the *Dame of Spades* by Peter Chaikovsky is on the programme. The title and the theme of the opera were borrowed from a short story written by Alexander Pushkin in 1834. Gardens occur quite often in his oeuvre, the poet always having a genuine affection for the great pleasure gardens of his time.

In his diary, Pushkin tells how he went to the Summer Garden for daily promenades during his years in St Petersburg. In this, he followed one of the great fashions of civil life in the capital. The general public had been admitted to the Summer Garden from the 1740s, only a few decades after Peter the Great (1682-1725) had created the garden, along with the whole city surrounding it.

3. *Peter the Great on the title page of the first Russian dictionary of symbols and emblems, published in 1705.*

The history of Peter's new city starts in 1703. He chose the marshy and monotonous area where the Neva flows into the Gulf of Finland for one of the greatest urban projects that has ever been accomplished. Having visited the West a few years earlier, he was determined to change the traditional orientation of Russia. In fact, Peter was to open the window to the West, as the Italian traveller Algarotti formulated it in the early 18th century. And this is how one anonymous Russian poet of the time characterized the process:

> Russia and Russia's strength lay hidden in dreary night;
> God said 'Let Peter be!' and then they burst to light.[1]

Not only was the new *stolitsa* (capital) placed in the westernmost part of the country, but it was also fashioned in Western style, and called *Sankt Pieter Burkh*, as a sign of Peter's admiration for Dutch culture and efficiency. In 1705, the city was made the Northern capital, while Moscow remained the other capital of the Russian Empire.

At this point, Russia had been at war for several years, and some of the first buildings in the newly founded city were erected to improve the offensive against Sweden. Thus, the Fortress of SS. Peter and Paul was begun in 1703, as too were the shipyards, soon to be called the Admiralty. But at an early point, Peter also took the initiative to create an Imperial summer residence and garden.

From 1704 a first version of the so-called Summer Palace took shape on the banks of the Neva. On this site an entire complex of gardens with many new and fashionable features was being developed in the first quarter of the century. The citizens of St Petersburg were invited for occasional parties and fireworks, and later, under Elizabeth (1741-62), weekly openings were organized. The alleys and bosquets, adorned with pavilions and numerous fountains, soon became the most popular recreational area of the city.

A Garden in the City

Peter's summer residence was placed on the south bank of the Neva. From here the Emperor, as Peter preferred to call himself as opposed to the tsar, the title used in Old Muscovy, could watch the new Fortress of SS. Peter and Paul. Ivan Matveev (d. 1707), the most prominent local builder, designed the first palace as well as some fountains, but his work soon proved inadequate. Peter wanted something Western, or more precisely, something Dutch.

The first major influx of Western influence on the arts in Russia dates back to the 15th century. Contact with Italy was then perhaps far more substantial than previously assumed.[2] Ivan IV had close con-

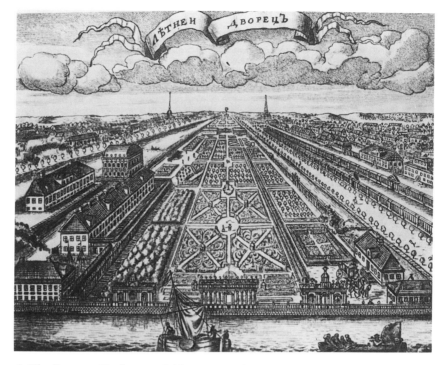

4. *The Summer Garden was laid out soon after Peter's foundation of St Petersburg in 1703.*

tacts with the North European Protestant countries, including Denmark, yet, contrary to his predecessors on the Russian throne, Peter decided to visit Europe in order to see the new and most ingenious creations in the fields of art and technology with his own eyes.

His European travel accounts from 1697, 1712 and 1717 bring clear evidence of how much first-hand experience with the great gardens of the Netherlands, Italy and France meant to him. Consequently, Peter sent out Russian artists to learn from abroad, and a hitherto unparalleled number of Western artists came to work in Russia. A massive ordering of Dutch and French literature on architecture and gardens was also carried into effect. Solomon de Caus' *Les raisons des forces mouvantes avec diverses machines tant utiles que plaisantes* (1615), which later had an immediate impact on the technology employed in the fountains in the Summer Garden and at Peterhof, entered Peter's library, and so did Dézallier d'Argenville's famous *La Théorie et la Pratique du Jardinage* (1709). General studies mingled with handbooks, richly illustrated albums and treatises. Depictions of all major French gardens were immediately accessible in a series of deluxe bindings.[3] Peter also initiated the translation into Russian of several foreign works on architecture, gardening and related subjects.

In view of Peter's fascination with the Netherlands, he employed surprisingly few Dutch artists.[4] However, in the case of the Summer Palace and Garden, Ivan Matveev was succeeded by an architect who had a sound experience in Dutch-inspired architecture, as well as by a Dutch gardener. The name of the first was Domenico Trezzini (c. 1670-1734), a Swiss-Italian, who had shown what Peter considered as the proper style and taste in his work for Frederik IV of Denmark.

For Peter, Trezzini then built a new palace (1710-12). That the building and its adjoining garden were surrounded by water on all four sides brought traditions of Dutch urban planning into memory, as did the asymmetrical siting of the palace and its relatively modest appearance. It was placed in the corner where the Neva meets the Fontanka, and formed as a single rectangular block of two storeys. It was not big and actually had little in common with the European princely residences of the time. It was modelled after the houses belonging to Dutch swells, as were Trezzini's houses for the St Petersburg nobility. Actually, Peter was not a man of great demands. His first residence in St Petersburg was a two-roomed wooden cottage (1703), not unlike a peasant's *izba* (cottage-like house). When a large house was required for entertaining, Peter borrowed one.

The collections of the Hermitage hold a plan of the Summer Garden which is usually ascribed to Peter and tentatively dated 1716. In all its simplicity, it gives a fairly clear idea of the geometric plan of the garden at this stage and of the division of the area into a pleasure garden, a vegetable garden, a big pond and a row of buildings, including the palace itself, along the Fontanka. Peter played a very active role as a patron. The annotation of a map of St Petersburg reads: "The tsar conducted all construction works, and for this he made sketches himself." At Peterhof, he worked energetically on the hydraulic systems for fountains and cascades, and made plans for the garden. The documents show that he also involved himself with some practical gardening. An inscription in his garden in Riga says: "Tsar Peter the Great, the founder of the fame and prosperity of Russia, planted these trees with his own hands in 1721."

For the Summer Garden, he personally ordered flowers to be moved from the Imperial gardens on the outskirts of Moscow, such as Izmaylovo where he had spent much of his childhood. Trees were moved from the nearby Baltic countries that had succumbed to Peter's army during the Great Nordic War. But in matters of design and the practical development of the Summer Garden, the professionals, not the Emperor, certainly had the most tangible influence. The Dutchman Jan Rosen and the Frenchman Jean-Baptiste-Alexandre Le Blond (1679-1719) were the key figures, and in due order, they proved faithful protagonists of their native garden traditions.[5] Mikhail Grigorievich Zemtsov (1686-1743), who had worked with Trezzini and Le Blond, was the first Russian to work in the Western style. It was he who completed Peter's Summer Garden.

Flowers and Fables

On the plan by Jan Rosen, dated 1714-16, emphasis is on the layout and adornments of the pleasure garden, with parterres and bosquets as the basic elements. The parterres unfold horizontally and dominate the upper part of the garden and the strip (not visible on Rosen's plan) between the Neva quay and the palace building. They are all flower parterres. The bosquets form a sort of frame around the central parterre, and consisting of lime or fruit trees, these green and relatively tall massives give relief to the whole design. A rigid system of avenues and alleys allows for promenades along and within these segments, while small open spaces formed as circles or squares and embellished with a fountain, a pavilion or a *treillage*, mark a temporary disrupture of these long walking and perceptional lines.

A few travel accounts from the early years of St Petersburg's history mention the Summer Garden. However one must turn to a description from the end of the 18th century to get a relatively precise characteristic of the general pattern:

This garden is laid out in the old or Dutch manner, it has straight alleys, that are cut by right, sharp and blunt edges, it has tall lime trees and maples the distance between which define natural or artificial groves and scrubs. One corner encompasses a small maze, another one holds narrow paths planted with Siberian peas, vegetables, and flowers.[6]

Basically, it was the flower parterres near the palace building which set a fashion in Russia to be associated with the Dutch garden tradition. Tulips, daffodils, lilies and roses embellished the parterres of the Summer Garden, whereas oak, maple, lime, juniper and fir were in the bosquets. For many decades to come, a *gollandsky sad*, that is a small garden in the Dutch manner, became a popular feature in the gardens of the St Petersburg and Moscow regions.[7] Russian gardeners were actually sent to the Netherlands for training. "Three men arrived from the Netherlands: Ivan Alabin, Ermolai Kratsev, Danilo Ovsyaninkov, who learned to make flowerbeds...", states a document of the Petrine period.[8]

5. The Summer Garden. Julius Caesar (left). Peace and Prosperity, commemorating the Great Nordic War (right).

Among the books and visual documents which Peter knew from various Dutch sources, many were not directly related to architecture and garden design, but touched upon iconography, ethics and classical literature. It appears though, that the impact of this kind of literature on the Petrine gardens was no less significant than the borrowings from the parterre tradition of Dutch 17th century gardens. An overall intellectualization of the arts took place under Peter. The introduction of allegorical sculptures and fountains in the gardens, *in casu* the Summer Garden, is evidently an outcome of this trend.

In 1705, Peter initiated the publication of the first iconographical dictionary in Russian ever (fig. 3). It was, of course, based on the well-known volumes filled with graphic depictions and explanations that had already been published in the West, not least the Netherlands, in the preceding centuries. Furthermore *Simvoli i emblemata* was first published in Amsterdam. A book of this type became a tool for the artists as well as for the public, and it may even be considered a precursor to the quite comprehensive buying of sculptures which Peter initiated. In any event, it was to have immediate consequences on how the Summer Garden looked by the mid 1720s.

Allegories of the arts and the virtues, the human characters and the time, mingled with mythological subjects. Statues of Vertumnus and Pomona referred to the art of gardening itself. Most of the sculptures were anonymous Italian 18th century pieces, acquired in Rome and Venice. One of the most prominent works was created on the Emperor's commission: To fit in with the praise of Russia's military power, alluded to in Andreas Schlüter's twenty-nine terracotta reliefs on the palace facade as well as in several large-scale paintings on the palace ceilings, Peter asked the Italian sculptor Pietro Barrata to do an allegory of Russia's victory in the Great Nordic War, "Peace and Prosperity" (1722). Busts of antique statesmen, commanders and philosophers served similar allusive purposes and helped to create in the Summer Garden an even more distinguished scene for the Russian Emperor's reception of foreign diplomats and other dignitaries.

Next to the sculptures the garden held several architectural pieces, the majority of which were created in the 1720s. There was a volière and a grotto sprinkled with sea shells, polychrome stones and fragments of glass, and there was a considerable number of *Lust-häuser* and fountains. With *Aesop's Fables* among Peter's favourite readings, Zemtsov took great care to refer to this classic for a number of the fountains to be inserted in the cabinets and niches both in the green maze for the Summer Garden and for Peterhof. A Russian edition of Jost Vondel's *Toneal des Menschlichen Levens* (1661) was another important source of inspiration to Peter and Zemtsov.

Bergholz, a Groom of the Chamber who served Peter the Great in the early 1720s, left a diary in which he included some very interesting remarks on the new gardens. On his way through the Summer Garden, he pays special attention to:

...a little pavilion, surrounded by water on all sides, where the tsar usually spends his time when he wants to be alone, or when he wants to drink well to somebody, because it is impossible to leave the island, from the very moment the boat which takes you to the pavilion, leaves the quay.[9]

This garden has just "...everything one can imagine for a pleasure garden to hold", Bergholz would argue.[10] The Summer Garden was, again in his words, partly *poteshny* partly *uchitelny*, that is partly pleasurable, partly didactic. This is about the first time garden elements, in Russian, were characterized with regard to the expected mode of experience. Just as Peter's gardens were laid out according to Western fashion, so the Russian language was obviously adjusted to this development. Yet, unlike Bergholz, most professional garden writers in 18th century Russia seem to have preferred the predicate *uvesitelny* to designate a pleasure garden.[11]

The basic utilitarian aspect of gardening was also offered considerable facilities at the Summer Garden, particularly in the early years. Here foreigners were in charge, as continued to be the case in most Imperial gardens throughout the 18th century. According to one source (1710-11):

The gardeners...included a German for the garden, a Dutchman for the orangery, ...and a Swede takes care of the extensive vegetable garden, which is laid out in a good way and contains a lot.[12]

A broad belt along the Moika Canal was laid out with neat vegetable beds. Long rows of fruit trees and bushes had also been planted here and there were several big greenhouses. The total yield was of course used in the Imperial household, exactly as in the days of Old Muscovy when the gardens of Izmaylovo and Kolomenskoe provided daily deliveries of fruits and vegetables.

Precisely this point has induced Russian and Soviet historians to argue that many features of the Moscow gardens of the previous centuries survived Peter's fervent desire to adopt Western patterns.[13] Yet, to grow fruit and vegetables was of course always an integral part of gardening, no matter how rich and splendid some pleasure gardens of 17th or 18th century Europe may seem.[14]

Suburban Splendour

Hardly two decades after Peter's first visit to Europe he had created himself a garden, the pattern and program of which stood for a world almost unknown to the contemporary Russian mind. The Summer Garden was as exotic as the entire city surrounding it. Yet Peter's fame as a great patron of pleasure gardens and as a renewer of the Russian tradition is most often connected with the creation of Peterhof, situated thirty kilometres west of St Petersburg, on the very banks of the Gulf of Finland. In his *Theorie der Gartenkunst* (1779-85) the German garden writer Hirschfeld was among the very first to sum up the importance of the Peterhof ensemble:

The largest and most splendid pleasure garden which Peter the Great had develop, though in the old formal manner, is undoubtedly the garden at the palace of Peterhof, ..., the traditional summer residence of the Imperial Court. This garden deserves to be named the Russian Versailles, by analogy

6. *Peterhof, the sumptuous suburban residence of Peter. The Great Canal leads the visitor from the sea to the main palace.*

with its precious and manifold buildings, the fountains, cascades, marble motifs in the grounds that are termed game reserves; in certain respects this garden has many advantages as compared to Louis XIV's sumptuous garden.[15]

Versailles set a pattern to be followed for centuries in practically all countries. This together with Peterhof's artistic qualities and immense scale are the main reasons for it having by and large overshadowed the Summer Garden.

Although Peter did not visit France until 1717, he had earlier been drawn to the French formal heritage. Apart from French book acquisitions, he had bought a model of the Versailles garden in 1712. Le Blond, a pupil and follower of Le Nôtre, was called upon in 1716 to lead the Imperial Building Chancellery. He made designs for St Petersburg's urban plan and Imperial gardens, including the drawing up of new plans for the Summer Garden. At Peterhof several architects of various origins were at hand, but Le Blond was to make the clearest mark on the extensive garden.

More than anything else, it was the water sceneries and the technologies behind them that had fascinated Peter during his visit to Versailles, Marly and St Cloud. That Russia under Peter had demon-

7. *The Hermitage in the Peterhof garden owes much to Peter's fascination with French building traditions.*

strated her military power at sea, was one more reason for letting Le Blond develop a garden at the new suburban residence, which allegorized water as one of its basic motifs. The Peterhof ensemble unfolds along one main axis, leading from the waters of the Gulf of Finland up through the Big Canal and the Big Cascade to the main palace building (J.-B.-A. Le Blond, 1714-21; B.F. Rastrelli, 1747-54), and further continued on to the Neptune Fountain in the Upper Garden. A secondary axial pattern links the Marly and the Monplaisir Palaces, including their respective gardens. Several fountains and cascades, some mythological or allegorical sculptures and a few water-squirting tricks similar to those at Versailles also adorn these gardens.

In comparison to the Summer Garden, Peterhof showed off a decisively more ceremonial pattern. The takeover of the great French manner, developed and refined under Louis XIV's patronage, marked the loss of a practicality and a relative intimacy that Peter had initially favoured, under the immediate spell of Dutch order, efficiency and *Grossbürgerlichkeit*. The names attributed to the palaces

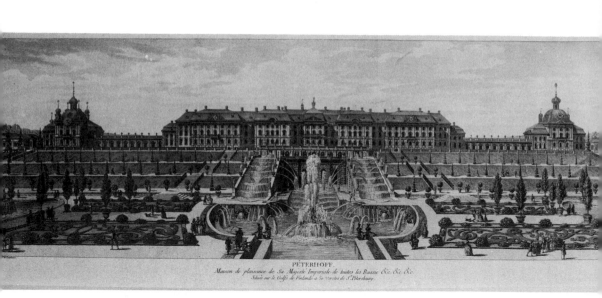

PÉTERHOFF.
Maison de plaisance de Sa Majesté Imperiale de toutes les Russies &c.&c.&c.
Située sur le Golfe de Finlande à 30 Verstes de St.Pétersbourg.

8. *Peterhof, the Palace and the Lower Garden. The palace was completed in 1754 under Elizabeth.*

and pavilions in the Peterhof garden also indicate that the old *gollandsky* manner had been replaced by that of French absolutism. Peter's confirmation of Russia's and his own power status made the substitution of one garden aesthetical model through another seem timely. In both cases, the West proved a satisfactory purveyor.

Catherine's Favourite Garden

The better taste in Russian gardens did not arise till the happy rulership of the present Empress Catherine II. (Hirschfeld, 1785)

Cold, cynical and power-seeking are some of the predicates often attached to Catherine the Great (1762-96). Her extensive warfare, her ambivalent relationship to the French Enlightenment, the growth of serfdom under her reign, and her innumerable erotic affairs are among the things that have caused many historians to look down upon this enigmatic woman ruler.

Of course, myths and stereotypes nourished by sexual as well as national prejudices enter this picture. The French have deprecated Catherine's passion as a collector because it deprived France of so many works of art.[1] But some have come up with another less crude view of Catherine. The British historian George Heard Hamilton claims that her character did not differ essentially from that of

9. *Catherine the Great during a promenade at Tsarskoe Selo, pointing at a military monument. Painted by V.L. Borovikovsky.*

10. Tsarskoe Selo. The Great Palace, now a museum, was built in 1749-52. Catherine the Great made it her summer residence in 1762.

other 18th century sovereigns. Enlightened despotism and military adventures were as much part of their ideological program as was theoretical liberalism.[2]

Catherine's way to power and her embracement of Russian culture is truly astounding. She was born Princess Sophia in the rather insignificant North German principality of Anhalt-Zerbst. In 1744 she came to Russia to marry the heir to the throne, and as tradition prescribed, she was re-christened in the Russian Orthodox Church. Catherine became her new name. Though a foreigner, she had a keen ambition of thoroughly studying the history and cultural traditions of Russia, in addition to the language. She was to remain persistent in these endeavours throughout her life. She once said: "I am drugged with the history or rather the chronicles of Russia which I love to distraction."[3] From 1783 until 1794, she regularly published essays on Russian history in St Peterburg's *Interlocuteur*. Extensive travelling throughout the Empire also formed part of her schedule.

Following the 1762 coup against her husband, Peter III (1761-62), Catherine unflaggingly worked on manifesting herself as one of Russia's great rulers and on legitimating herself as a rightful successor to Peter the Great. "Petro Primo, Catharina Secunda" runs the inscription on the equestrian statue in the Senate Square in St Petersburg. No reading of this heroic monument escapes the spell of Pushkin's *Bronze Horseman* (1833), in which the statue is seen as a symbol of majestic power and of humanity being haunted by natural and historical forces beyond its control.[4] But Catherine's motive for commissioning the French sculptor Étienne-Maurice Falconet in 1768 to create a statue of Peter the Great was very personal indeed.

Many of her political and legislative achievements should be seen in the line of the Petrine tradition. She expanded the Russian borders significantly, turning towards the Black Sea as compared to Peter's campaign on the Baltic shore. Her building program, too, was on a scale comparable to Peter's, and with the assistance of prominent foreign architects and some great Russian names, she made her mark on St Petersburg as well as on Russia's old capital, Moscow. All this in addition to founding a series of new cities.

Catherine's long correspondence with the Gallicized German Friedrich Grimm is an important source for her projects in art and architecture. In one of her letters she told him that "our craze to build is more fervent than ever before". And she continued in a nearly confessionary tone:

Building is a damned thing; it costs money, and the more you build, the more you want to build; it is an illness, just like drinking, or any other habit.[5]

The Imperial building program was marked by strong classicism. Most of the foreign architects were from Italy. Or, as Catherine told Grimm:

I wanted two Italians, beacuse we have some Frenchmen who know a lot and who design houses that look strange from the outside as well as indoors, because the architects know too much...[6]

But French art, culture and philosophy was otherwise at a premium in St Petersburg in the Catherine period. French became a badge of taste and caste. Grimm recommended the works of French artists and Catherine maintained an extensive correspondence with many of the French philosophers, although her relationship to their doctrines appears ambiguous. Nevertheless, it remains clear that Voltaire had a particularly strong impact on intellectual life in Russia in the last decades of the 18th century.

Yet the garden aesthetics which the Western élite in the second half of the 18th century were cultivating were neither Italian nor French, though elements of both traditions continued to survive and thrive. By the time Catherine became Empress, the English garden

11. *The Hermitage, built in 1748-52, at Tsarskoe Selo. The Great Palace is in the background.*

manner was literally sweeping through the grounds belonging to European monarchs and gentlemen, and like Peter the Great, she was ready to welcome the latest fashions. It mattered little that the landscape garden was a creation of the liberally oriented British society. The feudal countries on the Continent, and not least France, had taken this genre as a most welcome contrast to the pomp and parade of the formal garden tradition. As with the times, the ideological gap between the British and the rest of Europe did not hinder the acceptance of the very same aesthetical pattern. Following her Continental peers, Catherine placed Russia on this very map.

English à la mode

Originally, it was Peter who had discovered the site where Catherine the Great was to create her most splendid pleasure garden. The distance to St Petersburg was about the same as from Peterhof, some twenty-five kilometres, but Tsarskoe Selo lay south of the city. This forestry area was known under the Finnish name of Saari Mois, meaning an elevated site, until Peter decided to build a palace here for his wife, Catherine I. It was then renamed Tsarskaya Muza (the Imperial Muse) and later again Tsarskoe Selo (the Imperial Village).

Jan Rosen, who had previously worked in the Summer Garden and at Peterhof, is usually credited with having designed the first

12. *Tsarskoe Selo. The main axis of the formal garden as seen from the Great Palace towards the Hermitage.*

garden, with its ponds and canals, bosquets and bowers. The Dutch characteristics were somewhat veiled under the impact of the Italian architects preferred by Elizabeth. An imposing palace was built (Count Bartolommeo Francesco Rastrelli, 1749-52) and a series of pavilions, including a hermitage and a grotto, were added to the garden. Terraces were also featured. Under Catherine, a third source of inspiration, notably the English garden manner came to the fore, and an entirely new garden was developed in addition to the old one.

Documents from 1762, the very year Catherine was coronated, testify to her interest in modifying the layout of Tsarskoe Selo.

Do not cut the espaliers and the trimmed trees in the old garden and in the garden to be redesigned, except on the main way from the palace to the Hermitage...[7]

This was her first order to the gardeners at Tsarskoe Selo. At the very same time, building activities were started at Oranienbaum, situated on the Bay of Finland and not far from Peterhof. Oranienbaum originally belonged to Prince Alexander Menshikov, Peter the Great's chancellor. Like Peterhof, the palace was built on a terrace facing the sea. There was a harbour and a canal, and the sumptuous gardens

13. *The pavilion dates back to the Catherine period, whereas the pond is a relic from Peter the Great's Tsarskoe Selo.*

had been given a formal layout. In 1743 Grand Duke Peter Feodorovich (the later Peter III) had chosen Oranienbaum for his summer residence, and Catherine followed suit. Antonio Rinaldi designed a new palace for her, the so-called Chinese Palace (1762-68), with one part of the new garden featuring natural groves of a considerable size, and another given a formal design. Yet Catherine never spent much time at Oranienbaum. She preferred Tsarskoe Selo, and it was here that she realized her ambitions, as far as garden art was concerned.

Despite her fascination with the landscape garden, Catherine never went to England to see for herself what this genre was all about. She did not follow her idol, Peter, in his very practical approach to the artistic or technological inventions of the West. Neither did she partake in any specific design work. As a garden patron, Catherine was more of a mediator than a participant in a multi-disciplinary project. Through people, books and pictures she gained a fairly good impression of the garden aesthetics of the day, and is credited with having personally translated one of the most popular books on architecture and gardening into Russian.

The book was William Chambers' *Designs of Chinese Buildings,*

14. *Kadriorg near Tallinn. Peter's gardens had many features in common. This scenery may thus be compared to Tsarskoe Selo.*

Furniture, Dresses, Machines, and Utensils. To which is annexed, a Description of their Temples, Houses, Gardens, (1757). It had been published in English and French, and Catherine used the latter edition as the basis for her translation, which was published in St Petersburg in 1771. There are several other cases in which the Imperial Court and the St Petersburg élite made use of French as a filter in relation to the British world, including British art, literature and gardening. Richardson's sentimental novels, to take one example, were read in French.

The French had been among the first on the Continent to adopt the landscape garden, and a series of treatises and poems written by French admirers and connoisseurs of this genre were published in Paris from the 1770s. Over the years, some of these works became well-known in Russia. Some, including Réne-Louis de Girardin's *De la Composition des Paysages, ou des moyens d'embellir la Nature autour des Habitations, en joignant l'agréable à l'utile* (1777) and Jacques Delille's *Les Jardins, ou l'Art d'Embellir les Paysages. Poème* (1782), were also translated into Russian.[8] Gustav III of Sweden, for his part, carefully studied Catherine's project at Tsarskoe Selo to gain inspiration for his new garden at Drottningholm.

Up until the Catherine period there had been some business ties between Russia and Britain, but as far as horticulture was concerned only one instance of exchange is known to have taken place. Thus, one British gardener and naturalist of the early 17th century brought home a load of plants and a notebook on the Russian flora.[9] But Catherine changed this state of affairs. Hirschfeld informs us:

To lay out this garden [Tsarskoe Selo], which one day may surpass all works of this kind in Europe, she let knowledgeable men visit, and come from England.[10]

To further cultivate her taste for everything pertaining to the British garden heritage Catherine also acquired engravings with motifs from famous English gardens. Such a collection was hung at Tsarskoe Selo. Some of the scenes reappear in the famous dinner service which Catherine commissioned in 1773-74 from Wedgwood's. The design was known as the Green Frog and it was acquired for the Chesma Palace in St Petersburg.

Under Catherine, suburban life was no longer synonymous with festive masquerades and sumptuous hunting parties, as it had been under Elizabeth. Catherine's zeal was legendary, and when at Tsarskoe Selo, usually from April, she would work daily. Yet the Empress also took delight in unaffected pleasure. This is evident from V.L. Borovikovsky's portrait, which is so different from the many early official pictures of Catherine the Great, including those by the Danish-born Vigilius Erichsen.

Borovikovsky completed this portrait in 1794, just two years before Catherine's death, and here the elderly Empress is seen on a quiet promenade in the Tsarskoe Selo garden. She wears a coat and a hat without many trimmings, and the dog represented is one of the ones she called by an English name. As fashion prescribed, her beloved dogs were buried in the garden, and their names inscribed on the monument raised in their honour. The rostral column in the background, which Catherine points at, belongs to the group of garden monuments that commemorated the Russian victories in the First Turkish War (1768-74). The new developments at Tsarskoe Selo were at their peak when Catherine's commanders arranged for the borders of the Russian Empire to be moved further south, conquering the Crimean Peninsula, and thus gaining access to the Black Sea. It was a similar convergence of imperialist events marking the genesis of Peter's Summer Garden and Peterhof.

15. *Tsarskoe Selo. The pond in front of the Elizabethan grotto was made a centrepiece in Catherine's landscape garden.*

Landscaping the Grounds

In a much quoted letter from 1772, Catherine confided to Voltaire:

At present I love English gardens to distraction, I love curved lines, soft slopes, ponds and archipelagoes, and I strongly disdain straight lines and double alleys. I hate fountains which torture the water in order to make it change its natural course; the statues are relegated to the galleries, the entrance halls, etc; in short, anglomania dominates my plantomania.[11]

At Tsarskoe Selo, in a completely new layout on the south side of the Elizabethan palace and garden ensemble, Catherine saw her garden fantasies realized.

The big and very impressive palace which Rastrelli had built for Elizabeth remained the architectural nucleus of the Tsarskoe Selo ensemble. The old axial system was kept basically intact, as were the canals surrounding the Upper Garden, the parterres and bosquets, and the Italianate sculptural and architectural adornments. In terms of visual effectiveness however, the sumptuous grotto (Rastrelli, 1749-61) came to play a new and very significant role in Catherine's garden.

16. *Tsarskoe Selo. The Morea column recalls Catherine's war against the Turks. The cascades add to the landscape scenery.*

The pond in front of the grotto was considerably enlarged and the banks were made irregular. Small artificial islands were added, and winding paths were laid out among the trees, bushes and grasses adorning the banks of the pond. Out of this arose a provocative play between water, greenery and architecture. Consequently, the garden visitor would no longer rest passively in the grotto and indulge in the view over the pond. The new scenery invited for a stroll, in the course of which the viewer would discover the variety of the grounds and the grotto itself as one element of beauty and surprise among many other architectural motifs to be created along the garden route.

The grounds a bit further away from the Big Pond were laid out with artificial hills and slopes. Water from a natural source some sixteen kilometres away was led to supply the many small lakes that were gradually being created in the more remote parts of the garden. Some of the small islands were connected to the main paths by bridges, whereas others could only be reached by boat. Numerous trees and shrubs were planted (in fact more than 20,000 in 1772 alone). A big lawn from which gravel paths were banned was also fitted into the design. The grass carpet unfolded freely, adding air, relief and another tone of green to the horizontal pattern of small tree clumps alternating with massive groves.

These developments took place under direct Western influence. In 1770 or 1771 the Russian architect Vasily Ivanovich Neelov (1722-

82) had been sent to England for six months to study gardens. Immediately after his return, he was employed at Tsarskoe Selo along with one of his sons, Ilya Vasilevich (1745-93). Another son, Pyotr, who had accompanied his father to England, became architect at Tsarskoe Selo after the death of Ilya Vasilevich. In 1771, an English gardener by the name of John Busch (c. 1730-95) was also employed at Tsarskoe Selo.[12] He was born in Hanover, yet had moved to England where he owned a celebrated nursery garden.

As the research has focused on the great architects Catherine summoned to work at Tsarskoe Selo (Antonio Rinaldi, Giacomo Quarenghi, Yury Matveevich Velten, and Charles Cameron), neither the works of the Neelovs nor those of Busch have as yet been sufficiently analysed. Yet the fact that an English gardener was called in is significant in itself. Later, notably in the 1780s and onwards, the Court as well as a number of Russian noblemen saw to it that other garden professionals from England and Scotland were put in charge of their pleasure gardens. Thus, the Petrine tradition of hiring Western professionals for this kind of work continued to blossom, though now with England as the leading purveyor.

The main task of the English gardeners working in Russia was usually the cultivation of fruits, vegetables and flowers, and Busch's orangery is likely to have been one of the very best in Russia at the time. Lady Dimsdale, who visited Russia in 1781 with her husband Dr Thomas Dimsdale, known for his inoculation of Catherine and her son Pavel against smallpox, wrote about it in her journal:

The Green House was the largest I ever saw, containing several hundred Orange, Lemon & Citron Trees. I measured one of the Orange Trees round the body, and it was four feet four Inches in Circumference...There are a great number of Hothouses for all kinds of Fruits, and I think the best Melons I ever eat of Mr Bush's raising, and plenty of Water Melons, Peaches and Nectarines very good...Mr Bush shewed me the foundation of a hothouse which was building, of eight hundred Feet in length.[13]

Another early 19th century British source brings in another aspect of Busch's talents, crediting him with the creative design work at Tsarskoe Selo.

In *An Encyclopedia of Gardening* (1822; eight more editions before 1878), the garden specialist John Claudius Loudon recalls from his 1813 visit to Russia how Busch was asked to make a test design at a hilly site between St Petersburg and Tsarskoe Selo:

On entering the garden, and seeing a winding shady gravel walk planted on both sides, she [Catherine] appeared struck with surprise, and exclaimed

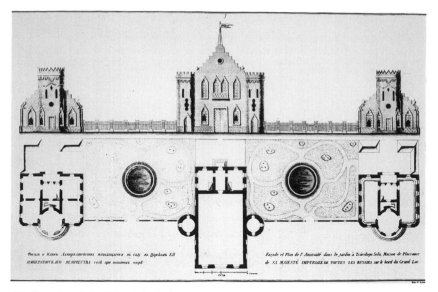

17. *Tsarskoe Selo. The Admiralty was used as a boathouse, and prints showing English gardens were on view in its salon.*

"This is what I want!" This walk led to a fine lawn, with gravel walks round it, which seemed to strike her still more forcibly, and she again said "This is what I have long wished to have". The following year the Tzarsco Selo gardens were given to the charge of John Busch, who carried on the improvements till the year 1789, when he left the service of the Empress and returned to England.[14]

No Russian or Soviet studies have given this passage any attention. Together with a Russian gardener by the name of Trifon Ilin, John Busch has been considered responsible only for the planting and the care of the garden.[15]

Drawing was part of the professional gardener's training program, and Busch drew a plan of the Tsarskoe Selo garden which previous studies have failed to mention. Judging from the architectural motifs Busch has included, the plan shows the garden of the 1780s. It comes very close indeed to a demonstration piece, and Busch may have drawn it and dedicated it to Catherine right before his departure. But this should not exclude the attribution of at least part of the landscape design to Busch. Future studies will cast more light on this.

When John Busch returned to England, he was succeeded by his son Joseph (1760-1838), who took over Tsarskoe Selo's much celebrated orangery. As for Catherine, her letters from Tsarskoe Selo testify to her deep interest in the garden project, although horticulture does not appear to have held the slightest interest for her. Peter the Great was different in this respect, as was Catherine's daughter-in-law, Maria Feodorovna. At nearby Pavlovsk, she would involve herself in all kinds of questions concerning her plantings and pots. Architecture, however, allowed Catherine to think big, which always became her extremely well.

More Than Mere Follies

Following the study tour, the Neelovs designed a broad variety of garden buildings and monuments at Tsarskoe Selo in the early and mid 1770s.[16] In concordance with the most fashionable English patterns, a blend of styles and meanings was featured. Each structure was accorded a specific arena, with the greenery, waters or area suiting the architectural design. Most of the garden buildings and monuments were placed in the vicinity of the Big Pond. The promenade along this piece of water and further on to the group of artificial islands at the Upper Ponds became the visual as well as the intellectual centre of the Neelovs' oeuvre. The subsequent addition of works by Rinaldi and Velten further strengthened this effect.

Leaving the Elizabethan garden by the splendid grotto, the promenade would first take the visitor to the Admiralty (V.I. Neelov, 1773-77). Like the nearby Kitchen (V.I. Neelov, 1774-76), the Admiralty was built of brick with white-coated ornaments. It was obviously patterned after some remains of medieval structures or so-called neo-gothic buildings which the Neelovs had studied on their visit to English gardens or in garden views. Lady Dimsdale wrote the following about the Admiralty:

There is a fine Building near the large piece of Water called the Admiralty, the first Floor only contains all the Boats, and places for the water Fowls to live in the Winter. The second Story is one large Room hung round with English Prints of Houses, and Views of different places in England, in it is a bow Window which looks full upon the Water...[17]

In fact, the picture collection inside the Admiralty did not leave anyone in doubt as to the models of the new Catherine garden.

At the far end of the Big Pond a pyramid (V.I. Neelov, 1771) was placed. The tall trees in this area induced the scenery with a rather sombre atmosphere, which, when Catherine's greyhounds later died, was found apt for the creation of a small cemetery. Parallels to this scenery existed not only in England, but also in some Continental landscape gardens. Hardly one hundred metres further ahead, the garden visitor would be surprised by the view of a marble bridge (V.I. Neelov, 1772-74) across a narrow piece of water. It echoed the

18. Chinese motifs abound at Tsarskoe Selo. The Creaky Pavilion was built in 1778-86.

art of Andrea Palladio, as did the famous Palladio Bridge (1737) at Wilton. No other work by the Neelovs followed the English fashion so closely.

Many more discoveries awaited the viewer when he penetrated into the area beyond the bridge. Here a monumental antique-inspired arch (Rinaldi, 1772-78) was built in memory of the work accomplished by Prince Orlov, one of Catherine's *Eagles*, as her favourites were also called, after a Moscow plague. The Ruin Tower (Velten, 1771-73), in turn, commemorated Russia's victory in the First Turkish War. Over the years, several more victory monuments were fitted into the landscape. But diversions and amusements were also thought of. Just as the English and Continental landscape gardens featured Chinese-inspired motifs, so too did Tsarskoe Selo. Bright colours and exotic-looking forms dominated the Chinese Village, several Chinese bridges and pavilions near the Lower Ponds and the Chinese Theatre. Some miniature mountain rocks and cascades were created to complete the scenery, but the many and varied architectural forms

19. *Tsarskoe Selo. Catherine often enjoyed her meals in the Cameron Gallery, while looking out on her pleasure grounds.*

20. *The Cameron Gallery epitomizes the use of antique political and aesthetic schemata during the reign of Catherine.*

remained the highlights of the garden promenade. The Chinese complex at Tsarskoe Selo was the largest of its kind in 18th century Europe.

It seems difficult to explain why one of the most popular motifs of the landscape gardens of the day, notably the antique-inspired rotunda, is missing from Catherine's Tsarskoe Selo. At some point the Empress was absolutely excited about the antique heritage as interpreted by the contemporary British and French artists. "I have all the works by the Adam brothers", she told Grimm, referring to *Works in Architecture* (1773-79).[18]

I feel excited, having for several days during all leisure hours contemplated Clérisseau's drawings, and I was not bored.[19]

She was particularly enchanted by the work of a Scottish architect, Charles Cameron (1743-1812), who joined the Imperial building staff by the end of 1778.

I here have an architect by the name of Cameron, born a Jacobite, trained in Rome; he is known for his work on ancient baths. This head, an enterprising one, greatly admires Clérisseau;...[20]

Works by Clérisseau and the Adam brothers actually served as models for Cameron's work in a series of palace interiors.

If Cameron did not design any antique-inspired garden pavilions for Catherine, he used his Roman background in a large-scale building complex which was added to the south side of Rastrelli's palace building. In a letter, written in 1779 to Grimm, Catherine said: "...here we are creating together with him [Cameron] a terraced garden with baths below and a gallery above; it will be beautiful..."[21] The complex comprised of the Cold Bath, the Agate Pavilion with a hanging garden and the so-called Cameron Gallery (1779-86). The whole was carefully integrated with the sloping hills of the adjoining landscape garden. The Cameron Gallery actually terminated in a sweeping curved staircase. Later a ramp was added at the back for the aged Empress to reach her garden in a wheelchair.

The bronze sculptures of antique philosophers and statesmen, set back between the Ionic columns of the open gallery, added to the classical serenity of this ensemble. Only one modern figure was included. But it was neither Voltaire nor Montesquieu, whom Catherine had studied so closely for her legislative reforms. Instead, the Empress wanted to honour an Englishman, Charles James Fox, for having categorically spoken in Parliament against a possible war between the two countries. Significantly, this was the last comment on the Russo-British relationship to be made in this ensemble so indebted to the British garden tradition.

It was Catherine who was the driving force behind the transfer of this pattern to Russia, and practically all of her gardens, whether in St Petersburg or Moscow, reflect the new and fashionable taste. Next to Tsarskoe Selo, Tsaritsyno on the outskirts of Moscow is particularly interesting. There was hardly any owner of a pleasure garden in Russia of the 1780s who would not dream of following this fashion, more or less convincingly, more or less sumptuously. Catherine's initiative indeed proved most decisive for the further course of Russian garden history.

Princely Gardens

Moscow... already boasts many gardens in the new taste. (Hirschfeld, 1785)

The fifth and last volume of Hirschfeld's *Theorie der Gartenkunst* includes a brief chapter on Russian gardens.[1] It begins with Peter the Great and closes with Catherine the Great, who was German-born, as too was Hirschfeld and was one of the garden patrons he most

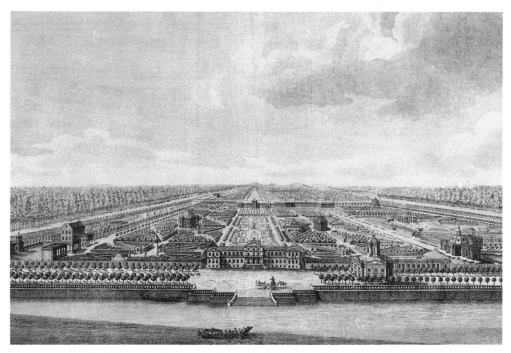

21. *Kuskovo's formal gardens. Kuskovo, built by serfs, was one of the Sheremetev family's Moscow estates.*

admired. Having never visited Russia, Hirschfeld based his chapter on the information he got from some of the garden plans and from a German diplomat. He explicitly refers to these two sources. Much more could have been said about the gardens of Russia, but Hirschfeld's comments are interesting in themselves and also as a signal of the growing exchange between Russia and Western Europe during the 18th century.

Tsarskoe Selo, "which in regards to costliness and taste may one day surpass all works of this kind in Europe", is accorded most attention.[2] But Hirschfeld also moves on to Moscow, although his level of information about the gardens here indeed falls far behind what he was able to tell his readers as far as the horticultural programs of the St. Petersburg region were concerned. Two gardens in Moscow are mentioned, Annenhof and Kuskovo. The first belonged to the Court, the latter to one of the most influential and certainly the richest noble family of the period, the Sheremetev family.

Annenhof goes back to the days of Empress Anna (1730-40), Peter's niece, hence the name of the palace and garden.[3] The architect B.F. Rastrelli whose name is closely linked to the history of the

22. *Kuskovo. Columns of the central portico. As with most Moscow buildings, the Kuskovo Palace, now a museum, was made of wood.*

Summer Garden and that of Peterhof and Tsarskoe Selo as well, had built a palace high above the Yauza river, thus allowing the residents and their honoured guests to admire "the surprisingly big city, which takes in the entire horizon."[4] The extensive gardens, "of perfect taste" as Hirschfeld characterizes them, were open to the public. Yet in Hirschfeld's time of writing, Annenhof had lost its original splendour and layout. In 1746 the palace had been destroyed by fire and the gardens soon became overgrown. Only the preserved mid 18th century plans testify to the intricacy of the parterres.

Thirteen kilometres east of the Moscow Kremlin lay Kuskovo, which Hirschfeld may have learnt about from descriptions as well as from a widely circulated series of engraved prospects. Kuskovo was in the possession of the Sheremetev family from 1623 right up till the Bolshevik coup. It was Field Marshal Peter Borisovich Sheremetev who by the mid 18th century had his serf architects and gardeners design an ensemble, which from early on made Kuskovo known as the Muscovite Versailles. Like the Annenhof gardens, the larger part of the grounds surrounding the neo-classical, wooden palace at Kuskovo was laid out in accordance with the Le Nôtre tradition.

23. *Arkhangelskoe. Anonymous painting showing the palace cum garden complex on the banks of the Moscow river.*

Some very elegant and well-furnished pavilions in the fashionable Western manner made this ensemble stand out even more among mid and late 18th century Russian pleasure gardens. In the early 1770s, a garden responding to the English landscape tradition was added to the formal garden.

Regarding pomp, splendour and fashionable Western-inspired features, another estate on the outskirts of Moscow should also have been mentioned by Hirschfeld. But news about the remodelling of the Arkhangelskoe palace and garden, situated twenty-six kilometres southwest of Moscow, barely reached Hirschfeld before he finished the fifth volume of *Theorie der Gartenkunst*. There is no doubt though, that even a few lines dedicated to Arkhangelskoe would have provided Hirschfeld's readers with more up-to-date information about Moscow's horticultural map than his reference to Annenhof (abandoned since the fire) and Kuskovo did. It took a Russian poet and translator, A.F. Voikov, to consider Kuskovo and Arkhangelskoe on equal terms.

In 1816 his Russian translation of Jacques Delille's didactic poem *Les Jardins,...* was published. In the sixty-five line eulogy on Russian gardens, Voikov wrote in order to complement the Western scene furnished by Delille's verses, it thus says:

> The example of the court is hallowed by the noblemen, the rich;
> In all of them a true passion for gardens arose:
> At Arkhangelskoe there are gardens, paths and alleys,
> Reminding of creation done by talented fairies,
> Whom wonder had sent to England.
> A great landlord, who practiced old Russian hospitality,
> Resided at Kuskovo,
> The people gathered for parties, and the mornings were calm.
> Sweet darling where a happy and well-lit house
> Mirrors itself in the silver pond.[5]

Under Catherine Moscow was experiencing a revival in many fields. Intellectual life, including publishing, was one such field. The Masonic lodges expanded significantly from the 1770s. Building activity blossomed as never before, and a great number of noble residences were erected on the banks of the Moscow and Yauza rivers and on the city outskirts. One French visitor reported:

One cannot picture to oneself the number of gentlemen in Moscow, whereas there are few in St Petersburg.[6]

These *gentilshommes* were the new and mighty builders and art patrons.

Artisanal workshops or even some type of industry were seldom connected with the large residential complexes outside Moscow. They became more and more common around 1800. At Arkhangelskoe, for example, a porcelain factory was opened in 1818. Yet, such enterprises were never physically integrated with the main house nor with the garden. The residence was basically created for pleasure, and the owner would frequently spend the summer months here, and return to the city by October.

Other highly enterprising garden patrons lived permanently in the countryside. Agriculture and forestry, more than official postings and industry, were the main sources of income for the members of the Russian gentry. And, as was repeatedly stressed in the garden literature of the period, the demands put forward by this group, with regards to their pleasure gardens, were typically rather modest, as were their financial means. This favoured the develoment of relatively simple landscape gardens or the adorning of an existing

24. *Kuskovo. The Grotto, built in 1755-61, by the Italian Pond. The interior is decorated with sea shells, stucco and glass.*

grove with a pavilion or belvedere, as opposed to the grand-scale, formal, and very intricate and work-consuming garden designs of the past.

Yet some of the Moscow patrons had the means at their disposal which allowed them to choose freely the kind of garden design to adorn their residences. The scale and layout of Kuskovo as well as Arkhangelskoe testify to the owners belonging to this group. They were princes, and their pleasure gardens were in harmony with their status.

Kaleidoscopic Gardening

As the mid-18th century palace had fallen into disrepair, Prince Nikolai Alekseevich Golitsyn (1751-1809) wanted to rebuild it to his personal taste, and in 1779 he decided to redesign Arkhangelskoe. The new palace and garden ensemble first of all came to echo the French formal tradition. Golitsyn clearly preferred the well-established aesthetics of the great mid 17th century gardens in *le bassin parisien* to the English fashion of his own time. During his European tour he had become absolutely enchanted by the gardens of Italy and France, just as Peter the Great nearly a century earlier.

Taking the Court as his model, Golitsyn hired foreign architects to realize his idea of a pleasure palace and garden. A French architect by the name of Chevalier de Guerney designed the classical palace complex (1780), apparently without ever visiting Arkhangelskoe.[7] Local serf-craftsmen carried out all work on the actual building site. Italian Giacomo Trombara created a terrace system which truly brought into evidence the gardens of the architect's own country. Besides, Trombara of whom little else is known, was the very architect whom Grimm had recommended in reply to a letter from Catherine, wherein she asked for two Italian architects; the other was Giacomo Quarenghi.[8]

The Arkhangelskoe Palace was placed on the most elevated site in the grounds. An earlier Dutch-inspired house had also been placed here. The garden facade of the new palace pointed south towards the Moscow river, and the terraces joined the palace with the big garden plateau. A brick wall closed off the southern part of this garden, with softly undulating meadows stretching further down to the river bank. Orangeries, greenhouses and vegetable beds were placed here.

Gradually, classically styled pavilions were erected in various corners of the garden, and Golitsyn also had a secondary residence built, in imitation of his French peers' preference for hermitages. All parts of the ensemble were subordinated to a central axis. It departed from the entrance porch, through the palace, the terraces and the grotto beneath the terrace staircase, and continued on to the garden plateau. As at Peterhof, the doctrines of d'Argenville were carefully observed in the layout of the garden plateau. Green parterres blended with flower parterres, and the trees bordering the plateau were alternately forming alleys and *treillages*. The bosquets of the earlier garden, developed in the 1730s, had been cut exactly the same way as those in the Upper Garden at Peterhof, and the same kind of trees were used.

Following a visit in 1782 to Sweden, Golitsyn called upon a Swedish engineer by the name of F.E. Norberg to create a hydraulic system that should outdo not only the one serving the fountains at Drottningholm, but also the intricate system at Marly outside Paris. Norberg came the following year and his success in Russia was honoured by his *Letter on the Hydraulic Machine at Arkhangelskoe* being published as a booklet in St Petersburg in 1787. Sculptures too were prime elements of the garden from its early years. Most were Italian 18th century pieces, covering as manifold an iconography as those of Peter's Summer Garden. The sculptures were placed along the gravel paths and in the parterres.

The number of sculptures increased significantly, when, after Golitsyn's death, Prince Nicolai Borisovich Yusupov (1751-1831) bought Arkhangelskoe. He was not only the Director of the Imperial Museums, but also a great collector himself, and his idea was to house and exhibit his art collection at Arkhangelskoe. Works were transferred from his other residences and he placed an order for dozens of new marble statues for the garden with Carlo Silvestro Penno, an Italian sculptor working in Moscow. The garden ultimately was to hold more sculptures than any other in Russia, complemented indoors by an outstanding collection of paintings and porcelain.

Yet, as one of the most prominent representatives of the Russian Enlightenment, befriended with French thinkers and fully *au courant* with European fashions, Yusupov also had some very clear ideas about how to make the Arkhangelskoe garden meet with the new aesthetics. Once more the Imperial gardens around St Petersburg served as examples, the interest now moving from Peterhof to Tsarskoe Selo and Pavlovsk.

The development of a new garden to the north and west of the palace was begun soon after the French troops had been forced to leave Moscow in 1812. Distinct groves, planted with trees typical of the Moscow region, were the main elements of this garden. Some natural ponds were integrated with the groves, and lended them their names. In one of the groves, a star-formed system of alleys led

25. Arkhangelskoe. Amongst its architectural motifs the formal garden boasts this pavilion dedicated to Catherine the Great.

to a marble statue of Apollo, the Greek patron of art, to whom Maria Feodorovna had already dedicated a similar monument at Pavlovsk. Centaurs similar to those on Pavlovsk's Bridge of Centaurs were mounted on the bridge crossing a deep chasm. Finally, some more monuments and pavilions, including a Temple Dedicated to Catherine the Great (Ye. Tyurin, 1819) were added to the old garden.

In result, when Pushkin visited Arkhangelskoe in 1830, it presented itself as a big and richly furnished ensemble. "I am suddenly carried away to the days of Catherine II", he said in his eulogy of Yusupov's estate. The blend of historical garden patterns somehow fitted in with one of the basic purposes of Arkhangelskoe under Yusupov, namely the palace and the garden being the private collection site of the prince. But such eclectism was far from confined to this ensemble. Similar methods were also applied in the planning of many other and less sumptuous pleasure gardens around 1800.

Muscovite Anachronisms

As opposed to Peter and most 19th century Russian rulers, Catherine had demonstrated a vivid interest in Moscow's layout, including the city's green zones. In 1775, the old fortifications around the city nucleus were replaced by a green belt. Lawns, lime trees, artificial ponds and gravel walks adorned what was officially named the *Bulvarnoe Koltso*, the Boulevard Ring. Gardens were laid out adjacent to the many new and fashionable palaces, including two new Imperial residences in the Moscow vicinity.

Not surprisingly, it was Catherine and the architects and planners in her service who served as models when Moscow was to undergo grand-scale development in the present century. Soon after the Bolshevik coup in October 1917, the new leadership decided to leave Petrograd, as St Petersburg was then called. The capital of Old Muscovy was preferred. In March 1918, Lenin took up residence in the Moscow Kremlin, and the people's commissars moved into the offices previously occupied by tsarist officials. With immediate effect, Moscow became the touchstone and the base of official city planning and landscape politics, just as St Petersburg had been since the Petrine period.

The idea of the public city park played a dominant role in a long series of urban projects, ranging from *A New Moscow* (1918) to the *General Plan for the Renewal of Moscow* (1935). Green belts were considered the ideal skeleton for joining the centre with the extensive forests surrounding Moscow. In tsarist Russia, many private gardens had been made accessible to the general public on specific days or on special occasions, but the very ideology of the public park was fostered only in the Soviet period. By contrast, during the 19th century, public gardens and parks were created in a considerable number in many European countries and in North-America, and a number of late 18th and early 19th century garden writers, including Hirschfeld, discussed the concept of the *Volksgarten* in length.

The idea of the first generation of Soviet planners, as stipulated by the Party, was to create a basically new landscape or garden genre under the key-notion *park kultury i otdikha* (park of culture and rest). Thus at a meeting on November 3, 1931, in the Central Committee of the Communist Party, the following resolution was passed:

The parks of culture and rest represent a new kind of institution that has numerous political and didactic obligations to fulfill, all of which are for the well-being of millions of workers.[9]

Historical paradigms were however to be used very extensively indeed.

Placed in the very heart of Moscow, the Central Park of Culture and Rest (1928), later better known as Gorki Park, was the very first public park of the Soviet period. A series of architects contributed to this project over the years, with Aleksander Vasilevich Vlasov (1900-62) as one of the early key-figures. The park was thought of as part of a grandiose axial system Stalin wanted to see realized across Moscow, from the Red Square to the Lenin Hills.

A monumental archway (replaced by a colonnade in 1955) marked the entrance to the park from Moscow's main traffic lane, the *Sadovoe Koltso*, the Garden Ring, the appearance of which was also a result of the Soviet renovation of Moscow.[10] The huge, flat area just behind the archway had originally been used for the First All-Union Agricultural Exhibition, organized in 1923 at the height of the New Economic Policy. It was called the Big Parterre, and the layout was, as the name indicates, indebted to the French formal heritage. Ornamental flowerbeds alternated with straight gravel walks, and a gigantic water bassin with fountains was placed to fit in with the axial scheme.

Vlasov thought of this part of the park as "the place for mass rest and the place for mass work."[11] On the long and relatively narrow strips of grassland between the parterre and the Moscow river on the north side and the Lenin Prospect on the south side, were a series of buildings destined for cultural events and political propaganda. The central axis of the Big Parterre continued into the main alley of the Neskuchny Garden. This name came from one of the two historical gardens in this part of Moscow that had been nationalized when the Bolsheviks seized power.

At one point, the Neskuchny Garden was one of Moscow's finest formal gardens. But, like the neighbouring Golitsyn Garden, it was severely modified in the 19th century. The natural groves were becoming dominant again. Gentle slopes, lakes, pavilions, and a grotto which, funnily enough, was called the Little Samovar, made Vlasov think of this area as a landscape garden. It was added to the Big Parterre to form the Central Park of Culture and Rest. To welcome the individual garden visitor or small, informal groups, as opposed to the masses assembling on the Parterre, winding paths were laid out and some more bowers were made.

In contrast to the first two segments of the Central Park of Culture and Rest, Lushniki sports facility was an entirely new creation. It was placed off the central axis, where the Moscow river bends and sort of returns back to the city. On this half-circle a huge sports complex was built, including an artificial lake.[12] And finally, a number of bridges connected Lushniki with the forestal Lenin Hills on the far side of the Moscow river. Promenades and skiing routes were the main attractions of this area, largely untouched by urban developers.[13]

In 1934 Vlasov insisted on the Central Park of Culture and Rest being "just as different from that of Coney Island as from that of Versailles."[14] Yet, in another place he argued that references to "the architecture of old Leningrad, with its green treasures: Pavlovsk, Peterhof and Detskoe Selo" were important as sources of inspiration, and all of these designs were offsprings of the western heritage.[15]

Many Soviet architects' understanding or interpretation of their projects in relation to the historical heritage was very ambiguous indeed. Contradictory arguments abound. The ambition to create something new and Soviet, though still with some connection to the Russian past but not to the Western universe, accounts for many of the contradictions. And the wish for something specifically Soviet happened to more and more exclude the invitation of foreign architects and gardeners to work alongside Russian specialists and workers, as practice had been in tsarist times.

Powerful Optics

Moscow's Central Park of Culture and Rest was a gigantic project. The contemporaries praised it greatly, and over the years it became a pattern for more than a thousand parks of culture and rest. In the first and so far the only general study of Soviet parks, published in 1940, the following was maintained:

On the basis of work on this park, a completely new socialist meaning was detected in landscape design.[16]

This was true with regards to how the park was being used:

Mass promenades and meetings, exhibitions of art and technique, various kinds of entertainment, amateur activities, mass sport, defence propaganda — all these activities, realized in truly natural surroundings, enrichen the feeling of rest among the visitors of the Soviet park.[17]

Yet, the aesthetical patterns of *in casu*, the Central Park of Culture and Rest, were essentially very traditional.

Just as the remains of the Neskuchny and the Golitsyn Gardens here were blended with some new developments, so practically all other Moscow parks of the Soviet period were placed where Russian

26. Moscow's Central Park of Culture and Rest, inaugurated in 1928 and for long called Gorki Park. Remains of 18th century gardens constituted the backbone of the Soviet design.

tsars and noblemen had previously gone hunting or enjoyed their pleasure residences and gardens. The dependance of Soviet landscape design on the Imperial heritage takes its beginning at this concrete level. But the Soviet architects also borrowed intensively from the tsarist past when landscaping new grounds and building new garden structures. The architectural vocabulary was indeed much indebted to 18th century Russian classicism, as even the toilets of the Central Park of Culture and Rest show.

The whole park was regarded as an element in a grandiose axial structure, the ultimate pattern of which was Louis XIV's route from the centre of Paris out to Versailles. In Stalin's program for Moscow, culminating in 1935 in the *General Plan for Moscow's Revival*, this axis was to depart from the People's Commissariat for Heavy Industry. This colossal building (never completed) was studded with political symbols and placed vis-à-vis the Lenin Mausoleum in the Red Square.[18] The Palace of Soviets (also never completed) was supposed to have been a second key monument on this optical line, before it continued through the Central Park of Culture and Rest up to the Lenin Hills.

One Russian precursor of this project should be called to mind. The place was St Petersburg, and the initiator was Peter the Great. "I never saw a more beautiful route", an English traveller reported, after having covered the route from St Petersburg to Peterhof.

I would have compared it to the road from Paris to Versailles, but no, this is better. Both sides of the road are adorned with big residences, shady forests, beautiful openings, gardens, and all this is designed in a remarkably elegant manner.[19]

The Peterhof Perspective, as this route was called, followed the coast. The Moscow project, however, was based on geometry and therefore closer to the French model, which indeed mirrored the pattern of political absolutism. This point ultimately confirms the relevance of looking into the similiarities between the garden program of the Stalin period and the gardens created by Russia's great 18th century rulers.

The Garden and the Gentry

Those books [Hirschfeld's *Theorie der Gartenkunst*] completely changed my views on gardens. (Bolotov, 1790s)

As ideas and concepts of the European Enlightenment became known and appreciated in Russia in the Catherine period, new philosophical and scientific traditions came into being. The Church was no longer the prime source of intellectual stimuli. St Petersburg and Moscow developed into centres of secular learning and distribution of knowledge. From several newly-founded printing houses an unprecedented number of books and magazines reached the élite.

Horticulture benefitted directly from this endeavour to enlighten the Russian readership. From 1780-89 a magazine entitled *Ekonomichesky Magazin* (The Economic Magazine) came out under the patronage of Nikolai Ivanovich Novikov, founder and head of Moscow University's printing house. Twice weekly, *Ekonomichesky Magazin* appeared as a supplement to the newspaper *Moskovskye Vedemosti* (Moscow News), gradually growing into a quite comprehensive opus which filled forty volumes, each some four hundred pages when bound.

The mind behind and main contributor to *Ekonomichesky Magazin* was Andrei Timofeevich Bolotov (1738-1833). In 1762 he had abandoned service in the Russian Imperial Army and returned to his family estate in the village of Dvoryaninovo, about one hundred and sixty kilometres southeast of Moscow. In so doing, he took advantage of an Imperial ukase issued that very year. The ukase freed the nobility and gentry from the obligation to serve the Court, as was otherwise stipulated in Peter's *Table of Ranks* of 1722. Bolotov's reaction to the ukase was sheer joy: "On that day I finished my fourteen years' military service and after my Abschied, I was forever a free man."[1] Many others also chose to retire and create a new life for themselves at the family estates they had left when summoned to the Imperial Court. Forestry and agriculture then became an important source of revenue. Apart from supplementing the household, gardens were very much appreciated for their recreational value.

In his horticultural writings, consulting and other informative activities, Bolotov addressed himself to his peers, that is, foremost the Russian gentry. The many new garden amateurs in this class could rarely afford to hire professionals, and Bolotov's advice was therefore very much in demand. With this in mind he repeatedly took care to underline the moderate size of the gardens belonging to his readers, and various economic considerations influenced his recommendations of specific designs, plants and methods.[2] In addition to Bolotov's own work at Dvoryaninovo, enabled by the said ukase, his continuous readings of Russian and foreign materials, and his plant experiments (which included cross-fertilization) all came together in his wide-

27. *Bogoroditske. Statue of A.T. Bolotov (1738-1833), one of Russia's most prolific garden writers and planners ever.*

ranging and energetic propagation of the latest discoveries in horticulture and garden aesthetics.

The subject of Bolotov's early writings (many of which were
published in the magazine *Trudy Volnogo Ekonomicheskogo Obshestva*
(Works of the Free Economic Society) and in *Selsky Zhitel* (The
Countryman), the precursor to *Ekonomichesky Magazin*) was practical
advice, explaining at length how, for example, to plant or graft apple
trees or currant bushes. He continued to write about such questions.
The same holds true of other garden writers of the Catherine period,
such as Nikolai Osipov and Vasily Levshin, who both published
comprehensive dictionaries and handbooks in the early 1790s. But
gradually Bolotov also turned to gardens that "are not only
utilitarian, but also for pleasure, and that could bring the owner
space and some kind of regeneration in the summer time."[3] This is
how he formulated his program of publications in 1782.

The scale and span of Bolotov's writings and his editorial work
in the horticultural field remain unsurpassed in a Russian context.
The first guide to Russian botany is due to him, as is a study of some
six hundred and sixty types of apple and pear, filling eight volumes
with text and another three volumes with watercoloured depictions.[4]
Significantly enough, both works were based on Bolotov's own
experimental work. For *Ekonomichesky Magazin* Bolotov wrote or
translated no less than 4,000 articles and notes. Apart from articles on
theoretical and practical gardening, he also squeezed in small notes
and reflections on a wide range of other matters. Suffice to mention
a discussion of fruit preservation, an essay on porcelain, the planet
Venus, dental diseases, extermination of cockroaches, breastfeeding
and recipes for making champagne out of birch trees. The spirit of
the Enlightenment literally pervaded this magazine.

Bolotov also wrote his memoirs, *Zhizn i priklyucheniya* (Life and
Adventures). They contain much information on the life style of the
gentry in the Catherine period, and confirm to what extent Bolotov
remained dedicated to the study of horticulture, agriculture and
forestry.

Initial Field Exercises

Having left St Petersburg before the English garden fashion was
introduced, Bolotov was not immediately in the position to bring
about the changes in the gardens of the Russian province which his
name is generally associated with, and which gave him the
reputation as creator of the Russian landscape garden.[5] At Dvorya-

*28. View dated 1786 from the Bogoroditske garden. Bolotov introduced the
landscape garden to the Russian province.*

ninovo, things looked very different from how they did in the two
capitals, where the provincial garden tradition by and large still
belonged to the old, pre-Petrine world order.

However, when Bolotov ventured to embellish the grounds and
the buildings at Dvoryaninovo, he did introduce several new
elements. One of his first ideas was to create a pattern of long,
straight alleys lined with forest trees. Yet fruit trees and fruit bushes
were planted between them, and the effect came quite close to that
known from the bosquets in early 18th century gardens. The alleys
led "to some dignified monument and place which deserves to be
contemplated", as Bolotov later said in one of his essays on the
Dvoryaninovo project.[6] Small pavilions, gates, ponds or glades also
served as motifs at the end of the optic axes. Some of the groves were
intersected by narrow paths, yet here Bolotov did not strive to "attain
too much symmetry".[7] Partly aesthetic, partly economic considerations confined the layout of a small parterre to the area in the
immediate vicinity of the house.[8]

Eventually, an important part of the garden at Dvoryaninovo
was redesigned in the English landscape tradition. But despite
continuous modifications, this is not the garden with which Bolotov's

29. *Bogoroditske. From the palace, now a museum, one may again enjoy the view of the landscaped grounds and the town.*

name is initially connected. The garden he created at Bogoroditske in the mid 1780s provides the clue.

With a certain status achieved through his publishing activities, Bolotov occupied a position as inspector of a number of *volosty* (administrative units in the language of tsarist Russia) from 1773 up to the accession of Catherine the Great in 1796. In this capacity, Bolotov was to design a number of gardens, similar to his own at Dvorya-ninovo. This position secured Bolotov a fixed income which, to judge from his own comments, he very much needed to support his large family.

Among Bolotov's responsibilities were the Bogoroditske and Bobrikovsky *volosty*, not far from Tula, famous for its metal resources and gun production. Both *volosty* belonged to Catherine and were destined for her son with Prince Orlov, Aleksey Grigorevich Bobrin-sky (1762-1813). For Bogoroditske, the famed St Petersburg architect Ivan Yegorovich Starov (1743-1808) had designed a palace in the neo-classical style (1771-76). But as was often the case with prominent artists commissioned to design buildings or art works outside St Petersburg, Starov actually never visited this provincial city.

In 1763 Catherine issued two ukases on the development of

30. *Bogoroditske. The now disappeared Echo Pavilion is among the garden monuments and follies painted by Bolotov in 1786.*

specific plans for urban structures and streets, and on the construction of public buildings in stone. In order to bring this program into effect, Bogoroditske was to be laid out anew, that is, according to the formal pattern which the Imperial Building Commission had designated. More than 300 Russian cities had their plans changed in the mid-1770s. Bogoroditske was split up into a geometric pattern, the centre line of which runs across the Big Pond right into the Big Oval Hall of the Starov palace. This design has recently been ascribed to Bolotov, and not Starov.[9] Bolotov may actually, through this example, have also influenced the schemes soon to be employed in other cities of the Tula region.

The forested grounds which surrounded Starov's palace and the little, trapezoid formal palace garden had fascinated Bolotov from the first time he visited Bogoroditske. But he very much regretted that people were indiscriminately cutting the birch and oak trees for firewood, and that cattle ate the remaining twigs. Bolotov thought this place deserved better, not least because of the impressive view from the palace hill across the lake to the town itself, but because he wanted to offer the future residents of the palace and their guests, in particular and not least noteworthy, the citizens of Bogoroditske, some interesting promenades and views. Picnics were also thought of, as is evident from Bolotov's essay "Practical Remarks about the

Transformation of Common Natural Groves into Pleasure Groves",
published in *Ekonomichesky Magazin* in 1784.[10]

Time and manpower were basically what was needed to
transform this tract of land into the Grove of Ceres, so Bolotov said.[11]
He focused on creating an interplay between the existing trees and
some new glades and ponds, as well as on trimming trees to open up
views over the natural slopes and the pond below the palace hill.
Besides this, the choice of Ceres, the Roman goddess of fertility, was
very popular among garden amateurs of the time. An obelisk was
erected when the grove was completed (1783), and some of the
glades were provided with small bowers or monuments.

Bolotov was subsequently commissioned to create a pleasure
garden of considerable size in immediate connection with the Bogoroditske Palace. His working conditions were unique. He was in a position to create a garden of his own choice because Count Bobrinsky,
for whom it all was intended, did not take up residence until after
Pavel had become Emperor, and the officials with whom Bolotov
dealt, only put forward their viewpoints when questions concerning
the planting of fruit trees and the emplacement of the orangeries
arose. Aesthetics remained Bolotov's domain.

In Russian and Soviet garden studies, few attempts have been
made to publish original plans along with the lengthy descriptions
of the historical gardens' architectural features. The studies on Bogoroditske are no exception. When writing about the new pleasure
garden at Bogoroditske, Bolotov concentrated on what was truly
novel in 18th century Russian provincial pleasure gardens, notably
his adoption of the aesthetics of the landscape garden. Due to this
focus, it has seldom been made sufficiently clear to what extent this
ensemble remained rooted in the formal tradition. That Andrei
Bolotov and his son, Pavel, did not depict the old-fashioned parts of
the garden in their many watercolours from the Bogoroditske garden,
has only supported the traditional approach to this question.

Yet three pieces of evidence remain which demand a different
approach. Firstly, Bolotov's original plan (c. 1784; part of the
collection of the Bogoroditske Palace Museum, housed in Starov's
palace building) shows an ensemble wherein various historical
patterns are combined. Secondly, Starov also made a plan (c. 1785;
kept at the Museum of Architecture in St Petersburg) demonstrating
the same. Thirdly, though the garden has been left to itself for decades, a promenade on the present grounds confirms much of what
can be deduced from these two plans. From the south, a long straight
alley showed the way through the old bell tower (early 18th century)
to the courtyard and the palace. This axis continued with a

monumental staircase and terraces leading from the Big Oval Hall down the palace hill. The geometrical layout of the city centre was the optical continuation of this line. The effect was that of monumentality and classical severity.

Big parterres and bosquets divided by gravel paths were created southeast of the palace. During the garden's development, Bolotov lived at Bogoroditske where he had a house and garden of his own, which apparently held the same features, though of course on a much smaller scale. In the grounds below the formal palace garden, facing the artificial island in the Big Pond, but still quite far from the Grove of Ceres, Bolotov was to conduct his first serious experiments in the landscape genre. This work took place from 1784 to 1786.

Bolotov's Vision of Nature

Some of Bolotov's articles which were published in *Ekonomichesky Magazin* prior to his design of the landscape garden at Bogoroditske, include sporadic comments on the charms of proposing different layouts in one and the same garden. Bolotov also compared the traditional and the modern way of designing gardens, that is the garden architect's approach versus the landscape artist's fascination with nature's own forms.[12] But it was a visit to Moscow in 1784 which made Bolotov discover, on a solid theoretical basis, the aesthetics of *"beautiful and natural gardens."*[13] In Moscow he bought the first volumes of C.C.L. Hirschfeld's *Theorie der Gartenkunst* (1779-85). Knowing German from his early military career when he had been posted to Königsberg, Bolotov was able to read this comprehensive work.

In the last issue of *Ekonomichesky Magazin* of 1784, Bolotov then published an essay entitled "Something about Gardens of the Modern Taste". It starts:

As many will know, the so-called English gardens are the most fashionable nowadays, and in Europe not only new gardens are laid out in this manner, also old gardens of the formal type are being modified, and such informal gardens are also becoming common here [in Russia]. But to avoid the defects the learned have discovered in Germany, I think it is a good idea to include a short and completely new, foreign text which tells about the essence of the new English gardens in Germany, and explains how such gardens should be made? From this it is possible to draw some conclusions with regard to our own gardens.[14]

31. *From Bolotov's album with watercolours from Bogoroditske. View of some of the garden pavilions, the old bell tower and the palace (above). The Grove of Ceres, with the obelisk commemorating the foundation of the garden (below).*

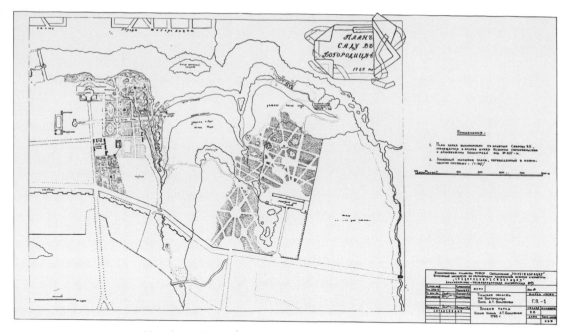

32. *Plan of Bogoroditske, 1785. Provincial estates typically incorporated several aesthetical garden patterns.*

Curiously enough, Bolotov did not mention his German source by name until two years later.[15] But the programmatic paragraph quoted above was immediately followed by translations and summaries of Hirschfeld's work in *Ekonomichesky Magazin*. Within two years, Bolotov created a landscape at Bogoroditske which was heavily indebted to the German armchair writer's interpretation of the English way of revealing nature and embellishing it. Parallel to his practical design work at Bogoroditske, Bolotov described his methods in writing. His articles form a counterbalance to the many largely theoretical contributions of foreign origin published in *Ekonomichesky Magazin*, especially from 1786 onwards.

Borrowing some of his terms from Hirschfeld, who of course again derived them from various English, French and German sources, Bolotov asserted that one of his ambitions was to create a series of beautiful and interesting garden *scenes* or *pictures*. The scenes were supposed to offer some attractive visual stimuli during the unrestrained garden promenade. Emphasis was on pleasure, not on any intricate patterns for which the reading would depend on the garden viewer's knowledge of ancient art, mythology and philosophy. The Bogoroditske garden was provided with a few buildings and monuments, such as a pyramid, a rotunda and a grotto. But the abundance of monuments and the connotative play which had been staged at Tsarskoe Selo for example, along with its weak imitation of the intellectualism of English gardens, was almost absent from Bogoroditske. The first reason for this is that Bolotov was always against high expenditures. Secondly, he preferred to use and play with the elements of nature. This allowed Bolotov to play an active part himself, as he had at Dvoryaninovo. Thirdly, no one in Bogoroditske was likely to have as high a level of education as the St Petersburg élite.

One of the tasks Bolotov set himself was "to assist Nature and to create waters with the help of art, where necessary".[16] He made way for a series of cascades and some small ponds in the narrow and rather steep gorge which lay just behind the formal garden, though closer to the palace than the Grove of Ceres. To give the cascades an appropriate background, it was necessary to find a mound of big stones, and out of these create a kind of stone hill with gaps and other irregularities. The profile and planting of every single bank was carefully considered. A number of banks were covered with meadow flowers, others were laid out as stone mounds with trees and bushes hanging over and reflecting in the water.[17]

To enhance the garden visitor's desire to move from one scene to another, Bolotov insisted on using motifs and effects that conveyed quite contrary impressions. From a densely planted grove where a black pyramid had been placed with an inscription to confer a melancholic mood, the garden path led on to a joyful scene. On a grassy hill stood a white, circular pavilion. This motif, which ultimately stems from the Temple of the Sibyl in Tivoli outside Rome, favoured so much by the landscape painters of both the 17th and 18th centuries, was extremely popular in the landscape gardens, whether English or Continental. Yet, in Bolotov's version it did not have any specific literary or mythological name. One of the illustrations accompanying Hirschfeld's text is likely to have served as a model for Bolotov. In his memoirs, Bolotov proudly states that dignitaries, including some from abroad, who had come to Bogoroditske to see its famous garden, singled this corner out for particular praise.

A strong desire for evocative, visual effects incited Bolotov to include painted views in the garden. On a hill above the flow of small cataracts and ponds, he painted architectural scenes on its rocky wall. His motifs were an old monastery and a ruin tower. But the fragility of such designs means that Bolotov's essay on prospective views is now the only source on this garden element.[18]

In another place was a scene, the main attraction of which was a huge stone block with multi-coloured veins, formed so by nature. Corridors, windows and doors were carved out in order to enable the garden visitors to study this extraordinary spectacle at close hand. The underground grotto was another fundamental surprise element in the Bogoroditske garden, and Bolotov dedicated an entire essay to it in *Ekonomichesky Magazin*.[19] Again much is due to Hirschfeld's work, but on certain points Bolotov acted independantly. He took particular delight in the use of mirrors and gleaming, multi-coloured stones to give the grotto a luxurious interior.

Though Bolotov claimed that he, to a very large extent, worked spontaneously and without the use of detailed plans, he is supposed to have made an album with sketches of how he wanted the Bogoroditske landscape to look. However, the whereabouts of Bolotov's album are still to be discovered.[20] The same holds true of the two drawings Bolotov sent to Catherine in the autumn of 1784, one showing a general view of the garden and the other the painted garden ruins.[21] Still existing, however, is the album Bolotov made with his son Pavel in 1786 upon completion of the garden. This currently belongs to the Museum of History in Moscow.[22] Together with a number of pencil drawings in the album, nearly forty water-colours form one of the most precious sources on Bogoroditske, one of the most elaborate pleasure gardens in the Russian province of the 18th century.

A National Appeal

While the general design and some architectural pieces of the Bogoroditske garden were indebted to foreign inspiration, the planting was based on local resources. The neighbouring woods provided what was needed at this point. Bolotov later concluded that such "old forest trees and groves once taught me how to lay out a garden."[23] Birch, oak and linden blended with aspen, maple, ash, willow and birdcherry trees. Birch was chosen for the imposing alley.[24]

Financial considerations may, at least to some degree, have influenced Bolotov's choice of local trees and plants. But in the case of planting, Bolotov, the great horticulturist, was eager to propagate a specifically national attitude. He found the Russian flora "particularly beautiful", as opposed to American or overseas trees "that the English use in their gardens".[25] Only in one early case did Bolotov try to accommodate those of the readers of *Ekonomichesky Magazin* who preferred to include "some foreign trees".[26] But the Bogoroditske garden and Bolotov's late, basically theoretical contributions to his

33. *Bogoroditske. Decades of abandonment and the luxuriant foliage of the Russian summer make today's visitor feel like an explorer.*

magazine show how beautifully varied landscape scenes could be created with the informed use of only a few types of tree. Besides, Hirschfeld had discussed this question at length. Much depended on the composition of the tree groups, the height of the trees, the shape of their leaves and their different green hues.[27]

The Russian or national motif appears again in a similarly programmatic form in a series of essays in *Ekonomichesky Magazin* in 1786. The most significant essay is entitled "Some Remarks about Gardens in Russia."[28] By way of introduction, Bolotov writes about Russia's old gardens and very much regrets that they are totally unknown elsewhere.[29] The modern gardens, on the other hand, have little to do with Russia's cultural heritage. They depend heavily on French and English traditions, he says. And foreigners, so Bolotov continues, are practically dominating the Russian garden scene. This calls for a serious attempt to

...create gardens of our own taste, and such that would correspond more closely to the main features of our moral character ... it would be disgraceful if we had English or French gardens, and not such that we had invented ourselves, and which we would therefore call Russian.[30]

This is Bolotov's conclusion, after having allowed Hirschfeld and several other foreign garden writers to thoroughly expound their aesthetic theories in front of the Russian readers.

Out of Bolotov's enormous production, these few lines have been quoted time and again in Russian and Soviet garden studies. I would even argue that, in some cases, Bolotov's argument has been understood as a convenient answer to one of the major concerns of Soviet historiography, namely the search for the supposedly national content of any form of art. Yet within the context of his own time, Bolotov was neither more nor less nationalistic than his Western colleagues, including Hirschfeld. A blend of national and international visions, or to employ the term preferred in the age of Enlightenment, a *cosmopolitan* system of references, was indeed a very typical 18th century approach. Hirschfeld as well as Bolotov basically favoured a blend of styles, usually French and English, though more of the latter than the former. Both typically characterized this solution as national, that is German and Russian respectively. This point justifies a more balanced reading of *Ekonomichesky Magazin* than that which focuses on the Russian aspect to the detriment of the basically enlightened or cosmopolitan spirit of Bolotov's work.

What *The Spectator* had meant for the formation of British garden amateurs' taste in the early 18th century, *Ekonomichesky Magazin* also came to signify to its Russian readership. Many concepts and recommendations were rooted in the British landscape tradition, but, as pointed out above, Bolotov's fascination with Hirschfeld and his publishing of hundreds of pages from *Theorie der Gartenkunst*, testify to Germany's role as a filter and mediator. Several of the garden motifs described or designed by Bolotov and like-minded professionals and amateurs, may in fact have been taken over from Hirschfeld, Grohmann and Mansa, among others. Yet for all Bolotov's dependance on Western idols and theories, his reputation as a great Russian garden publicist and artist is never likely to be threatened.

STYLES AND SEMANTICS

...every corner...bore witness to her [Grand Duchess
Maria Feodorovna's] taste, her preferences, and her
memories from travels abroad: There was the
Rose Pavilion, similar to the Trianon; there were
chalets like those seen in Switzerland; a mill and
some stables modelled after similar structures
in Tyrol, and gardens and terraces like Italian ones.
The theatre and the distant views correspond
to those at Fontainebleau, and artificial ruins had
been built in various places. (N.A. Sablukov, 1869)

In accordance with the main Western trend of the time, Russian
palace and country house architecture of the late 18th century was
rooted in the neoclassical tradition. So were the majority of the
garden buildings. A range of so-called exotic patterns also formed a
major source of inspiration to the leading garden designers of the
Catherine period. The assimilation of foreign patterns, including
Chinese, Turkish and Egyptian motifs, took place in close dependance upon the lessons propagated by the Western supporters of the
landscape garden. Thus, part of the philosophical and iconographical
apparatus contained in the *tableaux* of the Western gardens was also
adopted and transferred to Russian soil.

The following discussion of garden semantics focuses on the
buildings, big as well as small, and the monuments that form an
integral part of the garden scenery. The interplay between landscape
and architecture that was touched upon in connection with the
patrons and their choice of aesthetics, on the other hand, will
practically be left out of consideration. Examples of borrowings from
foreign sources are presented, partly in order to illustrate some of the
most characteristic features of the garden syntax and semantics, and
partly to bring more evidence as to the intense dialogue between the
West and Russia under Catherine. Even the cultivation of national
building styles, which in particular came to mark a number of gardens in the Moscow region and out in the province, was affiliated
with modern Western practice. The use of elements of 17th century
Moscow architecture eventually evolved into a many-stringed
adoption of medieval forms from various foreign sources.

34. *Muranovo near Moscow. Many of Russia's old gardens still allow for nature, history and poetry to blend profusely.*

In Russia, literature was the key eye-opener as to how to approach and understand the imagery and allusiveness of 18th century gardens. A series of foreign garden writings and poetical works became well-known among members of the Imperial Court, the nobility and the gentry as well. Jacques Delille's *Les Jardins, ou l'Art d'Embellir les Paysages*, a lengthy didactic poem, was particularly popular. Extracts from this work are juxtaposed with garden scenes and monuments in order to further characterize the classically inspired universe. Examples are mainly taken from noblemen's gardens in the Moscow region.

In the subsequent discussion of the antique-inspired language of the Scotsman Charles Cameron, focus then moves back to the Imperial pleasure grounds near St Petersburg. Cameron worked for Catherine at Tsarskoe Selo and for her son and daughter-in-law, Grand Duke Pavel and Grand Duchess Maria Feodorovna, at nearby Pavlovsk. When staging the numerous temples, pavilions and ruins in the landscape garden at Pavlovsk, Cameron used his Roman experience as a primary source. The analysis of this imagery includes comments on the Russian adoption of Arcadia, the pastorale and a few more basically antique concepts.

Next to Delille's poem, William Chambers' writings on Oriental gardening offered a very popular source of inspiration and understanding. His *Designs of Chinese Buildings, Furniture, Dresses, Machines, and Utensils. To which is annexed, a Description of their Temples, Houses, Gardens, &c.* will be used as a key to the more exotic cavalcades of Russian 18th century gardens. Apart from discussing various Chinese-inspired garden scenes, this chapter also proposes to go into some of the motifs originating in the fashion for the Islamic World and for Egypt. How exoticism was treated in contemporary Russian garden writings is also mapped out.

The so-called *gothic* trend represents yet another aspect of 18th century Russian as well as Western garden iconography. This matter is analyzed in the context of the national ideologies, historicisms and medieval allusions, the use and popularity of which increased most significantly in the gardens of Moscow and St Petersburg towards the very end of the 18th century. The discussion of the oeuvre of a single artist shall again be proposed. As a counterpoint to Cameron, the work of Italian-trained, but Russian-born Vasily Ivanovich Bazhenov is thus to be dealt with, prime motifs being freemasonry, chivalry and martial architecture. Besides, Bazhenov's plans for a palace outside Moscow, commissioned by Catherine and named Tsaritsyno, may also help to draw more attention to the life and work of this architect.

From Paradise to Mount Parnassus

> Thus fountains, marble, all that pomp supplies,
> Art's splendid ornaments fatigue the eyes;
> But landscape breathing gratitude and joy,
> Nature's unfeigned perfections never cloy.
> Still in your gardens then her charms prefer,
> Your model choose from Him who cannot err.
> (Delille, 1782)

Paradise is probably the metaphor to be encountered more often than any other in the language of garden poets, architects and patrons. Where and whenever gardens were created, terms designating an ideal world have been in regular use. This tradition also has a long history in Russia. The chronicles show that the gardens of medieval times inspired Biblical allusions, whether they were made to the orders of the Church or the tsar.[1] Long after garden art had become a purely secular affair, a similar vocabulary continued to be used.

To the members of the late 18th century nobility and gentry, the garden was a privileged and rather intimate place. It was a world apart, and precisely this seemed to justify the use of the words *Paradise* or *Eden*. Many of the names given to the new pleasure grounds or country estates included such metaphors: *Raek* or *Otrada*, meaning Little Paradise and From Paradise respectively; *Priyutino* or *Pribezhishche*, meaning Asylum and Place of Refuge respectively, and so forth. One poet compared the garden to a fragment of Eden transmitted through the ages.

The classical opposition between life in the city and life in the country occurs time and again in the letters and memoirs in the Catherine period. One nobleman thus asked:

In what city can we spend our time in such a simple and happy way? The theatre of nature is the best place for any kind of celebration of friendship.[2]

Near some country houses so-called ideal villages were created for a number of peasants to live in and to assist their master when guests were coming. But misunderstandings and conflicts frequently arose between the local peasant population and the gentlemen. There was an immense gap between the reality of serf life and the gentlemens' craving for idylls.[3]

"I live exactly like in Paradise", says a letter written at Sukhanovo, some twenty-five kilometres south of Moscow, by another member of society's high ranks. It continues:

35. *Pavlovsk. 18th century painters and poets looked upon this landscape garden as a recreation of Arcadia.*

I am not busy going anywhere, I do not have any duties, I do what I like, all day I am occupied with various things concerning the house and the garden, I am making a road in the park, I write instructions for the administrator.[4]

Time and space ceased to be fixed categories. And the motifs, in particular some of the architectural structures adorning the landscape garden, allowed for a mental journey into antique Arcadia.

Delille's Gardens

It was Virgil who in his *Eclogues* invented the idea of Arcadia. Since Antiquity this easeful life of the shepherds had become synonymous with felicity and social perfection. Allusions to this happy state of existence occur in various forms in the Russian landscape gardens, either in individual motifs such as a Shepherd's Grotto or in the naming of an entire garden such as Arcadia. The creation of such classic allusions in the botanical and architectural developments of the gardens was successively followed up by a pastoral trend in

Russian poetry. Nikolai Karamzin and other poets carefully studied the works of their European contemporaries, and the same foreign works appeared in the libraries belonging to the learned garden patrons.

Jacques Delille's *Les Jardins, ou l'Art d'Embellir les Paysages. Poème* (1782) was particularly well known and appreciated. Though many of Delille's readers knew French, this didactic poem was published in Russian in 1814, and again in 1816. Delille also had a poem in the pastoral genre published in Russian in 1804.[5] His popularity never ceased, and even some Soviet handbooks on horticulture include quotations from him.

In the first song in *Les Jardins,...* the painter-poet announces his program:

> I sing how Art the imperfect landscape aids,
> Directs the flowers, the waters, lawns, and shades.[6]

Delille basically aims at a universal portrayal of the elements of garden art, but it is clear from the outset that his ideals are strongly rooted in English landscape art: "...Kent bids Nature wear a smiling mien".[7]

> But ere you plant, ere your adventurous spade
> In the maternal soil a wound has made,
> To form your gardens with unerring taste,
> Observe how Nature's choicest works are traced.
> ...
> From the most striking be your models drawn,
> And learn of landscape, landscape to adorn.[8]

References to specific gardens, palaces and country houses occur frequently in Delille's eulogy of the landscapes of his own time.[9] On the outskirts of Paris, he found a garden corresponding perfectly to his ideals: The Moulin Joli.[10] The same ideals as those of the owner and creator of this garden, Claude-Henri Watelet, a nobleman, art connoisseur, traveller, amateur artist and the author of a popular book on garden aesthetics, *Essai sur les Jardins* (1774). Besides, also Watelet's treatise was well-known in Russia.

But then, Delille dwelt on garden semantics to a much higher degree than any Russian garden writer of the period. If he had ever visited a place like Sukhanovo, he would have likely become as enthusiastic about this landscape as he was about Moulin-Joli. A promenade through the Sukhanovo garden, with *Les Jardins,...* as a fictious guidebook fully confirms this.

36. Sukhanovo near Moscow. The cult of the antique made white rotundas very popular in 18th century Russian garden scenes.

Allusions to Arcadia

The Moscow senator Aleksei Petrovich Melgunov, known for his interest in archaeology and science, had bought Sukhanovo in 1769. In the 1780s he set about to renovate the site in accordance with contemporary aesthetics. Concurrently, dozens of other summer residences situated mainly south or east of Moscow were being rebuilt and new gardens were being developed.

At Sukhanovo, no major attempt was made to change the profile or the character of the forestry grounds. Natural hills, gorges, and plenty of water remained principal characteristics. The garden was laid out on the grass-covered, rather steep hill which ends at the pond soon to be renamed the Pond of Dreams. Practically all trees were felled in a broad belt to open the magnificent view from the classically styled main building[11] across the water to the opposite embankment with its clumps of birch and fir trees. On both sides of the broad grassy belt, the natural woods were partly thinned out, partly enriched with new plantations, and straight alleys alternating with winding paths were formed.

> Happy the man possessed of ancient groves,
> Happier who plants his trees, while Time improves,
> And forms their beauties to reward his care;
> He like great Cyrus cries, "I placed them there".[12]

So Delille said, considering the tree the most beautiful element of the garden.

At Sukhanovo, old and new trees intermingled, and a certain picturesque approach is evident.

> Endeavour then judiciously to use
> These numerous greens of ever varying hues.[13]

And the waters were no less varied and beautiful.

> And ye streams, rivers, lakes, and fountains, thence
> New life, new freshness every where dispense.[14]

As for the paths, Delille recommends:

> Ill can their lines in infant plans be traced,
> In finished grounds the eye selects with taste.
> When through improvements you conduct a friend,
> You mark what pleases, shun what may offend,
> ... [15]

The paths served two functions. They made the landscape more accessible and they helped to accentuate the sporadic pieces of architecture which alluded to the world of antiquity.

A white rotunda in the Doric order was partly hidden in the dense greenery. Built sometime in the 1780s by an unknown architect, the temple lacks the grandeur of, for instance, Cameron's neoclassical structures; however, it is still a fine antique-inspired building. It was called the Temple of Venus, although the statue below the cupola was not Venus but the Roman goddess of spring, said to be looking after Venus' gardens. This statue works together with the bas-reliefs on the entablement, which depict various scenes of rural work, giving the temple an overall horticultural theme. The cultivated garden visitor of the Catherine period is likely to have reflected on the *locus amoenus* tradition, and possibly also on Alcinous' garden, as described by Homer. Both sources formed part of the material often employed in the British and Continental landscape gardens.

Delille would have praised this garden building. He was of the opinion that garden buildings should be applied with great care.

> Ye graceful forms of Architecture, hail!
> ...
> With judgement vary; be not too profuse;
> Employ these treasures, but without abuse.
> Far from our gardens that unmeaning crowd,
> In modern scenes by prejudice allowed,
> Those temples Roman, Arab, Greek, Chinese,
> Absurdly raised in every clump of trees;
> Where without aim or choice a chaos reigns,
> And on disfigured spot the globe contains.[16]

At Sukhanovo, there was practically no violation of the stylistic similarity between the main building and the other structures. Only the kitchens followed a medieval pattern, not unlike that of the Admiralty at Tsarskoe Selo. When some more garden structures were created in the 1810s and 1820s with one of Melgunov's daughters as the new originator of projects, they were all marked by the same restrained use of forms and emblems. Therefore the wooden Temple of Solitude, placed near the lake, was also in the Doric order. Classical architecture, including that in which the French landscape painters of the 17th century had indulged, contained all that was needed in terms of form and content to match the idea of the idyllic garden landscape.

Delille followed the early British protagonists of this genre in referring to the work of Poussin.

> He paints the shepherds, and the village maids
> Dancing at festivals beneath the shades,
> And near a tomb, where rudely graved, remain
> These words, "I too was an Arcadian swain."
> This trace of fleeting pleasures seems to say,
> "Mortals, enjoy, be happy while you may;
> Dance, mirth, and shepherds soon will fade away."
> ...
> Give these effects, nor in your pictures fear
> To let a sacred urn or tomb appear,
> A faithful monument your grief reveal:
> Who is not doomed some cruel loss to feel?[17]

The inclusion of tombs and urns allowed for more allusions to the ancient world, and equally important, such motifs also furthered the sentimentality so important to the spirit of the age.[18]

In Virgil's interpretation of the Arcadian universe, the stress placed on the idyllistic shepherd life by a harsher world was continuously felt, with even death breaking into Arcadia. In Nicolas Poussin's famous painting "The Arcadian Shepherds" (c. 1650), referred to by Delille, the inscription "Et in Arcadia Ego" reminds the beholder of this ever lurking menace. Several 18th century gardens, the most famous of which was Shenstone's Leasowes, featured exactly this motif. Other examples are the French Bois de la Garenne and the Polish Arcadia, near the palace-cum-garden at Nieborów. In Russia, however, the cult of death in a garden setting took on another character, and specific references to "Et in Arcadia Ego" apparently do not occur.

Memorials to late friends, lovers, heroes, poets and even the beloved dogs do occur, yet these scenes lagged far behind British and especially Continental fashion's popularity.[19] The death of close relatives even less frequently motivated garden monuments — for 18th century Europe as well as for Russia. One of the Russian garden patrons to move in the opposite direction was Grand Duchess Maria Feodorovna. The landscape garden at Pavlovsk came to have several sepulchral monuments dedicated to Maria Feodorovna's closest relatives. And the erection of a mausoleum to Prince Dimitry Petrovich Volkhonsky makes the Sukhanovo garden stand out among the contemporary gardens, though for some slightly different reasons.

Yekatarina Alekseevna Melgunova, who inherited Sukhanovo from her father, made her mark on the garden during her many years here; she died in 1853. The mausoleum (1813) was built in memory of her late husband. It was placed in a remote part of the garden, near the edge of a gorge which further dramatized this garden motif. As with the Temple of Venus, a number of attributions have been suggested.[20] It was an ensemble of a considerable size, and it testified to the architect's clear feeling of how to adopt the classical vocabulary to a suite of spaces, the most important of which was the central rotunda with a slightly protruding Doric portico. The proportions of the portico in relation to the building height correspond to the Golden Section so that the spirit of the Roman Pantheon somehow mingles with that of some of Bernini's church buildings.

The ashes of the late prince were transferred to the mausoleum in 1814, and a church room with the traditional Russian-Orthodox appointments was created in the rotunda. The structure was thus turned into a place of religious worship, completely overruling the intellectual play with Arcadian allusions that had originally motivated the creation of garden pavilions at Sukhanovo.

37. *The Mausoleum at Sukhanovo. In Russia, tombs and memorials only occasionally occurred in the sentimental garden scenarios.*

Russian Rotundas

In an early poem with the expressive title *Épitre sur les Voyages* (1765), Delille declared:

> Travel, You Friend, this is the empire ruling over us.
> It is by this means that we breathe the air of the entire world.[21]

A considerable part of Russia's leading social and cultural circles adopted this philosophy. Travel came into fashion, and Russian gentlemen increasingly showed a preference for having European pictures in their collections. "It looks as if all Europe had been sacked to create museum stores in Moscow...", one European visitor to Moscow noted.[22] In gardening, a similar phenomenon was evident.

Europe not only furnished some general aesthetical patterns for the planning of gardens, but it also played a fundamental role as an iconographical point of reference. Maria Feodorovna remains unique in her conglomeration at Pavlovsk of garden motifs commemorating the European cosmos she had been raised in and which she experienced on her Grand Tour with Pavel. But less could suffice the journey into the unspoiled sphere of nature and art as united in the noblemen's landscape gardens.

Count Nikolai Petrovich Sheremetev (1751-1809) was very much concerned with demonstrating his fine tastes when he created the theatre palace and garden at Ostankino, twelve kilometres north of the Moscow Kremlin:

> When I embellished my village Ostankino and presented it to the viewers in an enchanted form, I thought that, by realizing something great, a real surprise and a thing that would delight the visitors and show off my knowledge and taste, I could forever enjoy the calm that my work has resulted in.[23]

The idea was to have an ensemble that could accommodate larger and more complicated theatrical performances than Kuskovo ever could. Like Golitsyn's and Yusupov's Arkhangelskoe, Ostankino was conceived of as a refuge for the muses and for those who cultivated them.

A number of talented serf architects, including Pavel Argunov, Aleksei Mironov and Grigory Dikushev, designed an ensemble which was to be referred to as a fairy tale.[24] A picture gallery, called the Italian Hall, and a concert hall in neo-Egyptian style were important features, next to the theatre itself (1792-97).[25] The Ostankino garden was also laid out in view of Sheremetev's wish to entertain on a large

38. *Plan of Ostankino, 1793. As fashion prescribed, sinuous paths, a hill and a belvedere were added to the formal garden.*

scale. As opposed to Sukhanovo, this was a princely garden, just as the projects of the Sheremetev family had always been, and although fashion had changed, the parterre solution was also found suitable for Ostankino. Alleys and avenues divided the adjoining bosquets into geometrical segments, and mythological and allegorical sculptures were carefully distributed.

39. *Marfino, the Temple of Apollo (left). Tsaritsyno, the Temple of Ceres (right).*

The northernmost part of the Ostankino grounds, however, contained quite different motifs. This part was full of natural contrasts, including small hills, the little river Kamenka and several ponds. Given that Nikolai Petrovich Sheremetev in 1793 wanted his English gardener, "as he best could", to choose "a special place where I can go and be by myself, unnoticed by everybody", this area was ideal for individual promenades and rest.[26] Here, an Alley of Sighs, planted with lime trees, became a main feature. A garden plan by Mironov and another one by Argunov have survived, both of which include a number of interesting features, for example a small landscape garden next to the Egyptian Hall and a sinuous pattern of narrow paths around an open-air theatre at the Italian Hall. However, few of these elements actually ever left the drawing board. Yet attention should be paid to one particular motif, notably an artificial hill which, as Argunov proposed, was placed east of the palace. It was called the Parnassus. Today, no more than a hillock remains.

Artificial hills had been featured in a number of Russian gardens of the preceding decades. They may generally have been created for the dual purpose of presenting a nice view and for offering enjoyable

40. *Tsarskoe Selo. The remains of the Parnassus are best seen during the long, cold winters.*

sledging. Interestingly enough, the Russian taste for this garden motif is mentioned by the Polish garden writer August Fryderyk Moszyński in his *Essay sur le jardinage anglais* (1774).[27] Elizabethan Tsarskoe Selo is a prominent example, and two absolutely charming variants, each with a fine serpentine walk, are seen in an anonymous watercolour (1830s) belonging to the Museum of History in Moscow. One later example is found in the garden of Leo Tolstoi's Moscow residence.

The Russian sources do not seem to mention celebrations or ceremonies in connection with such sceneries. Nor do they tell about any allegorical meaning. Such was otherwise common whenever rocky or earthen hills occurred in the gardens of European mannerism, so that a motif like the Pratolino Parnassus was probably created to celebrate the men who dedicated their lives to the pursuit of virtue by service to the Muses. Since the Ostankino hill was called the Parnassus, its original meaning perhaps came quite close to this. Moreover, Nikolai Petrovich Sheremetev's qualifications were of a nature to give sense to such an interpretation.

On top of the hill stood a white rotunda (c. 1795) of the type encountered in dozens of gardens of the time. Apparently, it did not

41. Hills allowing for nice views in an unknown garden of the Russian province. Anonymous watercolour.

relate to the Parnassus iconography, as a temple dedicated to the Muses or to Apollo would have done. It seems to have been called the Temple of the Beautiful View. Serf architects were at hand and although they — as seen in the case of Ostankino — demonstrated great talent, their iconographical knowledge was of course seldom comparable to that of the learned St Petersburg and Moscow professionals. What could have been a perfect celebration of Nikolai Petrovich Sheremetev's art patronage turned into a composite motif, with the hill alluding to one historical pattern loaded with meaning, and the temple simply offering a nice view.

Several architectural and iconographical dictionaries of Western origin were known in Russia in the Catherine period. One version of Ripa's work was translated, and Osipov and Lem mentioned allegorical sculptures in their books. But semantics was generally not a subject of particular interest to the Russian garden writers. Practical horticultural matters were accorded much more attention, and Bolotov, to name the most diligent garden writer of the period, never felt inspired to discuss any antique or other sources in length.

In one of his articles in *Ekonomichesky Magazin* on garden architecture he said:

...garden buildings, in particular, assure the gardens of the newest fashionable manner a great appearance, they primarily comprise pavilions formed like temples; out of these, the best are the circular ones with cupolas; such a building should be placed where a wealth of other motifs already bring life to the scenery and it will bring great beauty and an uncomparable view to various places.[28]

The article ends:

Practice has taught me that such buildings [pavilions formed like temples] are necessary in gardens to frame views, and especially to cut dull and unpleasant views.[29]

Not surprisingly, Pleasant View, Beautiful View and Magnificent View were names frequently given to such pavilions.

The Ostankino temple belongs to this group. Another group is formed by pavilions dedicated to the Graces, the Muses, Venus, Apollo, Ceres, Bacchus or other mythological figures. In the Moscow region, Ceres and Bacchus were particularly popular. Finally, structures that were placed in a remote corner of the garden would typically be named Temple of Rest, of Love, or of Friendship. The cases of Sukhanovo and Ostankino show that dedications, and with them the iconographical subject matter, were being cherished in a relatively relaxed manner. The unifying element was the more or less generalized antique form. This in itself may often have served as the main bearer of allusions to Arcadia.

Classical Quotations

...a home of one's own, a colonnade, a temple at Pavlovsk brings me more pleasure than all the beauties of Italy... (Maria Feodorovna, 1782)

Most of the foreign and Russian architects working for Catherine were great connoisseurs of the classical vocabulary, with the Italians' background particularly appreciated. The Russian Vasily Ivanovich Bazhenov commissioned to redo the Kremlin in Moscow and to design a new Imperial summer residence outside the old capital (notably at Tsaritsyno, 1775-85), had spent nearly a decade in Rome. Back in Russia, he translated the first two books of Vitruvius' voluminous work on architecture, thus creating the basis for the Russian understanding of the antique heritage. Following its first publication in 1785, Bazhenov translated the remaining books by

42. *Bogoroditske. Bolotov was eagerly propagating modern echoes of the so-called Temple of the Sibyl in Tivoli.*

Vitruvius from French. This work then came out in St Petersburg in 1790-97.

Books and manuals destined for the architectural students of St Petersburg's and Moscow's new academies or art schools were also indebted to the classical sources. Two such examples are *Kratkoe Rukovodstvo k grazhdanskoi Arkhitekture ili Zodchestvu* (Brief Guide to Civil Architecture or Building, 1789) and Ivan Lem's *Teoreticheskaya i prakticheskaya predlozheniya o grazhdanskoi arkhitekture* (Theoretical and Practical Comments on Civil Architecture, 1792-94). The lessons and works of Palladio, Serlio and other Renaissance architects were also made known through the same channels.

The attention accorded to Charles Cameron (1743-1812), the Scottish architect who worked in Russia for 30 years and was patronaged by the Imperial family, is another prominent example of the Russian homage to classical aesthetics. In London, in 1772, Cameron had published a treatise on Roman baths, *The Baths of the Romans, Explained and Illustrated, with the Restorations of Palladio Corrected and Improved*. To later generations of Russian, as well as to Soviet architects and planners, Cameron's buildings for Catherine the Great at Tsarskoe Selo and also for Grand Duchess Maria Feodorovna at nearby Pavlovsk, came to embody the native classical heritage.

In the same way that Rome's political past in many respects held the same tremendous power of fascination upon the Soviet leadership as it did upon the rulers of the Russian Empire, so Rome was very often referred to in the written essays accompanying the Soviet architects' anthology of historical layouts and forms. Whether completed or not, the large majority of the designs which the omnipotent state patron commissioned his favourite architects to create was indebted to the antique. Significantly enough, Vitruvius' work on architecture was republished along with the new *socialist-realist* manifestos. In a number of cases though, the Soviet exploration of the antique derived not so much from the old sources as from the careful studies which numerous archaeologists and artists of the Catherine period had undertaken of the Roman scene.

Cameron was frequently cited, occasionally even idolized, when the classical orders were once more given pride of place. The architects of the 1930s were in search of inspiration which could eventually inspire them to build a city not unlike their patrons' vision of the Third Rome. In conscious opposition to modernism, it was maintained that only the basic and traditional concepts in architecture were valid. Architecture was an Art and the classical orders were one of its foundations. In 1934 the doctrine of *socialist realism* was thus advanced in all artistic areas, including architecture, and it soon became the only line to enjoy official support.[1]

To provide the professional architects with the adequate historical and formal reference systems, *Arkhitektura SSSR* (The Architecture of the USSR), the official magazine of the Union of Architects (founded 1932), was regularly publishing articles on projects and works by the great neoclassical architects of the Catherine period. The articles appeared amidst theoretical writings on Soviet Utopia, descriptions of Moscow's new buildings and summaries of the Central Committee's decisions on urban matters. In 1935 an article on Cameron's treatise was published in *Arkhitektura SSSR*, where it said:

...although it was written more than a century ago, it is of equal significance...the translation and publication of C. Cameron's Roman Baths will enrichen Soviet architects with the most precious artistic material.[2]

Several years later, notably in 1939, the treatise was published in a Russian translation and so was the first monography on the Scottish-born neoclassicist.[3]

Cameron's Archaeological Approach

Cameron arrived in Russia by the end of 1778, bringing with him his thorough classical training. During his study years in Rome, he was directly involved with the first wave of antique discoveries. It was while excavating the Baths of Titus that he was inspired to write his treatise. Cameron also went to Pompeii where systematic excavations had begun in 1763. This experience was an important supplement to the knowledge of antique architecture and interior decoration which he gained from Clérisseau, his primary mentor, the Adam brothers, as well as from publications such as Sir William Hamilton's four-volume *Collection of Etruscan, Greek and Roman Antiquities* (1766-67).

It remains unclear how Catherine's attention was brought to Cameron's work,[4] but it was he, the author of *The Baths of the Romans...*, who realized the Empress' idea of having a Graeco-Roman structure built at Tsarskoe Selo. Prior to this, notably in the days of Old Muscovy, Aleksei Mikhailovich is known to have invited Italian architects to build baths in his palace at Kolomenskoe. While Cameron was adding a sumptuous bath and gallery wing to Rastrelli's palace building at Tsarskoe Selo, Catherine took much delight in various aspects of the antique heritage which her art advisors were so diligently supplying her with. Next to architecture and sculpture, painting was indeed much favoured by the Empress, and she greatly appreciated the Roman motifs by the Frenchman, Hubert Robert.[5] Several of his paintings were to be hung at Tsarskoe Selo, while Cameron imported Wedgwood china and other examples of neoclassical imagery for the palace interiors.

Not only Catherine was to take advantage of Cameron's talents for creating classical structures and sceneries. The larger part of the work he did during his more than thirty years spent in Russia is tied to Pavlovsk, the *dacha* of the Grand Duke Pavel and the Grand Duchess Maria Feodorovna, that is, Catherine's son and daughter-in-law. Yet Cameron lived at Tsarskoe Selo, in the British gardener Busch's apartment above the orangery, and he married one of Busch's daughters. Her name was Catherine!

Pavlovsk, situated just three kilometres from Tsarskoe Selo, took its name from Pavel, who as a young man had enjoyed hunting in the forests. Newly married, he and Marie Feodorovna were to spend their first three summers at some former hunting lodges at Pavlovsk. When Catherine's first grandson, the future Alexander I (1801-05), was born in 1777, she presented the young couple with a tract of land for them to build their own pleasure palace. She subsequently also took the initiative to let Cameron work at Pavlovsk.

43. *The Pavlovsk Palace is heavily indebted to the Palladian tradition so favoured by English country house owners.*

In 1778, part of the forest was cleared and the construction of two wooden houses began: Paullust and Marienthal. A Dutch-inspired flower garden was laid out and next to the Slavyanka river some artificial ruins were erected, along with a Chinese kiosk and some Chinese bridges. Yet Cameron propagated a classically inspired vocabulary from the moment he took charge of the design. He worked at Pavlovsk in two periods, 1779-96 and 1800-3.[6] Over the years he designed a new palace, no less than twelve major garden structures, numerous bridges, orangeries, service wings, and more. Cameron's first designs concerned the garden. In fact, Paullust and Marienthal were not replaced by the new palace until the new appointments of the landscape garden made Maria Feodorovna consider the building of a more fashionable residence.

The Pavlovsk Palace (1781-86) remained Cameron's largest commission ever. The building was in the Palladian manner that had been *en vogue* for English country houses since Lord Burlington built his villa in Chiswick around 1725. For the interior, Cameron may

44. *The landscape scenario of Pavlovsk deserves reputation as the finest work in this genre in Russia.*

have been obliged to use engravings by Adam for inspiration, as he at Tsarskoe Selo had to copy Clérisseau. Thus the Italian and Greek Halls at Pavlovsk have several features in common with Adam's Rotunda and Great Hall at Kedleston (1760). The palace was enlarged by Vincenzo Brenna (c. 1750-1804), the architect of Pavel's own choice, but the heart of it is Cameron's work. Compared to his elegant garden structures though, this building block gives a quite different and very massive impression.

Traditionally, the landscaping of the grounds known as the Slavyanka Valley has also been ascribed to Cameron.[7] Yet it should be mentioned that Loudon suggested a different attribution after his visit to Russia in 1813, just as he did in the case of Tsarskoe Selo. His hypothesis was that the celebrated Capability Brown, the master of some of England's greatest landscape gardens, furnished the design for Pavlovsk, and that the English gardener Gould, who worked for Potemkin, one of Catherine's favourites, brought this project to Russia.[8] This has not been further researched, but the extensive undulating greens, which at this stage were quite unusual in Russian

45. Pavlovsk, the Cascade. Several generations of Russian landscape painters have been inspired by this garden.

landscape gardens, seem to have been shaped by an artist with a painterly vision. An architect like Cameron basically belonged to another school. If he did in fact contribute to the development of the Slavyanka Valley, he is likely to have studied some British examples.

The names of Brenna, Rossi and some other foreign as well as Russian architects are connected with the layout of parterres, alleys and terraces near the palace area. Most of this work was done in the 1790s, when Maria Feodorovna and especially Pavel, had a strong preference for a much more formal, partly Italian and partly Dutch-inspired garden program. The areas called the New and the Old Silvia also date back to that decade. Ultimately, a unique suite of landscapes was to be created on the extensive grounds surrounding this core: the Great Star, the White Birch Area and the Parade Ground. Here an Italian-born theatrical painter by the name of Gonzaga literally transferred the aesthetics he honoured as a painter to nature.

Family Memorials

The first description of the Pavlovsk garden, published in 1843, states:

The Family Grove consists of young birch trees. A bronze plate hangs on every tree, with the name of a member of the Imperial family, the year of birth, and on some plates, also the year of marriage. These birch trees, planted on the occasion of happy events in the August family, form a kind of live chronicle of the Imperial family. In the center of the grove is a pedestal with an urn, that one may call the urn of fate.[9]

Not far from the palace was this so-called Family Grove. One of Maria Feodorovna's basic concerns when creating the Pavlovsk garden was to feature and pay homage to her family. Contrary to Catherine, who in her position as Empress embraced a tremendously wide range of affairs, Maria Feodorovna was primarily interested in her family and domestic life.

At Pavlovsk she wanted to create a home for her family, to plant trees and erect garden pavilions in memory of her relatives. When in Rome during her tour of Europe with Pavel, she was yearning for her children and she very much missed the immediate contact with her ambitious palace and garden creation. She preferred her own garden temples to the Roman marvels, as she said in a letter from the Holy City. Pavlovsk grew into a life-long passion for her. After Catherine's death, it replaced Tsarskoe Selo as the official Imperial summer residence, though Pavel preferred the medieval atmosphere of the Gatchina Palace (Rinaldi, 1766-81; enlarged by Brenna, 1790s). At Pavlovsk, Maria Feodorovna would continue making plans right up till shortly before her death in 1828. Over the years, a very personal and sentimental iconography came into being.

The Slavyanka river winds slowly through the Pavlovsk landscape, and on a little peninsula Cameron placed the Temple of Friendship (1779-83). It was his very first work for Maria Feodorovna. Besides, this yellow and white neoclassical rotunda has often been referred to as the first structure in the Doric order on Russian soil.[10]

Dozens of such neoclassical rotundas had been designed for the British and Continental landscape gardens by the time Cameron began work at Pavlovsk. Initially, the popularity of the rotunda motif in the English landscape garden depended very much on the painters' discovery of the so-called Temple of the Sibyl in Tivoli near Rome. After Claude, several generations of French, Dutch and German artists paid homage to this place when on their Grand Tour. The rather dramatic scenery around the temple, with steep rocky walls

46. *Pavlovsk. Obelisk commemorating the foundation in 1777 of this summer
residence for Grand Duke Pavel and Grand Duchess Maria Feodorovna.*

47. Maria Feodorovna had the Temple of Friendship built at Pavlovsk in honour of her mother-in-law, Catherine the Great.

and the nearby cascade, developed into one of the most popular emblems of the antique, and was widely used by the painters and landscape artists of the 18th century.

Like the Temple of Ancient Virtue at Stowe (1734), the Temple of Philosophy at Ermenonville (c. 1770) and many other examples, Cameron's Temple of Friendship allude to this tradition and taste. Yet, however important the antique allusions are, they only represent one aspect of the meaning inherent in this structure. Maria Feodorovna much regretted the chronic discord between Pavel and Catherine, and the temple was conceived as a demonstrative act to patch up this incompatibility. Significantly enough, dolphins symbolizing friendship and vines decorate the metopes. Allegories on Fame, Friendship, Gratitude and Justice are also included in the scheme.

Though Maria Feodorovna's temperament and her interests were quite different from Catherine's, the two women liked each other.[11] Both had a remarkable understanding of how to create a sumptuous residence and how to fill it with the best art objects of the day. However, in previous studies, not much has been said about Maria Feodorovna, though many have agreed with Loudon that Pavlovsk

48. *Pavlovsk. The Apollo Colonnade is one out of a series of garden motifs dedicated to the Greek patron of the arts.*

"represents the best specimen of the English style, in the neighbour-hood of the Russian capital, or indeed in the empire".[12]

Import of the Vernacular

Along with her comprehensive knowledge of art, Maria Feodorovna was also very much of a horticulturist. Her father was her first mentor in this field, and later at Pavlovsk she much desired to include elements commemorating the garden experiences of her childhood and youth in the Duchy of Württemberg. The garden belonging to the family's summer residence at Étupes, not far from Basel, was laid out in 1771 as a landscape garden with natural grottoes, classical temples, Chinese bridges and vernacular buildings. Le Rouge thought Étupes worthy of being included in his *Détails des nouveaux Jardins à la mode; Jardins anglo-chinois à la Mode* (1776-87). Maria Feodorovna's nostalgia for Étupes made her have plants and plans sent from home. Thus in 1782-83 Cameron found himself copying the Chalet, the Dairy and the Charcoal Burner's Hut from Étupes.

49. *Pavlovsk. The Dairy is a copy of a similar structure in the childhood garden of Grand Duchess Maria Feodorovna.*

Cameron's Dairy (1782) still exists. It is a thatched structure made of granite boulders, which originally held a stable, two small tiled rooms where the milk was kept, and an elegant hall for gatherings. The cultivation of rustic life and vernacular architecture was particularly dominant in French landscape gardens. Maria Feodorovna's desire to have a small *hameau* at Pavlovsk may have been furthered by the visit in 1782 to Marie-Antoinette's much celebrated rustic ensemble at Trianon and to the Prince de Condé's Chantilly. News about the rustic elements of the Pavlovsk landscape reached Hirschfeld, and he liked them very much. He praised Pavel's and Maria Feodorovna's ability, "as of now rarely cultivated by influential people,...here to enjoy this calmful and happy country life."[13]

Semen Feodorovich Shchedrin, the foremost Russian landscape and garden painter of the period, who had learned about the pastoral tradition during his study years in Rome, included cows, sheep and a few shepherds in his idyllistic gouaches of Pavlovsk. Through engravings, Shchedrin's motifs set a pattern for a whole generation of painters. At the same time, translations of contemporary Western pastorals inspired the Russian poets in their first experiments in this genre. Some of the poets were befriended by Maria Feodorovna, and

50. *At the far end of the Pavlovsk landscape garden, ruinous structures remind the visitor of the decay of all things.*

in the early 19th century Pavlovsk became one of Russia's prime literary asylums.

Next to the *hameau*, the urns, tombs, sepulchral monuments and ruins were garden elements that alluded to the antique heritage and to Maria Feodorovna's memories from home and abroad. Just as the happy events in life were commemorated in the garden, so too was death. Sentimentality was a key notion of the period, and the inclusion of the urn in the Family Grove points to the attraction to sorrowful motifs, so characteristic of many British and Continental landscape gardens. Contrary to a significant number of contemporary patrons in the West, Maria Feodorovna never invented stories or accepted any motifs not immediately tied to her family life as inspiration for such scenes.

In 1786-87 Cameron designed a monument dedicated to Maria Feodorovna's late sisters. As with the Temple of Friendship, he also elaborated here on a typically Roman temple form, notably an edicule. White and rose marble gave it a very elegant look. Two columns and two pilasters in Doric order carried the entablement, with rosettes ornamenting the coffered ceiling of the niche. Initially, only the memorial plates would allude to the death of Maria Feodo-

51. *Pavlovsk. This Ionic pavilion with the Three Graces adorns Maria Feodorovna's Privy Garden.*

rovna's sisters, yet the subsequent addition by Thomas de Thomon (1754-1813) and Ivan Petrovich Martos (1754-1835) of a sepulchral monument to Maria Feodorovna's parents in the niche itself, together with a sacrificial altar and other emblems of death on a square in front of the pavilion, made the meaning of this family memorial utterly clear.

Age hindered Cameron from submitting a design for a mausoleum to Pavel who put an end to his life in 1801. Instead, a number of younger architects were asked to submit projects. Monumental temple-like solutions were the majority, and Maria Feodorovna ultimately chose a design marked by the gloomy spirit so characteristic of some of the building projects Pavel had his favourite architect Brenna realize. The granite mausoleum (de Thomon, 1803-10), the fronton of which bears the inscription "To the benevolent husband", was placed in a remote corner of the garden, called the Old Silvia. Dark tall firs surrounded the monument and a narrow path wound up the slope. As recommended in the garden literature of the time, the trees had been planted to emphasize the melancholic atmosphere prevailing in this place.

At the far end of the Slavyanka Valley, in another remote part of

52. *Pavlovsk. Following her husband's death, Maria Feodorovna had this mausoleum built in a sombre part of the garden.*

the Pavlovsk garden, were some artificial ruins. Representing the fugacity of time, such motifs were supposed to, according to contemporary literary sources, awaken melancholic connotations. The question of authorship has not been settled in this case, but the ruins clearly form a complement to the transience alluded to in Cameron's and de Thomon's antique-inspired memorials. Fragmentary copies of antique sculptures lay scattered on the ground beneath the brick structures, serving to complete the meaning of this ruinous scenery.

One mid 19th century writer proposed to read the Pavlovsk garden as an echo of the places and collections seen by the *Duc du Nord* and *Duchesse du Nord* during their Grand Tour in 1781-82.[14] Indeed, the garden comprised many such copies and loans, not least from antique sculpture. A copy of the Apollo Belvedere was the main piece in Cameron's Apollo Colonnade (1780), as it was in Brenna's Old Silvia (1793). An Apollo Mousagetes was placed in Brenna's New Silvia (1800), and the Three Graces embellished Cameron's Ionic Temple (1800). One obelisk (Cameron, 1782) was erected to commemorate the foundation of Pavlovsk, and another was placed on the garden periphery and named the End of the World (Cameron, 1783).

This garden formed an entire universe to its creator. Maria Feodorovna's memories from home and from abroad blended ingeniously in the pavilions and monuments Cameron and other prominent neoclassicists designed for her. These structures induced the Pavlovsk garden with a specifically sentimental touch, soon to be much praised by Zhukovsky, a contemporary and equal to Pushkin. To the larger Russian public however, Pavlovsk took on a special meaning when, in 1814, Maria Feodorovna organized celebrations to commemorate the Russian victory over the French under her son, Alexander I. From having served as a family retreat with pastoral overtones, Pavlovsk became a national symbol. Personal concerns blended with Russian national interests, as had previously occurred when Catherine commissioned war monuments for her pleasure garden at Tsarskoe Selo.

In contrast to other garden pavilions and monuments in Russia, Cameron's works, not least the Doric Temple of Friendship, gained a reputation that far exceeded the St Petersburg region. Cameron set a norm to be widely copied and his interpretation of the classical form ideals, as formulated by Winckelmann, was soon followed up by other antique-inspired garden structures, one of the finest of which is the Temple of Ceres (Bazhenov, c. 1780) at Tsaritsyno. However, the name of Catherine's and Maria Feodorovna's Scottish architect soon fell into almost complete oblivion.

Scenes of Exotica

The Chinese excel in the art of laying out gardens. Their taste in that is good, and what we have for some time past been aiming at in England, though not always with success. I have endeavoured to be distinct in my account of it, and hope it may be of some service to our Gardeners. (Chambers, 1757)

Hadrian's villa ranked among the antique landmarks which artists and patrons most frequently visited on their Grand Tour, and the monuments from all corners of the world which adorned the garden came to serve as prototypes for many landscape architects of the late 18th century. One of the most perfect replicas of the Roman Emperor's setting is Parc Monceau (1774-79) in Paris. Carmontelle, the prime force behind this project, defined the idea as being that of making "all times and all parts of the world cohabit in one garden."[1]

Hadrian's villa and garden was also frequently referred to in the architectural writings of the time. This is what the Scottish architect

53. *Oranienbaum. Catherine had this Chinese Palace built at her ill-fated husband, Peter III's favourite summer residence.*

William Chambers (1723-96) said by way of introduction to his highly influential *Designs of Chinese Buildings, Furniture, Dresses, Machines, and Utensils. To which is annexed, A Description of their Temples, Houses, Gardens, &c.* (1757):

Variety is always delightful; and novelty, attended with nothing inconsistent or disagreeable, sometimes takes place of beauty. History informs us that Adrian, who was himself an architect, at a time when the Grecian architecture was in the highest esteem among the Romans, erected in his Villa, at Tivoli, certain buildings after the manner of the Egyptians and of other nations.[2]

From around 1750, the propagation of exotic styles played an increasingly dominant role in architectural theory as well as in practical building. Egyptian, Turkish and Chinese accents intermingled with antique patterns, and the same artists often excelled in a broad spectrum of styles.

Chinoiseries as part of a sumptuous indoor palace decoration had been *en vogue* since the beginning of the century. Following the taste of his Western peers, Peter saw to it that a Chinese porcelain and lacquer interior (1721-22) was created in one of the cabinets of the Monplaisir Palace at Peterhof.[3] It was Peter's impressions from his visit to Monbijou near Berlin in 1717 which served as his inspiration. Forty years later, when Catherine as newly crowned Empress set

54. *Oranienbaum is one of the last Imperial gardens to undergo restoration. Yet the grounds offer nice and quiet strolls.*

about to modernize the palace and garden at Oranienbaum, probably the greatest single contribution to the history of *Chinoiseries* on Russian ground was made. A new palace, called the Chinese Palace (Rinaldi, 1762-68), was built. Its sumptuous interior and decorative art collections call to mind the tea-house (1754-57) at Sans-Souci and the Kina (1753-69) at Drottningholm. The Imperial gardens, however, were not to hold any Chinese-inspired pavilions or landscape scenes till Chambers' *Designs of Chinese Buildings* became known.

Chambers made himself a great name as a Palladian architect, but he was also a fervent propagator of Chinese garden aesthetics. Trade had brought the Swedish-born author of *Designs of Chinese Buildings* to India and China several times, before he changed his course and decided to study architecture. Following the same pattern as most architectural students of the time, he turned to Rome to get a proper training. Yet the impressions from Canton of the 1740s never failed, and Chambers continuously moved between two poles: Antique and Chinese. Confucius' House (1745-48) in Kew was his first royal commission, and while he was still working on the pioneering development of Oriental and Turkish scenes in Kew Gar-

55. *Tsarskoe Selo, silk tapestry. Chinese-inspired interiors had a great vogue in 18th century Imperial Russian residences.*

dens (1757-62) in London, George III appointed him Royal Gardener.

Designs of Chinese Buildings was Chambers' first work based on his impressions from China. The first edition was published simultaneously in English and French. His second and more extensive work, *Dissertation on Oriental Gardening* (1772), which is a fable on the Chinese manner, was also published simultaneously in English and French, and in 1775 it was available in German.[4] Both works became widely known and echoes of Chambers' interpretation of how the

56. Tsarskoe Selo. The Grand Caprice answered to the recommendations
described in contemporary books on Chinese aesthetics.

Chinese used a variety of scenes and pavilions in their miniature
landscapes are found in late 18th century gardens in Spain, Poland,
Sweden and many other countries, including Russia.

    Generally, the British country house owners and garden patrons
regarded the new landscape manner as a politically loaded alternative to the princely gardens of the past and they tended to look
down upon Chambers' close ties to the Court. However, the reception

he received from the élite on the Continent and in Russia, whether princely or noble, was different. Still, a number of Chambers' colleagues, including Hirschfeld, were of the opinion that his empirical material was highly insufficient, and much was in fact based on an earlier French book about China, notably Du Halde's *Description géographique, historique, chronologique, politique de l'Empire de la Chine* (1735). In practice, however, no other propagator of Chinese aesthetics was as successful as Chambers.

Prompted by the publication of Catherine's Russian translation of the French edition of *Designs of Chinese Buildings* in 1771, this work was one of the first foreign books to shape the Russian garden patrons' taste for exotica as part of the landscape. At this very point, new and large-scale developments at Tsarskoe Selo were being realized, and some of Chambers' recommendations were being carefully listened to.

Chambers and Chinese Caprices

"The perfection of their gardens consists in the number, beauty, and diversity of these scenes", Chambers asserted with regard to the Chinese taste for gathering and staging a variety of motifs in their landscapes.[5]

Various are the artifices they employ to surprise. Sometimes they lead you through dark caverns and gloomy passages, at the issue of which you are, on a sudden, struck with the view of a delicious landscape, enrichened with every thing that luxuriant nature affords most beautiful. At other times you are conducted through avenues and walks, that gradually diminish and grow rugged, till the passage is at length entirely intercepted, and rendered impracticable, by bushes, briars, and stones: when unexpectedly a rich and extensive prospect opens to view, so much the more pleasing as it was less looked for.[6]

The creation of visual surprises was a key notion, fitting in perfectly with the aesthetics of the British landscape pattern which Catherine was determined to follow in her new garden at Tsarskoe Selo. A series of structures created with the materials of nature and some fanciful buildings were erected to add visual and emotional variety to the grounds.

Two remarkable archways were placed on the road leaving the south side of the palace courtyard. This road marks one of the borders between the old Elizabethan garden and the new landscape garden, and in the Catherine period it was all the more important because the traffic between St Petersburg and the Imperial summer

57. *Tsarskoe Selo. Crowned by a pagoda-like pavilion with Ionic columms, this motif embodies Catherine's garden fantasies.*

residence went along this route. The Little Caprice (1770-72) and the Grand Caprice (1772-74), as the archways were called, served as signals to the numerous and highly fashionable attractions of the Empress' new garden at this early point in the visitor's *entrée*.

The architect Vasily Neelov, who had been sent to England to study gardens, and who designed the majority of the structures at Tsarskoe Selo, was responsible for the erection of these caprices. Yet some engineering technology was also needed, and a German specialist by the name of Johannes Gerhard was attached to the project. A number of his preparatory sketches are at the Russian Military Historical Archives in Moscow. They indeed bring some interesting evidence as to how Gerhard was experimenting with the elevation of the stone massive of the Grand Caprice. The entwined lines of movement even disguise his aiming at a certain elegance.

The archway is some seven metres high and five metres wide, with the rocky massif consisting of irregular blocks of stone. It gives the impression of the mountain structures which, according to Chambers' description, the gardeners and painters of the Middle Kingdom had modelled, using the natural landscape as their prime source. "Nature is their pattern, and their aim is to imitate her in all her beautiful irregularities."[7] So Chambers said. And later:

58. *Tsarskoe Selo. The Cross-Shaped Bridge is characteristic of the impact of European 'jardins anglo-chinois' under Catherine.*

They likewise form artifical rocks; and in compositions of this kind the Chinese surpass all other nations...When they are large they make in them caves and grottos, with openings, through which you discover distant prospects. They cover them, in different places, with trees, shrubs, briars, and moss; placing on their tops little temples, or other buildings, to which you ascend by rugged and irregular steps cut in the rock.[8]

As *point de vue*, a lofty pavilion with an exaggerated Chinese pagoda-like roof was placed on top of the rock massive. Antique-inspired elements were also used, as in the six Ionic columns bearing the roof. The application of bright colours to this structure added to the visual effect of the entire scenery.

The archways literally opened the way to several other Chinese

59. *Tsarskoe Selo. The multi-coloured pavilions making up the so-called Chinese Village have recently been restored.*

motifs. All of them were placed so as to enliven the rather densely planted area to the west of the Big Pond. A variety of bridges were created to span the many small, irregular ponds and the canal surrounding the Upper Elizabethan Garden. The little and rather simple pavilion on the Cross-Shaped Bridge (1776) makes this one of V.I. Neelov's most charming works. A much more complex Chinese repertoire, including dragons, ornamented sculptures, vases and coral motifs, characterized the bridges Cameron designed, and which V.I. Neelov helped to realize in the 1780s. The Creaky Pavilion (Velten, 1778-86) not only struck a decorative chord, but also a humoristic one. Each building segment was given an intricate decorative scheme, with geometrical patterns, floral motifs and legendary animals in multi-coloured carvings. The pavilion's emplacement on a narrow strip of land between two small irregular ponds further added to its prominent role as a visually stimulating piece of architecture.

The most ambitious Chinese-inspired projects at Tsarskoe Selo were the Chinese Theatre and the Chinese Village, the latter consisting of more than a dozen buildings. Plans for these ensembles, to which Cameron, Rinaldi and V.I. Neelov all contributed, go back to the early 1770s, when the caprices were also still under construction.

Work on the village continued for several decades and underwent many changes. Given the size of this ensemble, it was not supposed to be discovered as a surprise piece during the meditative garden stroll. In this it differed from the caprices, the bridges and the Creaky Pavilion, which corresponded perfectly to Chambers' doctrine:

The banks of their lakes and rivers are variegated in imitation of nature... In some places flat..., in others steep, rocky, and forming caverns... Sometimes you see meadows..., and sometimes groves, into which enter, in different parts, creeks and rivulets, sufficiently deep to admit boats; their banks being planted with trees, whose spreading branches, in some places, form arbours, under which the boats pass. These generally conduct to some very interesting object; such as a magnificent building, places on the top of a mountain cut into terrasses; a casine situated in the midst of a lake; a cascade; a grotto cut into a variety of apartments; an artificial rock; and many other such inventions.[9]

Comprising living quarters, halls and many other facilities, the Chinese Village could be rather likened to a secondary palace ensemble. Denying any endeavour to compete with the antique vocabulary and syntax, Chambers had recommended the use of Chinese elements "...in extensive parks and gardens, where a great variety of scenes are required, or in immense palaces, containing a numerous series of apartments..."[10]

This was the idea that enchanted Catherine most in her reading of Chambers, and which resulted in Tsarskoe Selo receiving as many Chinese-inspired garden structures as no other garden ever in Russia. However, Chambers' lengthy discussions of the Chinese landscape architects' approach to effects based on nature's own elements found little echo. Some cascades, small gurgling streams and articificial islands were created and harmonized with the natural landscape scenery, but such *tableaux* were far less important than the architectural motifs in Catherine's garden at Tsarskoe Selo.

The same tendency can be detected in most other Russian landscape gardens of the Catherine period. Architecture, rather than nature was featured as the main surprise element, with the softly undulating landscape, the waters and the groves forming a harmonious setting for various antique or exotic buildings. Chambers' disctinction between "three different species of scenes, to which they give the appellations of pleasing, horrid, and enchanted", appears not to have found any major audience in Russia.[11] Caves, grottoes, ruins, deformed trees, exotic birds, and vehement torrents did occur in the new gardens of St Petersburg, Moscow and the Russian province, but there were never many such motifs in any one garden, nor were any gardens developed in view of proposing a specific route through such contradictory emotional stages. Programs of this type, like the one implemented in the Désert de Retz (1774-84), remained a Western phenomenon.

The popularity of Chinese motifs lagged far behind that of rotundas and other antique-inspired emblems, and neither Catherine's higher officials nor the Russian gentry spent large sums on exotic garden structures. There is apparently no evidence of any prominent architects having been commissioned to do such structures for the nobility's gardens. Here the taste for something foreign and bizarre was reduced to the creation of relatively simple Chinese pavilions in wood, and hence painted in bright colours.

The Sheremetev family knew what was fashionable and customary, and the landscape gardens that were developed adjacent to the formal gardens at Kuskovo and Ostankino are known to have comprised of examples of simple oriental imagery. The designs were made by serf artists. Their work basically relied on pattern books and graphic illustrations, of which there were plenty in the well-stocked libraries of the two palaces. Significantly enough, Peter Borisovich Sheremetev's book collection also included the French edition of Chambers' first book on Chinese garden aesthetics, *Traité des édifices, meubles, habits, machines et ustensiles des chinois. Compris une description de leurs temples, maisons, jardins, &c.*

Islamic Inspirations

When designing Kew Gardens, Chambers had simultaneously applied architectural motifs of Chinese and Islamic origin. His Mosque (1762) set the example for the use of an Islamic vocabulary in many other gardens of the second half of the 18th century. Along with *la Chinoiserie, la Turquerie* was one of the styles most frequently featured by royal and noble patrons at the zenith of European rococo. The costumes and appointments used for the sumptuous masquerades of that period were typically styled in the Turkish manner.

Constantinople, the successor to Rome and the cradle of the Orthodox Church, was the city to which Kiev and Moscow, Russia's two first capitals, had felt the closest kinship. Russian artists, including garden architects, had been looking to this culture for inspiration. The popularity of the hanging gardens with the Russian rulers, including Peter and Catherine, may be seen as an example of this exchange. During Catherine's reign, Russia had strong political and military interests in the south, in contrast to Peter whose prime military goal was to establish Russian control on the Baltic coast.

60. *Tsarskoe Selo. The Turkish Bath commemorates the Third Turkish War. The Palladio Bridge is seen to the far right.*

Catherine and her commanders turned towards the areas bordering on the Black Sea and ultimately won the First Turkish War (1768-74). This came to have a significant impact on the artists' use of allusions to the Islamic world.

One of the most noteworthy monuments in the Tsarskoe Selo garden is the Chesma Column (1771-76). It commemorates a successful sea battle, which took place on June 26, 1770 near Chesma on the Black Sea. Yet Rinaldi, who also designed two other victory monuments for this garden and one in the Gatchina garden, chose classical forms. The very use of columns and obelisks, with appropriate attributes and inscriptions, was a continuation of the antique tradition of monumental art. Had Rinaldi used an Islamic vocabulary, empha-

61. *The church next to the Chesma Palace, St Petersburg, reflects Catherine's ephemeral interest in Islamic aesthetics.*

sis would have been on where the battles had been fought, and perhaps not so much on the outcome. Faced with Rinaldi's antique monuments, the learned garden visitor was indeed likely to think of suitable prototypes for the Russian military victories.

Few Islamic motifs found their way to Catherine's gardens. At one point Tsarskoe Selo boasted a Turkish pavilion, modelled after a structure in the sultan's garden at Constantinople. Prince Repnin, who in 1779 was appointed ambassador to the Sublime Porte, procured the necessary plans and information. The largest building to exemplify Catherine's momentary interest in Islamic architecture was the Chesma Palace (Velten, 1774-80), situated a couple of kilometres south of the St Petersburg Admiralty. The flattened domes that crown the palace building are however not particularly convincing emblems of Turkish inspiration. The Palace Church (Velten, 1777-80) which lies opposite the palace itself also has several rather bizarre features such as white stripes on a pink background and pinnacled lanterns. It is obvious that no serious studies of the sources were undertaken.

Turkish pavilions occasionally appeared in the gardens of the Russian nobility of the time. Prince Kantemir, from whom Catherine bought Tsaritsyno in 1775, had a Turkish-inspired structure in his garden. A number of gardens situated somewhat further away from Moscow, such as Yaropolets and Shablykino, also boasted such motifs. In some cases a tent made of fabric proved sufficient as a more temporary installation. There is no reason not to believe that at least some of these Turkish-styled garden structures owed their existence to fashion as well as to the Russian victories in the Turkish Wars.

The fact that such pavilions were more popular around Moscow than in the St Petersburg region may be indicative of this. After all, it was Moscow which had been the centre of great festivities at the end of the First Turkish War. Besides, one of the most popular plays performed by the serf artists at the Ostankino Theatre, Kozlovsky's *The Conquest of Izmail* (1792), was also inspired by the Islamic world, and towards the end of the century, Turkish masquerades were a very popular element in the repertoires offered at various summer residences.

Exoticism in Theory

Out of the exotic garden elements which Chambers mentions in his writings, the Egyptian motif came to play the less important role in Russia. Yet Catherine could not do without this, and a pyramid was included in the Tsarskoe Selo garden. The four marble columns at the corners of the pyramid and the urns and vases in the interior, however, made the scenery look rather heterogenous.

On Russian ground there does not seem to be any parallel to the contemporary European fashion for Egyptian-inspired garden imagery. The connections to the cult of one of civilization's first nuclea, as practiced by the freemasonic lodges, have been detected in some French and German gardens, but experiments with such meanings or similarly intricate iconographical programs were apparently never aimed at by the Russian garden patrons and their artists, neither in the Catherine period nor later. Only the allegorical sculptures and fountains of the Petrine gardens matched some Western counterparts in regard to comprehensive emblematics.

A few palace interiors of the late 18th century held rather prominent examples of the use of Egyptian motifs. The Music Hall at Ostankino was fashioned in this manner, as was the Hall which preludes the sumptuous stylistic cavalcade of the Pavlovsk apartments. The slightly later central buildings of the Kuzminki Estate on the Moscow outskirts (originally from the mid 18th century, then rebuilt in the early 19th century) comprised of a so-called Egyptian Pavilion (Andrei Nikiforovich Voronikhin, 1811). Later, the Napoleonic excavations of the Pharaonic tombs did not pass unnoticed in the Russian townscapes. An enormous Egyptian Gate (Adam Adamovich Menelaws, 1827-30) was built on the main entry way to the town of Tsarskoe Selo. This structure, one of the world's largest neo-Egyptian monuments, was covered with scarabea, sun emblems and mythological scenes that had all been patterned after drawings published by French archaeologists.

Discussions of the Egyptian and Turkish garden elements played as limited a role in the horticultural writings of the Catherine period as such elements did in the gardens. Bolotov was one of the few Russian writers, if not the only one, to mention these exotic forms. Following the discovery of Hirschfeld's *Theorie der Gartenkunst* and some more garden publications of foreign origin, he dedicated almost an entire volume of *Ekonomichesky Magazin* to a historical survey of the national schools of gardening.[12]

The Turkish region is praised because of its climate and the natural flora. "Nature there is beautiful and generous", Bolotov asserts.[13] Most 18th century garden writers and architects focused on the kiosks and tents as main attractions of the Islamic gardens, but in the case of Bolotov, the Northerner's enthusiasm for the lemon trees and sparkling water meant that only a few lines were dedicated

62. *The pyramid in the Tsarskoe Selo landscape garden was the last resting place of Catherine's favourite greyhounds.*

to architectural adornments. As for the Turkish gardeners, they were even characterized as rather incompetent, and Bolotov did not approve of their aesthetic language. Their creations "cannot be said to be particularly beautiful", he claimed.[14]

This is one of many points on which Bolotov shared his attitude with Hirschfeld, his German idol. Bolotov's negative attitude to Turkish culture, if not to the natural landscape, may have been further supported by his having written his articles for *Ekonomichesky Magazin* in the aftermath of the Turkish wars. Still, not one sentence in his writings testifies to Russia having had any connection with the Oriental heritage, neither in the convent gardens of medieval times nor in the pleasure gardens of Catherine's age. When writing about Turkish-inspired garden architecture, Bolotov obviously forgot or simply did not bother to complement the ideas he imported from various theoretical sources of foreign origin with the history of garden plans and pavilions on Russian soil.

The Chinese gardens, however, were dealt with in considerable length and from various viewpoints in *Ekonomichesky Magazin*. Echoing contemporary Western ideals and colleagues, Bolotov considered the Chinese tradition important because of the impact various descriptions and depictions of Chinese gardens had had on the landscape garden:

No other such [foreign] gardens of our time have been praised as much as the Chinese gardens...These gardens not only awoke much surprise, but also much esteem, and whereever the new English garden manner was introduced, news about Chinese gardens were of much help.[15]

Bolotov's main source is of course William Chambers.

We are grateful to Chambers, Architect to the English King, for having supplied the first seductive description of Chinese gardens and for a general eulogy.[16]

Because of Catherine's interest in Anglo-Chinese gardens, the chapter entitled "Of The Art of Laying out Gardens among Chinese" from Chambers' *Designs of Chinese Buildings* had been available in a Russian translation since 1771, and Bolotov chose this very text for *Ekonomichesky Magazin*. It was published *in extenso*, with small editorial changes, such as "Englishmen" being systematically substituted by "we", that is the Russian public.

Bolotov also added some personal comments as well as remarks he had literally taken over from Hirschfeld. In *Theorie der Gartenkunst*, Hirschfeld had exposed his personal scepticism about the empirical basis of Chambers' impressions and judgements, and Bolotov allowed for a considerable part of Hirschfeld's text to follow after Chambers' appraisal of "the art of laying out grounds, after the Chinese manner".[17] He subsequently used Hirschfeld's brief summaries of some other European accounts from the landscapes and gardens of China.

Bolotov's publishing in 1786 of extracts from Chambers' and Hirschfeld's writings on Chinese gardens meant that this ancient, and suddenly extremely fashionable culture became known to a greater readership. From having been a concern of the Imperial court in St Petersburg, the *Anglo-Chinese* garden manner became a notion to which the members of the Russian nobility and gentry could relate. The local serf artists' subsequent experiment with pagoda-like roofs and ornate bridges show that they, in practice, had grasped one of Chambers' basic lessons, although few of these artists are likely to have consulted his writings personally.

Masonry and the Middle Ages

I think it is impossible to regale oneself for the empire in a more useful way than by elucidating and planning its very history. (Catherine the Great, 1784)

All Russian Grand Dukes, Tsars and Emperors were crowned in the Cathedral of the Assumption in the Moscow Kremlin. The founding of St Petersburg in 1703 might have signified the end of this tradition, but it did not. Nor did it cause the rulers to disregard Moscow in other spheres of politics, religion and art. The *heart* of Russia, as Moscow was traditionally called, never lost its aura and its importance as a powerful social and cultural centre in the Petrine age and later.[1]

Yet neither Peter nor Elizabeth sponsored any building projects in Moscow that bear comparison with what was being created in St Petersburg and the surroundings at the time. German-born Catherine, on the other hand, felt very much obliged to Moscow. Having no legal claim to the throne, she had to identify herself with the present as well as the past of her adopted country. She frequently visited Moscow, describing it to Voltaire as "a world, not a city".

Already in 1762, when in Moscow for her coronation, Catherine had visited the Imperial palace ensemble at Kolomenskoe (1667-71), situated ten kilometres southeast of the Moscow Kremlin. Drawings and a model of this magnificent religious and secular complex were to be made before the wooden palace was destroyed. Several years later the Empress' attention was focused on the prime emblem of Old Muscovy, the Kremlin itself.[2] In this, Catherine most demonstratively complemented her archaeological and archival interests for the city, being the first one out with an important series of building projects.

A new palace was commissioned. This time a Russian-born architect, Vasily Ivanovich Bazhenov (1738-99), was chosen to make the designs. Bazhenov belonged to a generation which benefitted from the new Western-inspired educational establishments of Moscow and St Petersburg, including the Academy of Arts. A five year stay in Paris and Rome had given him a thorough first-hand knowledge of the latest European trends.

His designs for the Great Kremlin project (1767-75) were indebted to the classical manner, or rather the leading French neoclassicists' interpretation of it. In fact, de Wailly had been his tutor in Paris, and Bazhenov also used elements from the works of Perrault and Soufflot. However, his radicalism in creating a new Kremlin may have been too pronounced,[3] and the economic resources

63. Tsaritsyno. The Adorned Bridge was aimed to be the entrance to Catherine the Great's Muscovite summer residence.

of the Russian Imperial Court were, though abundant, not completely without end. The project remained a Utopia, evoking enormous praise especially from foreign visitors to an exhibition in the old Kremlin Palace where Bazhenov's model, made from the finest pieces of wood from the demolished Kolomenskoe Palace, were displayed for a number of years.[4]

By spring 1775, Catherine took the first step towards the creation of two new Imperial residences on what was then the city outskirts. One was completed seven years later, the other one never. Named after Peter, the Petrovsky Palace (Kazakov, 1775-82) was placed northwest of the Kremlin, on the way to the Northern capital. The layout of the palace and the adjoining garden show that Palladio and the formal heritage were still in favour. But the decorative scheme was unusual for an 18th century building. The ornaments had been borrowed from old Muscovite architecture.

The place destined for the second project lay close to Kolomenskoe. It was called Chornaya Gryaz, which literally means Black Mud, but it was renamed Tsaritsyno when work on the Imperial residence began. Bazhenov was in charge, and he set about to create a palace ensemble for Catherine, which was even more indebted to the architecture and emblems of the pre-Petrine period than Kazakov's Petrofsky ensemble.

However, as with the Great Kremlin project, Bazhenov's talents were not fully honoured by his sponsor this time either. Construction was already well under way when, upon her first inspection of Tsaritsyno in 1785, Catherine decided to replace Bazhenov with Kazakov.[5] The latter then worked at Tsaritsyno, though almost exclusively on the Big Palace, until the early 1790s. Yet, Tsaritsyno remained a torso, albeit a truly gigantic one. Neither Pavel nor any other Russian ruler felt inclined to complete what Catherine had initiated here. A Scottish gardener by the name of Francis Reid (d. 1798) was also hired in 1785, but he was only involved with the grounds and not with the garden buildings. Reid's contribution should be compared to that of Busch at Tsarskoe Selo and Sparrow at Gatchina. Furthermore, it brings some additional evidence to the influx of Scottish professionals and workers in the Catherine period, following Cameron's example.

The first decade, when Bazhenov was working on the Tsaritsyno project, is revealing with regard to the new taste for medieval allusions. Bazhenov left behind him an important corpus of drawings, and an analysis of this material and the remains of the palace and garden ensemble makes it evident why he has been compared to Thomas More, the utopist, as well as to Lomonosov, one of the most erudite men of the Russian Enlightenment.[6] He masterminded an ensemble which eventually could have become Catherine's Muscovite Tsarskoe Selo.

Ivan Feodorovich Michurin (1700?-63), Prince Dmitry Ukhtomsky (1719-74?), Karl Ivanovich Blank (1728-93) and a few other Moscow architects had also been influenced and used certain motifs from the old cityscape in their church and palace buildings from around 1750. But Bazhenov's project for Tsaritsyno formed part of a much more comprehensive cultural trend, embracing taste, tradition and politics alike. As in the case of the Petrovsky Palace, the development and design of Tsaritsyno was planned to visualize what Catherine thought of as a very important link between her new Russia and the past. Both projects must furthermore be regarded in connection with some very specific politico-military events that affected Russia's external relations as well as the country's internal stability.

Bazhenov's National Project

Russia emerged victorious from the First Turkish War. Vast territories in the south became Russian dominions and were soon to be called

64. Tsaritsyno. The Great Palace remained a torso. Catherine thought it looked like a coffin surrounded by candles.

Nova Rossiya. The newly gained access to the Black Sea also meant that the Russian Empire moved closer to the Oriental world. But the Imperial Court faced several serious threats from within the borders of the extensive country during the great peasant rebellion under Pugachev (1773-75).

The reformist zeal of Peter had never been welcomed by the partisans of the old ways, and a series of peasant insurrections took place in the early 18th century. Under Russia's subsequent ruling Empresses, the peasants put the blame for their worsening living conditions on the rulers being women. The leader of the peasant rebellion under Catherine, the hetman Pugachev, was regarded as the miraculously returned figure of Peter III, Catherine's slain husband and her predecessor on the throne. Viewed from the Northern capital St Petersburg, the location of which symbolized Russia's westward orientation, all this seemed extremely far away. What Catherine needed was a practical and symbolical strengthening of the Imperial Court's presence in Moscow, thus reversing the course Peter had taken about a century earlier.

In the first place, the end of the First Turkish War gave rise to large-scale public celebrations in Moscow in 1775. Bazhenov was

65. Tsaritsyno. The Adorned Arch is one out of a series of decorative structures set up in the landscaped scenery.

asked to create a landscaped replica of the new Russian possessions in the south. Catherine had become tired of monuments, of "silly heathenish temples", as she frankly admitted.[7] The time had come for something different. "Truly enough, it is meaningless to place the sea on hard soil", she told Bazhenov, "but don't focus on this drawback, then the rest will appear very reasonable".[8] Anyway, two triumphal arches and no less than fourteen obelisks were also erected on the southern city border, with Kolomenskoe as a highly allusive background. These monuments were closely related to the obelisks and columns which Catherine had ordered for Tsarskoe Selo while the war had not yet come to an end.

Many elements in Bazhenov's design were based on national building traditions and imagery. Among the many decorative patterns on the Tsaritsyno palaces, bridges and other structures, several emblems with a distinct historical significance also appeared. The Adorned Bridge (Bazhenov, 1780s) is the first structure the visitor sees when approaching Tsaritsyno from Moscow.[9] It spans a chasm and leads right into the greenery of the pleasure ground. None of the characteristics of neoclassicism or the exotic styles which characterized the archways and bridges at Catherine's Tsarskoe Selo mark this bridge. Values other than those of the newly Europeanized Russia seemed more appropriate in the context of Old Muscovy. At Tsaritsyno, Bazhenov seems to have been guided by the ambition to create an ensemble that could challenge comparison with neighbouring Kolomenskoe.

The Adorned Bridge is made of red brick with limestone trim. It is crowned by a gallery with pointed openings, all framed by trim stone. This motif repeats itself in the imposing, tooth-edged tower on the side which leads on to the Tsaritsyno grounds. Opposite this is a slope, scanned by a series of likewise heavily ornamented pinnacles. Finally, the limestone was used to set off the St George crosses on both sides of the archway. St George, who inspired the baptism of thousands of people by heroically rescuing a maiden from the dragon's jaws, was one of the most popular figures in the medieval frescoes of Old Rus and in icon painting. He was the patron saint of Moscow, and he also appears in the national coat of arms.

A monumental drawing, executed by Bazhenov in 1776, displays the intention of the Tsaritsyno project. The panorama comprises no less than three palaces, two for Catherine and one for her son Pavel. There are several structures for the officials, the guards and other staff members of the Court, in addition to two imposing bridges, an opera house, two hermitages, an orangery, a number of garden pavilions and utilitarian facilities including kitchens. The church and

66. *Tsaritsyno. Despite its traditional Moscow-inspired building materials, the Great Bridge echoes Roman aqueducts.*

part of the formal garden, which the previous owner, Prince Kantemir, had developed along with his palace, remained as it was.

The main as well as the secondary buildings were spread over a vast area. Some clearing of the natural woods and some planting was done, and a parterre was created in front of the Great Palace (Kazakov, 1787-93; on the remains of Bazhenov's earlier project). Yet, as for example at Sukhanovo, the main features of the surrounding pleasure grounds were the natural gorges, the lakes, islands, and the alleys and paths that crisscrossed the woods and invited the garden stroller to contemplate various views, pavilions, as well as the entrance bridges and gates. Thanks to the dense plantation, even the major buildings appeared as surprise elements in this comprehensive palace and garden ensemble.

The majority of the structures depicted in Bazhenov's more than three metre long panorama were actually built, and other motifs were later created in the garden to diversify the promenades. Examples include the Temple of Ceres (Bazhenov, 1780s), the Adorned Arch (Bazhenov, 1780s), the Belvedere (Yegotov, 1803) and the ruins on one of the artificial islands. The Temple of Ceres is the only structure at Tsaritsyno for which Bazhenov chose an antique form.

67. The remains of an arch motif in the Tsaritsyno garden. Winding waters and pathways allow for a variety of pictures.

A comparison between Tsaritsyno and the fortified walls and towers of the Donskoi Monastery in Moscow, the walls of the Kremlin or the fragments of Kitai Gorod, testify to 16th and 17th century Muscovite architecture's particular importance as a source to Bazhenov at this stage. Bazhenov had experimented with similar forms in some early church buildings, but the scale and variety of Tsaritsyno far outrivalled any previous examples of a medieval revival in 18th century Moscow architecture. As the allusions of the red brick architecture are complemented by the use of various symbols and emblems, the appearance of the St George cross on the Adorned Bridge is echoed in the Great Bridge (Bazhenov, 1784) across a deep ravine and in Catherine's Little Palace.

The double-headed eagle which can be seen on the Opera House (Bazhenov, 1776) is another case in point. By marrying Sophia Paleologos, a niece of the last Byzantine Emperor, Ivan III (1462-1505) had brought the former Byzantine coat of arms with the double-headed eagle to Russia. From then on the Grand Duchy of Moscow used the symbol in its efforts to compare itself to the Christian empires of antiquity and to legitimate itself as the Third Rome. Similar political and ideological considerations may also explain the occurrence of the sun emblem in structures such as Catherine's Little Palace, the Men Servant's House and the Great Bridge, the latter patterned after the Roman tradition of aquaducts.

Following the French Royal tradition, Catherine actually used the sun metaphor in one of her mottoes. There may however be more to this aspect of Bazhenov's lush décor. Indeed, it is tempting to relate the sun and the star motifs of the Tsaritsyno ensemble to traditional freemasonic imagery. The sun, the moon and the stars, however, nearly always occur along with other freemasonic emblems, such as the pillars of Jachin and Boaz, the pyramid, the sundial, and so on.

Readings and Rituals of Medieval Patterns

The history of Russian freemasonry begins under Elizabeth. As fashion had it in most Western European countries of the time, not least in France, members of the social and cultural élite in St Petersburg were drawn towards the moral philosophy, the social and educational ideals and, also, the ceremonial life which was performed by the members of the masonic lodges. Under Catherine, lodges were created in Moscow and in several provincial towns.

In fact, some foreign writers called her a patron of freemasonry.[10] The Russians, however, were of a different opinion. Catherine's initial indulgence towards the freemasons may, at least partly, be a result of her occupation with many other and much more urgent affairs. In the 1780s, however, Catherine changed her attitude and she took a number of concrete measures to cut back the influence of the freemasons. In a very categorical way she would often link their writings and doings to various mystic teachings and personages, like Swedenborg and Caliostro, thus expressing some of the most common prejudices against freemasonry. This is evident in Catherine's letters to Grimm, in the essay entitled "The Secret of the Free Society" and in three of her comedies: *The Siberian Shaman* (1785-86), *The Deceived* (1785-86) and *The Deceiver* (1786).

Like numerous other influential men of the arts and letters in the Catherine period, including the publisher Novikov, Bazhenov was a freemason. This did not have as tangible consequences on his architectural designs as it had with many Western architects of the time, but it has certainly had a remarkable effect on the way his work at Tsaritsyno has been regarded. Thus in Russian and Soviet studies, Catherine's dislike of Tsaritsyno and her dismissal of Bazhenov in 1785 has again and again been interpreted in light of her criticism of what she thought freemasonry represented.

Still, no analysis has yet been conducted to investigate the supposedly masonic imagery in the Tsaritsyno ensemble, let alone in the Russian architecture of the period. Research along those lines was, for self-evident ideological reasons, practically unthinkable in Soviet times. On the other hand, arguments on the role of freemasonry in the case of Catherine's dismissing Bazhenov were energetically put forward in the studies published under Stalin and later. A reason for this may have been the desire to cover up that aspect of Bazhenov's oeuvre because it did not fit into the mould of Soviet architectural ideology. Like Charles Cameron, Bazhenov was a connoisseur of the antique tradition, and in the Stalin period both were very much appreciated for having made this tradition known in Russia in writing too. Buildings by Bazhenov were thus said to "represent an outstanding school of architecture to Soviet architects."[11] Yet only his neoclassical works, and among these primarily the unfinished Kremlin Palace and the Pashkov House in Moscow (1783-87), were taken into consideration. Neither Tsaritsyno nor Bazhenov's church buildings were ever discussed at length.

In 1787, Bazhenov is known to have been something of a go-between, introducing the coming Emperor Pavel to some of the books from which the Moscow Martinists, headed by Novikov, drew their ethics.[12] Tradition has it that already at the architect's third visit concerning these spiritual matters, Pavel told Bazhenov that he only took an interest in him as an architect, not as a Martinist. Yet Russian-Soviet posterity has judged Bazhenov as well as Pavel severely for their contacts in this question, and Pavel's subsequent use of Bazhenov's artistic talents has been interpreted as a betrayal against the Catherine heritage.

Truly enough, Pavel was up against Catherine in practically all matters. He dismissed Cameron from Pavlovsk and asked Brenna to continue the work instead. After Catherine died he reinstated Bazhenov. For the third time in his career, Bazhenov was commissioned to design an Imperial residence, notably the Engineers Castle (1797-1801) on the southern side of the Summer Garden. Here too, however, much remains to be said about the extent to which freemasonic emblems were used.[13] The Engineers' Castle was destined to be the Emperor's prime residence, and the square just south of the castle was used for his favourite pastime, which was drilling troops.[14]

Pavel shared his military passion with his slain father Peter III, but neither of them ever conducted any battles outside the model fields they created in the vicinity of their palaces. Characteristically, a number of structures were erected at Pavlovsk and Gatchina in

68. Pavlovsk. This castle was built to respond to Pavel's passion for martial structures and ceremonies.

response to Pavel's fascination with military and knightly orders. Among these structures was a medieval-like castle called Bip (Brenna, 1794-97). Pavel had this castle built on the very same site as Marienthal, which had lost its significance due to the construction of the new palace by Cameron. Bip was supposed to serve the Emperor as something of a toy, yet by spring 1798 the meaning of the structure was modified upon Imperial orders, and Bip became a working fortress. The bridges spanning the moat went up for the night and guns were heard during the day.

Brenna also made some less comprehensive designs for the garden at Pavlovsk, such as transforming an existing water mill into a tower (1797). The structure known as the Peel Tower was placed where the water of the Slavyanka form a small waterfall. The facades of the tower were later painted by the Italian theatrical painter Gonzaga to give the structure a partly ruinous look, consisting of a timber frame, timber windows and various similar ornaments in the rustic style. Gonzaga supplied other patterns, as can be seen in a series of sketches at the Hermitage, including a spiral staircase on the outside which led the way to the first floor where a luxuriously furnished *salon* awaited the visitor. Such a contrast between the exterior and the interior appeared in numerous other garden pavilions of the period, from the Cottage (1780s) at Louis XVIs Rambouillet to the Birch House (c. 1798) at Pavel's Gatchina.

Given Pavel's flirt with freemasonry and that Brenna, like Bazhenov, was a freemason, it might be tempting to suggest an affinity between the tower in the Pavlovsk garden and those towers in Western landscape gardens which somehow allude to the Biblical Tower of Babel and thus embody a link with masonic imagery. However, there is probably not much substance to this, as the new appearance which Brenna and Gonzaga gave the tower makes it akin to the pastoral motifs in Maria Feodorovna's landscape garden. The tower should also be perceived as an interesting *point de vue* in its own right, as perhaps the structure, by its very tower-like appearance, was also thought of as a motif touching upon military matters, thus serving as a kind of pendant to the Bip Castle.

Surrounded by sentries and barriers, the Gatchina complex contrasted strongly with the overall country atmosphere of Pavlovsk. Not surprisingly, it became Pavel's favourite residence. Here he created a martial microcosmos for himself, finding particular pleasure drilling a toy army of no less than two thousand troops dressed in Prussian uniforms. Instead of some garden structures bearing allusions to martial life, the extremely bare architecture of the castle itself held references to what the owner of this place appreciated most.

As King of Poland after Catherine's death, Pavel set out to re-establish under his personal guidance the Polish Priory of the Catholic Order of the Knights of St John of Malta, created in the 11th century as a European defence against the Turks. By guaranteeing the Priory an annual subsidy, Pavel was declared protector of the Knights, so that when Malta fell to Napoleon in 1798, St Petersburg became the temporary headquarters of the Knights of the Order and Pavel became the Grand Master. In gratitude he asked Nikolai Aleksandrovich Lvov (1751-1803), architect, landscape architect, poet, and inventor, to design a building at Gatchina which could serve as a seat for the Order. The Priory (1798-99) was placed on the far border of the so-called Black Lake, which formed part of the garden layout. This ensemble clearly illustrates Pavel's fascination with a medieval world order, and like the Bip Castle it was an offspring of the Emperor's often naive approach to life.

By contrast, the medieval tendencies of the Catherine period seem to have had a serious and indeed very concrete significance. They were of a different order. Not only did Bazhenov and other

69. *Sukhanovo, the Kitchen. Red brick and limestone, turrets and pointed arches were much in line with medieval buildings.*

prominent architects again and again make studies of Old Muscovite architecture, but a look into the political climate of the Catherine period supports the theory that the Tsaritsyno ensemble owes its very existence to the Empress' desire and demand for reviving the old capital to some of its past glory.

Russian "Gothic"

In Bazhenov's speech at the laying of the foundation stone for the never completed Kremlin project, he discussed the main sources of his own stylistic experiments, mentioning the impact from 17th century Moscow architecture. In referring to it as "Russian gothic",[15] it is clear he wished to designate something national and old. Any connection with the etymological meaning of *gothic* as pertaining to the Goths, or with French, German or English gothic architecture can not be acclaimed in this context. Nor did Bazhenov's understanding have anything to do with the correlation between gothic ruins and the architecture of grottoes, which is encountered in a number of

70. *Voronovo near Moscow. As the foreign models prescribed, the Dutch House was placed next to a pond and flowerbeds.*

English and Continental mid and late 18th century writings on garden art. Examples of the latter usage are found in Decker's *Gothic Architecture* (1759) and Wright's *Grotesque Architecture* (1767).

Modern studies of Russian 18th and 19th century architecture and gardens have moved a good part away from Bazhenov's terminology. *Gothic* is of course applied to such structures as the Gothic Arch (ascribed to Velten, 1778-79) in the Tsarskoe Selo garden, which is made of wrought iron and overloaded with typically English perpendicular ornaments, and is likely to have been copied from an illustration in a book on architectural styles.[16] In Russian, it seems

71. *Tsaritsyno, the Ruin Tower. Similar motifs are to be encountered in numerous landscape gardens of the time.*

gothic is used to designate at least four types of architectural forms, with the terms *pseudo-gothic* and *neo-gothic* used quite as often with the same intent.

Bazhenov's use of the term primarily concerns those of his and Kazakov's buildings comprising quotations from 16th and 17th century Moscow architecture in the form of ornamental patterns and emblems and in the use of material. The palace ensembles, Tsaritsyno and Petrovsky epitomize this tradition. The characteristic use of red brick with limestone trim has induced some authors to a rather senseless use of the term *gothic*, as when the Dutch House (1755) in the garden at the Voronovo estate, situated seventy kilometres southwest of Moscow, is referred to as "only one footstep away from *gothic*".[17] In reality this building, like the slightly earlier Dutch House (1749) at Kuskovo, was patterned after typical Dutch town houses, in commemoration of the first Dutch influence under Peter the Great.

A second gothic line is embodied in a number of secondary, utilitarian brick structures in the pleasure gardens of the early and mid 1770s, on the outskirts of St Petersburg and Moscow. This phenomenon is directly connected with the study of the English

72. *Marfino near Moscow. The Palace is studded with quotations from English architecture.*

landscape garden and the use of gothic or gothicizing elements in its architectural motifs. The Neelovs had been sent to England to study gardens and garden architecture, and the impact this trip had on their subsequent work at Tsarskoe Selo appears in the Admiralty and the Kitchen, among other places. Elsewhere, such as in the Kitchen at Sukhanovo, inspiration came either from imported visual and written sources on the English landscape garden or from the new St Petersburg gardens, or perhaps from both. Uncoated red brick was the preferred material, which may have had something to do with it being a relatively cheap and fully adequate solution for such utilitarian facilities.

In landscape gardens of the last quarter of the 18th century, natural looking grottoes and bridges, rocky hills with cascades, and artificial ruins became standard elements. All these features were part of the vocabulary discussed and illustrated at length by the protagonists of the landscape garden, whether they were English, German, French, or Russian. And because the British fused these structures into one category called *natural* or *gothic*, it has become accepted among Russian and Soviet historians to refer to these generally simple garden structures in the same way.

The fourth type of buildings to which *gothic* is generally applied concerns a group of pleasure palaces and garden buildings which appeared in Russia in the 1820s. Similar to Tsaritsyno, these structures were modelled after medieval castles, but the decorative scheme was not so much inspired by national Russian sources as by 12th to 14th century Western architecture. The occurence of this type of building coincides with the popularity of Walter Scott's historical novels and Thomas Gray's nostalgic poetry in the first half of the 19th century. Examples are found in a wide radius from Moscow as well as St Petersburg.

The palace ensemble Marfino, situated thirty-five kilometres north of Moscow, was literally conceived in the shadow of the late 18th century revival of Old Muscovy architecture, but the main building, the arch and the bridge (Mikhail Dormidontovich Bykovsky, 1830s) all bear ornaments that were obviously borrowed from English Tudor. The hiring of foreign architects could in itself be a sound guarantee of getting the desired syntax from abroad. Thus, when Count M.S. Vorontsov, as newly appointed general governor in Nova Rossiya, set out to create a residence for himself in Alupka (1832-51) on the south coast of the Crimea, he chose English and German architects and garden designers (Edward Blore, William Hunt, et al.). As son of a former Russian ambassador in London, Vorontsov had spent his youth in England, and this may in itself have strengthened his desire for having a large Tudor-inspired palace. The facade towards the courtyard, however, was inspired by Islamic architecture.

Towards the middle of the 19th century, eclecticism was gradually developing into a major trend, and a more distinct diversity in the sources used by the Russian architects was being felt. The architecture of Western Europe and that of Russia seems to have been interrelated in spirit, form and meaning as never before. Both the Gothic Chapel (1829-32) and the Gothic Stables (1847-55) at Peterhof could have been erected in almost any Western country of the time, the first having been designed by the German, Karl Friedrich Schinkel and erected under the supervision of the Scot, Adam Adamovich Menelaws. At this stage, there was absolutely no remains of the philosophy conceived under Catherine that Russia needed a national *gothic* building program.

USES AND USERS

Remember how they used to live in Ancient Rome: never in humiliating idleness, always either in active service to their fatherland or in solitude, in a remote and serene place, managing on their own and providing themselves with new mental forces, new knowledge and new talents; this is how they now live in many European countries. (Kurakin, 1790s)

Since antiquity, the creation of a residence out in the countryside was regarded as a privilege, and in the course of the 18th century, Russian writers and noblemen became increasingly conscious of the dichotomy between life in the city and life in the country. A much discussed theme in fiction and non-fiction, it was parallel to the assimilation of antique building forms in new palace and garden projects; the life pattern enjoyed by the antique rulers and higher officials at their suburban residences was also often referred to in writing. Just as this pattern was thought of as ideal, the villa tradition of the Renaissance was also considered a model of its kind.

The quotation above from a letter by Chancellor Aleksander Borisovich Kurakin to his brother is characteristic of the time. Kurakin was the owner of the Nadezhdino estate, situated northwest of Moscow, and his enthusiasm for the recreational life in the countryside knew no bounds:

You must not think that I will come back; no, your urban life does not at all attract me. It is a pity that you and so many of my friends believe that I left in order to enjoy the solitary life in the country and stayed here with the sole purpose of saving money; truly enough, it is very nice not to have empty pockets, but believe me, peace of mind is more precious, and I need it more than money.[1]

In other cases, the country house and its garden also served as a place for the host to entertain a large number of guests. And some noble families were not averse to competing with the Imperial Court when staging musical and theatrical performances.

Following the discussion of this interplay between recreational and ceremonial life, the aim of the present chapter is to look into the intense cultivation of the gardens as practiced by the poets and the painters of the late 18th century. The poets and the painters were among the most frequent users of the gardens, and the works they created, often under the immediate spell of the *genius loci*, throw revealing light on the semantics of the garden scenes. It should be noted that many such works in themselves constitute an important source as to how the historical gardens once looked.

In the chapter entitled "Poets and Promenades", focus is on the poets' discoveries of nature as an aesthetical motif and as an object of philosophical meditation. The elements of nature being subject to constant change and ultimately to decay inspired the poets to sentimental readings of the garden universe, the painters to garden *tableaux* alluding to vanity and death, and the garden owners to the common idea that their properties were places of rest, recreation and death. Thus, the notion of time is fundamental in all three readings. Zhukovsky, whom posterity has generally placed in the shade to the benefit of Pushkin, is the poet whose works are most explored here.

Since the early days of British landscape gardening, painting had been considered a tool and a source of inspiration in the practical design of a garden. William Kent had set the example, and in Russia, an Italian-born theatrical painter Gonzaga was to create a unique series of natural garden *tableaux* at Pavlovsk. Analyzing this creation opens the discussion of the painters' perceptions, thus adding one more piece to the jigsaw puzzle concerning the dialogue between East and West.

Painting was first of all a much preferred medium in which to interpret impressions of the surrounding landscape or garden. The leading Western schools of the time set an example to the young generation of Russian painters, the most talented of whom were offered the possibility of completing their training abroad, in Rome or Paris. Works by Semen Feodorovich Shchedrin are discussed to illustrate this point. Landscape paintings by some foreign artists were also at a premium, and the Frenchman Hubert Robert's popularity with the Russian public is discussed.

Politico-historical iconography represents an important aspect of the ceremonial program contained and performed in the gardens of the tsars. Later this tradition has been echoed in Soviet and post-Soviet garden design. The analysis of garden *tableaux*, created with a specific political intent, will therefore include examples from the 18th century as well as from more recent times. Reaching back to the subject and line of thought in Part One, "Patrons and Programs", the analysis of political emblems will also confirm to what extent the builders and the artists, together with the users, may constitute the basic framework of a garden hermeneutical approach.

73. *Marfino. Promenades, boating, games and parties were popular pastimes in the pleasure gardens of the tsarist epoch.*

Parties and Other Pursuits

...while walking along my lanes and paths, I admired once and again all the pleasures of nature, then I used to take a book out of my pocket and, secluding myself in an overgrown corner, read some deep reflections, and my spirit soared high up in the sky. (Bolotov, 1790s)

For the tsar or for the humblest serf or peasant, the practice of Christianity was an integral part of life in 18th century Russia. People flocked to the churches for services which lasted for several hours. The holy icons were incessantly addressed while candles were lit in front of them, and the traditional bowing and kissing repeated itself again and again. The influx of Western ideas and patterns did not change this, and the development of pleasure palaces and country houses naturally included the construction of a church.[1]

No matter how fundamental the religious ceremonies were in the life and routines of a Russian gentleman and his household, and however popular the new meditative approach to nature was, secular festivities were also considered very important. Traditionally, hunting was a favourite pursuit among the members of the country's leading circles, which like the vegetable gardens and the orchards, had a utilitarian purpose. But the splendour of the hunting parties occasionally seem to have outrivalled the richness of the very event itself. When Elizabeth resided at Tsarskoe Selo, this also seems to have been the rule.

Revelling was one of Russia's favourite pastimes. When parties were scheduled, it was the moment to enjoy various outdoor attractions, whether in summer or winter. Merry-go-rounds, seesaws and slides were very popular attractions in the gardens developed under Peter and Elizabeth, as were fields for various kinds of games. Sliding and sledging were so popular as amusements, that the so-called *montagnes russes*, or sliding hills, attracted many a garden visitor.

At Oranienbaum, Catherine had Rinaldi design a sumptuous two-storeyed garden pavilion (1762-74). Banquets were held here, and from the south side of the pavilion guests could glide down a 532 metre long switchback in small carriages. According to a contemporary source, the slope was thus used:

...a small carriage containing one person, being placed in the centre groove upon the highest point, goes with great rapidity down one hill; the velocity which it acquires in its descent carries it up a second; and it continues to move in a similar manner until it arrives at the bottom of the area, where it rolls for a considerable way.[2]

In most places though, a wooden slide proved sufficient. Other outdoor pursuits which the male members of the country house community and their guests enjoyed were archery and ball games.

The local peasants were often asked to dress up in their very best clothes and to contribute with some kind of entertainment. Songs, dances and games which originated in the old Russian peasant culture were performed at the host's command. From one of the parties given at Marfino in the 1840s, a Moscow student named Alexander Lvov reported that the peasants would throng beneath the balcony of the palace, and cascades of coins were offered to them after their performance.[3]

Sometimes a gentleman would hold big parties for the mere sake of festivity. In one place no less than eighteen social gatherings were held in three weeks,

...with fireworks and music in the garden; the surrounding factories stopped working, because the workers spent all night around the house and in the

74. Oranienbaum, the Sliding Hill. On the south side of the pavilion the guests could glide down on a long switchback.

garden, and the prior of the neighbouring monastery was unable to manage the monks who, instead of attending morning prayer, stood on the walls of the monastery and looked at the fireworks, and listened to the gypsies and to the horn music.[4]

This is far from the only report of its kind. Truly enough, excessive partying was not in immediate tune with the philosophy of rural rest propagated by the poets, the garden writers and some of the country house residents, but however beautiful and varied the garden landscape was, and however interesting books and pieces of music could be enjoyed, life in the countryside occasionally became somewhat monotonous. A tone of regret over the lack of entertainment was frequently heard amidst the many verbal celebrations of country life. Revelry was taken to be a convenient way of overcoming dullness, at least temporarily.

A party would often begin with a service in the church. Afterwards the host would welcome his guests in the main building. According to Lvov's description of the party at Marfino, this welcome would take place from the balcony, decorated for the occasion with laurel wreaths and flowers, and many serf musicians and singers would stand along the route from the church to the palace. Following the first meal, hunting was next on the morning's program. At lunch time hundreds of peasants entertained, and afterwards a number of orchestras played till the elderly started leaving to take a rest, and the young guests went into the garden to dance, to watch theatrical performances and to ride the merry-go-rounds. In the evening, the garden was illuminated and the party continued. Lvov concluded:

This was how the glorious count gave parties at his Marfino; pleasure and joy were omnipresent at the Russian landowner's temple of festive hospitality.[5]

Some parties lasted for several days, and sometimes participants were of a great number — from one hundred to three or four hundred people.

Whenever guests were invited, the host took care to exhibit and offer the best his gardens produced. What amazed foreign guests most was the amount and the variety of fruits.

At the tables of the nobility, there is generally an abundance of the finest fruits: pines, peaches, apricots, grapes, pears, cherries, and even lemons and oranges, none of which can be obtained here, in perfection, without the assistance of hothouses.

Great care is devoted to these orangeries, which are frequently superintended by individuals retained for the purpose, who are under the direction of an English or German gardener. Indeed, there are instances of individuals (Germans) kept for no other purpose than to attend to the pine-apples.[6]

This is how the Englishman Robert Lyall described his impressions of life at the pleasure palaces in suburban Moscow, with which he included a catalogue of plants found in and around Moscow in his book entitled *The Character of the Russians and A Detailed History of Moscow* (1823). Lyall continued:

The test of the gardener's knowledge is the quantity and the quality of the fruit produced; therefore he is, in general, stimulated to the greatest exertions, to render himself worthy of his place. Indeed, he sometimes has a higher interest. Many of the nobility have a much larger supply of fruit than they consume, and a quantity is sold in town, upon which the gardener himself has a certain percentage; or sometimes he gets the third part of all the fruits to himself.[7]

Most often, the gardener managed his affairs rather independently. It was he, not the patron, who was the specialist. But there were exceptions.

Horticulture as a Hobby or Business

At Pavlovsk, Maria Feodorovna supervised all planting and took an active part in the care and protection of the flowers and trees. She not only had the ambition to duplicate architectural scenes from some of Europe's landscape gardens, but was also determined to overcome the restraints the northern Russian climate put on planting and to create a garden that excelled in beauty and lushness.

Familiar with many garden theoretical works of the day, she often personally decided which plants were required, her vast botanical knowledge permitting her to specify the varieties. Seeds and cuttings were ordered from many countries for the Pavlovsk orangery and the many hothouses. Fruit trees were brought from Moscow, pineapples from Peterhof, linden trees from Lübeck, bulbs from Holland, and in 1795 a collection of one hundred and twenty-six plants from the hothouses in Kew Garden was sent by George III, including new plant discoveries from the South Seas. Maria Feodorovna's passion for flowers was reflected in a wealth of pots in the palace interiors, the greenhouses and the luxuriant parterres of the Private Garden.

When Pavel and Maria Feodorovna set out on their Grand Tour in 1781, the Archduchess typically wanted to be kept informed about

75. *Kuskovo. Gardeners at work in the parterre garden. The orangery is seen in the background.*

the gardens back home. Kuchelbecker responded to her wish in a letter of March 2, 1782:

The gardener went to town to present a flowering rosebush to Their Imperial Highnesses [the children had been left in St Petersburg]...I would like to bring them a cherry tree in bloom. There are several trees, a peach tree, an almond tree and plum trees in flower. The violets have passed. If the snow and the ice did not remind us of it, one could forget that this place is at 60 degrees latitude. The grapevines and so many other trees are in flower, the daffodils, the primroses, the hyacinths are already blossoming and soon to do so the lilacs, the buttercups and the oreilles d'ours [aromatic primroses]...the rosebushes in bud in our greenhouses make us regret each day that the springtime in our hothouses is not seen by Your Highness.[8]

How Maria Feodorovna involved herself with the Pavlovsk garden on a practical level is evident from the following letter of hers, from April 20, 1786. It is about the long linden alley.

I have arrived from Gatchina at this moment and have examined with the most scrupulous attention the way of planting trees (especially the lindens and rose trees) of Sparrow [the English gardener at Gatchina] and I confess

76. *Sheremetev's orangery at Kuskovo produced some of the finest fruits in 18th century Russia.*

that I was very surprised to see the difference between the care he gives to it and the little Visler [the German gardener at Pavlovsk] brings to it. Sparrow, after having planted the lindens in black earth puts more on top of the roots and every two days has each linden watered and the roots covered with many pine branches. He does the same with rose trees and so all of these are green...It is women who are used to water the trees. Try and find some for this work and starting tomorrow water my new planted lindens and roses.[9]

And in another slightly later letter to Kuchelbecker:

I am told that it is in Finland that one will most easily find a fine oak; that one could take it in the early spring, with all the roots and earth. We must at present dig the hole which will receive it and then cover it so that snow does not fall into it and when one plants the tree, which we will transport on a sledge, put a good layer of Holzerde [wood mold].[10]

It was a time when scientific results were emerging from the serious study of plants. Among the analyses known also in Russia was Linné's system of classification. Kuchelbecker bought a copy of the book for Maria Feodorovna, and at one point he even promised to furnish her with "the catalogue of the plants at Pavlovsk".[11]

In the central Russian provinces, fruit growing and forestry were

77. Pavlovsk. Grand Duchess Maria Feodorovna took a very active part in the planning and care of her garden.

main sources of income at numerous estates. To meet the demand for professional advice, Bolotov dedicated the larger number of his writings to topics in this field. To cultivate one's land was an old and very basic command, and from the last quarter of the 18th century it received more theoretical attention then ever before in Russia. Concurrently, the Catherine period for the first time saw the publication of a number of guides to utilitarian gardening for individual households.

An anonymous work entitled *O poleznykh iskusstvakh i khudozhestvakh dlya sadov* (Practical and Artful Gardening, 1779) was the first example in this genre.[12] All of the one hundred and fifty pages were filled with practical advice. The first subject to be dealt with was "How to Prepare a Good Soil for All Kinds of Plants?", the second "How to Improve Bad Soil?", and so on. Soon after this book appeared, Nikolai Osipov and Vasily Levshin wrote and published a number of handbooks and horticultural dictionaries.

One of Osipov's titles, *Novoi i sovershennoi ruskoi sadovnik* (A New and Entirely Russian Handbook on Gardening, 1793), is particularly interesting in the sense that the author so strongly emphasized that it was a Russian and not a foreign work. But in *Karmannaya kniga selskago i domashnyago khozyaistva* (A Handbook on Household and Garden, 1791), he openly admitted to having included ideas from various foreign sources. In some of Osipov's and Levshin's works, comments and explanations on features pertaining to pleasure gardens were also included. But the readers would have to consult other sources if they had any ambitions of developing gardens in the landscape manner. In terms of aesthetics, more than a generation separated Osipov and Levshin from Bolotov and Lvov.

Not surprisingly, Russia's first botanical garden had already been founded in St Petersburg under Peter, and many Russian botanical studies had since been published. A complete catalogue, in Latin as well as Russian, according to the principles laid down by Linné, was the result of a study undertaken by the academician P.S. Pallas in a central Moscow garden during the summer of 1781. The garden was founded in 1756 by P.A. Demidov, the son of one of Russia's most influential metal industrialists.

...the river border [the Moscow river] was totally unfit for developing a garden; but for two years 700 people worked on levelling out the hill above the river, ...Then the owner of the garden decided to use it for fruit growing, and subsequently for botany, and he built many different hothouses in it.[13]

So Pallas tells. He ends his catalogue of the 2,224 plants contained in the garden with the hope that this place may be protected in memory of its knowledgeable founder and that it will help in "furthering the study of the Russian Empire's botany".[14]

Demidov's own correspondence gives a number of interesting clues to his interest for the greenhouses, the fruit trees and the many birds and animals he, like Maria Feodorovna, had imported from abroad. His letters resound with the joy he found in gardening:

Tell me where to find some warm weather: we have very cold nights, as if there was a light frost, and it is gloomy during the day, and there were no more than two warm days this month. Outside, any delicate plant fades. Moreover, it is very windy almost every day. What can be done to get a climate which is good for your health? My only joy is plants; they delight me, I am very thrilled about them.[15]

The scientist Pallas knew very well the answer to Demidov's request for a milder climate. He himself went to the Crimea to enjoy the natural delights of Russia's southernmost corner.

It was Grigory Potemkin who in 1783 had fulfilled Catherine's ambitions of conquering this beautifully situated peninsula. Potemkin himself did not hesitate to show a keen interest in horticultural matters, as long as he could stay in the Crimea. The title of Prince of Tauris, the antique name for the newly conquered land, was be-

78. Portrait of P.A. Demidov, founder of great botanical collections. Demidov
once wrote: "My only joy is plants".

79. *Pavlovsk, the Privy Garden as it looks today. Maria Feodorovna had trees, cuttings and seeds sent from abroad.*

stowed upon him after the victory, and in St Petersburg Catherine ordered a palace (Starov, 1783-89) with a landscape garden to be built for him. However, Potemkin was too active a person to follow the pattern of the many meditative garden strollers among his peers in the Northern capital. Instead, he set about planting and exploring vast territories on the southern coast of the Crimea for commercial purposes.

Fig, almond, laurel, pomegranate and cypress were found in the private garden of the Prince of Tauris. With the much milder and warmer climate on the very borders of the Black Sea, garden owners were able to enjoy plants, flowers and fruits which in the north were only seen in orangeries and hothouses. Moreover, the peninsula had a natural flora which astonished anybody coming from St Petersburg or Moscow. Potemkin contributed to this exotic look by importing plants and trees from Constantinople, so that from the mid 1780s extensive olive and mulberry plantations were developed on the lands near the old Tatar towns of Foros and Sudak.

Some forty years later, with the help of French professionals, Count Vorontsov founded the first large-scale vineyards on the peninsula. The area near his Alupka Palace became a nucleus in what later turned out to be one of Russia's biggest successes in viticulture. In the 19th century, dozens of such businesses and pleasure residences developed where formerly the khans had been delighting in their artistic garden imitations of Paradise.

The Garden as Theatre

Birthdays and the arrival of friends and distinguished guests were good pretexts for organizing large-scale festivities at the country houses. The arrival of as prominent a person as the Emperor or the Empress gave rise to special ceremonies, and was generally commemorated by the erection of a monument. Revelling, which otherwise was basically ephemeral, suddenly turned into a phenomenon of historical significance.

Of course, very few of the gentry were so fortunate as to receive, if only once in their life, the Russian ruler as their guest. When such an event did take place, sadly it was rarely described in the detail that would allow for posterity to imagine the scenario. The lack of information on Catherine's visit to Bogoroditske is much regretted. Some more information however has been left regarding the visits she paid to Kuskovo. When in Moscow in 1775 for the celebration of the end of the war against the Turks, Catherine visited the ageing

80. *Kuskovo, the obelisk commemorating Catherine the Great's visit to Count Sheremetev's Muscovite summer residence.*

Field Marshal Peter Borisovich Sheremetev at Kuskovo and donated a monument.

The obelisk, which was placed in the parterre garden, was crowned by a statue of Minerva, the Roman goddess of war. For the day of Catherine's arrival, Sheremetev ensured that a sumptuous outdoor celebration was organized. "For this specific day the triumphal arch had been erected on the Kuskovo Prospect..."[16] The source of this quotation, an anonymous book entitled *Kuskovo i ego okrestnosti* (Kuskovo and Surroundings, 1850) continues:

While the festive Imperial procession moved along the broad road, the girls who wore white dresses and had wreaths on their heads walked in front of all others and covered the road with flowers. When the procession approached the lifting bridge, the ship with twenty guns and other ships on the lake saluted for the sovereign guests. In the evening, following the performance, firework was lit and all Kuskovo was splendidly illuminated.[17]

The celebrations on the occasion of Catherine's successive visits to Kuskovo in 1785 and 1787 were no less overwhelming. The pattern repeated itself, when Pavel in 1797 came to Moscow for his

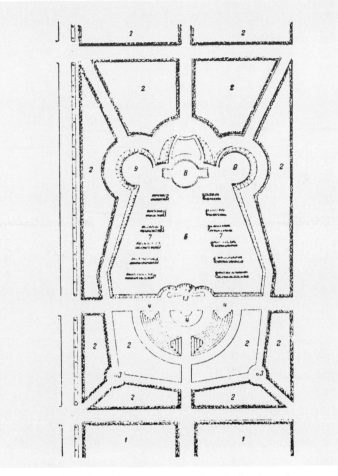

81. *Reconstruction of Kuskovo's green theatre. Serf actors, dancers and musicians gave lustre to the Sheremetev theatres.*

coronation and visited Nikolai Petrovich Sheremetev at the latter's new theatre palace at Ostankino.[18]

Even more than such festivities, it was the theatres at Kuskovo and Ostankino that lent these suburban residences their renowned society atmosphere. Serf theatres were quite popular in the late 18th century, with sources mentioning nearly two hundred such theatres in twenty-four provinces.[19] Performances were given in the most varied places, but a few troupes had a proper scene at their disposal and performed there regularly. The Sheremetev theatres enjoy a special place in the very early chapters of Russian theatrical life. They were considered among the best.

The first Kuskovo Theatre was established around 1763. This was an open-air theatre placed northeast of the Italian House so as to balance with the field for games and attractions near the Dutch House. Like its Western counterparts, such as the theatre at Marie-Antoinette's Trianon, it was made with the same materials as the surrounding gardens. Bosquets of birch and fir trees bordered by lower espaliers surrounded the theatre. Particularly charming was a covering of strawberry plants of the soil between the trees. The scene, the orchestra pit and the coulisses were also defined by espaliers. The painted decorations were movable, and a special box and an amphitheatrical space with about one hundred seats were established for the Count and his family, and the invited public respectively. Flowers added to the natural charms of this ensemble.

As for the question of authorship, the names of some serf architects, gardeners and painters have been proposed.[20] But the sources have not previously allowed for any precise attribution. Due to its fittings and size, the Kuskovo Theatre was rather intimate. Motifs for the small operas and musical plays were often inspired by the local setting. Among the titles were *Gulyanie, ili Sadovnik Kuskovsky* (A Promenade, or the Kuskovo Gardener) and *Nimfa Kuskovskaya* (The Kuskovo Nymph). Some modifications were made to the theatre when Peter Borisovich Sheremetev in 1769 took up permanent residence at Kuskovo and built himself a luxurious new house called the House of Solitude. Later, the young Nikolai Petrovich Sheremetev built an indoor theatre at Kuskovo. Yet regular performances continued at the green theatre all through the 1770s and 80s.

Kuskovo also boasted its own orchestra, which at the time was referred to as a hunting orchestra. Each of the ninety-one horns in the full orchestra made only one sound, the note of which depended on the length of the horn, a fact which once prompted a foreign traveller to assert:

It is a serious and festive music, but only serfs can play this kind of music, because only serfs can be taught to produce only one sound.[21]

This particular genre also found its way to some musical works composed for the scene, but generally it was enjoyed as part of the entertainment in a mid or late 18th century garden setting.

The Sheremetev family's theatrical and musical programs, by and large, outrivalled what other noblemen could produce to entertain the guests at their residences in the Moscow surroundings. Prince Yusupov was the only competitor when he at Arkhangelskoe invited the Moscow society for performances at his new theatre (Gonzaga, 1818). Cultural life out in the province was on another scale. Al-

82. *Pavlovsk, the Aviary. The birds, however, soon gave place to exhibitions of antique treasures and flower displays.*

though the owners of moderately-sized pleasure palaces and country houses usually had some musicians, singers and actors of their own, the ensembles performing at Kuskovo and Ostankino counted some of the country's leading artists. Only the traditions of Tsarskoe Selo, Pavlovsk, Gatchina and other Imperial residences were on the same level. As for Pavlovsk, it was Pavel's fascination with theatre that made Maria Feodorovna arrange for dozens of plays and operas to be created there. Later, Pavlovsk came to be associated with the best of Russian music life. A "Vauxhall" (from which *vokzal*, the Russian word for railway station, is derived) was built, and the train connection from St Petersburg enabled more citizens to spend a day in the country.

Solitude and Eternal Rest

Vanity, hollowness and haste were used as synonyms of city life. Such a life pattern hindered everybody from being at rest with themselves.

I live in the country now, knowing no vanity, doing whatever I wish, whenever it pleases me. I live the way I want to, and not as somebody else asks me to. I am not forced to want what others want. There is nobody to make me express joy or make me cry or laugh.[22]

This was a poet's attitude. The point was to escape from the city and to spend some time in peace.

Figures occur in practically all garden pictures of the time, yet the scenes are not thronged with people as had been the standard way of representing gardens until the last quarter of the 18th century. The idea of nature as a positive force was new. The manners of the garden visitors changed in consequence, as did the visions of the painters. One could submerge oneself in nature and restore the tired spirit, but to accomplish this, a certain measure of solitude was required. Sometimes only a single figure is present in the garden scenes. Most often, though, groups of two or three persons are shown walking on the winding paths, admiring a small cascade or enjoying a pavilion on the bank of a lake from a boat. To add a touch of Arcadian life to the garden views, herds of grazing cattle or sheep were occasionally included. Shchedrin's scenes from Pavlovsk represent the utmost in this genre.

Next to promenades and the simple being in the midst of nature, or rather a garden, reading was a much favoured pursuit. If outdoors, a bench in the shadow of an old tree or an airy pavilion offered a perfect setting. On a rainy September day in her early years at Pavlovsk, Maria Feodorovna wrote: "I read, write, study music and do a little work...In the evenings I play cards."[23] Later in the same autumn:

We usually have supper at 4 or 5 o'clock...after supper we spend time reading and in the evening I play chess until 8 or 9 o'clock...Then three or four of us make 100 circles of the room; at each turn Lafermier [Franco-German librarian to Pavel] pulls a seed from his hat and with each dozen he makes an announcement to the room in a loud voice.[24]

Although Maria Feodorovna was no ordinary representative of Russia's country house residents, these brief descriptions of hers undoubtedly correspond to what was customary.

On the other hand, it is also clear that she was much more concerned with horticultural questions, theoretical as well as practical, than the large majority of country house owners. Many preferred some other kinds of outdoor activity next to the peaceful promenades. Angling, sledging and various kinds of games were quite popular pursuits. This can be seen in many garden paintings of the period, including the album with watercolour views from the garden at Bogoroditske, painted by Bolotov with the help of his son.

Yet strangely enough, no one here is occupied with practical gardening.

To the watercolour painter Andrei Timofeevich Bolotov, the main point in garden life was "rest and independence, or said in another way, comfort".[25] The French terms here employed come from Alexandre Delaborde's *Description des nouveaux jardins de la France et de ses anciens châteaux, mêlée d'observations sur la vie de campagne et de la composition des jardins* (1808), a much read work in which the author includes a characterization of the rural pattern of life during the French Enlightenment.

Many scenes in Bolotov's album also include people who are being shown around. Bogoroditske was much admired in those days, but the figures also represent, by projection, the beholder of the watercolours. The album was, after all, conceived as a demonstration piece, an evocative visual document. Finally, what Delaborde termed "meditation and contemplation" was something quite essential for Bolotov to demonstrate in his garden views.

Individual figures are shown in deep thoughts and in equally deep admiration of the landscape. In his memoirs Bolotov wrote:

O God! How many truly joyful and pleasurable moments did I experience when being among Nature's favourites, while they were making up spring's first greenery! How I admired the variety and different hues of the leaves and grasses![26]

Bolotov was far from being a poet, but as a learned man and a publicist, he had at his disposal a language in which to speak about his impressions of nature and about his garden activities. His memoirs thus communicate a fine portrayal of a gentleman's daily life at a Russian 18th century country house.

In the following extract from his memoirs, it is summer and the place is Bolotov's native Dvoryaninovo.

...my life at that time was rather special and so monotonous and simple that I can describe it with a few words. Waking up every morning at sunrise, I first of all used to open the window facing my flower garden, I sat down at the window and admired the beauty of Nature and all the pleasures of a spring morning...[27]

After lunch, Bolotov again went to the garden, and

...sitting in some nice shady corner, I plunged myself into a pleasant book, or took my brushes and paints and continued painting right up till when I had to work again.[28]

83. View from the Bogoroditske garden. The air of this scenery is in harmony with Bolotov's memories from his family estate.

Bolotov's summer day also ended outdoors, in a lyric mood.

> I devoted pleasant evening hours to admiring the beauties of nature; in order to admire them comfortably and to enjoy myself, I used to go to the old, lower garden from where I could watch the whole place...There, sitting on the soft grass and with a nightingale's loud song from every grove, I admired the sunset, the cattle passing the river and running from the fields to the stables, the murmur of water that runs over small stones in our beloved and beautiful river Skinga.[29]

Whenever Bolotov wrote about the practical work in the garden and on the estate as such, he characteristically did it in a positive way, but others looked upon it differently. Some regretted that farm work, economy, family and other obligations left too little time for pleasurable pursuits, including writing. "...the ploughmen, the harvesters, the cutters and the threshers are our muses", one poet concluded.[30]

As time went by, many a higher official made preparations for spending his last years in the countryside. Gardens which for already at least a decade or two had been compared to scenes of antique idylls, and where ruins and graves alluded to the perishability of all worldly things, gradually turned into sites of eternal rest. The Chancellor Bezborodko expressed his purpose this way:

I remain faithful to my desire to quit the big world and to settle in the country where I have built an asylum for myself, ...where I intend to spend my last days and those that come after death.[31]

In Delille's poetic interpretation it says:

> Here Man come to commune with his heart retires,
> And of the future and the past enquires;
> Thinks on the good and ill the Gods bestow,
> Of prosperous guilt, and undeserved woe;
> And oft reverts, and mid the circling hours,
> As blown in desert waste some scattered flowers,
> Recalls those moments, short, alas! but dear,
> Marked by past bliss, now blotted with a tear.[32]

Poets and Promenades

> I bid thee welcome, O, sequestered nook,
> Refuge of quietude, of toil and inspiration,
> Wherein my days meander like an unseen brook,
> Sunk in oblivious elation,
> I'm thine — I have exchanged those shameful Circe's yokes,
> Luxurious merriment, carousal, dissipation,
> For the quiescent fields, the peace of murmurous oaks,
> For heedless idleness, the friend of inspiration. (Pushkin, 1819)

The garden creations of the Russian rulers and their architects were occasionally celebrated in the poetical works of the pre-Petrine period. Garden poetry, though, experienced its first real blossoming in the late 18th century, at which point garden owners and poets not only began to indulge in each other's company more than ever before, but an entirely different relationship between them came into being. Officially commissioned appraisals were complemented by a cult of friendship and intimate feelings.

The garden landscape with all its allusive or sentimental overtones was described and praised in what turned out to be the first Russian experiments in a new genre. So that in the same way the new attitude to nature brought about a landscape painting which was based on an immediate encounter with nature, it also gave rise to new motifs in the literature of the time. "For a very long time my soul did not enjoy such a complete solitude, such a complete free-

dom. I am alone — alone with my thoughts — alone with nature...",
it said in Nikolai Karamzin's short story "Derevnya" (The Countryside, 1792).[1]

The elements of a garden were compared to natural groves, virgin
forests, and natural lakes. As Karamzin pointed out, such natural
scenery was "better than French and English gardens".[2] Like most of
his poet colleagues, he could not escape the aesthetics of the
landscape garden.

The little river gurgles and invites me to its sides — I go — the water jets
are enticing, they attract me — I cannot resist this yearning and throw
myself into the fluid crystal. The pavilion above me is interlaced with two
willows — the helpful gardener brings me a basket full of fragrant rasp-
berries...The heat passes — I go to the meadow to botanize.[3]

The majority of the literary texts praising nature were not created
under the impact of virgin land. In fact, the garden refuges in suburban Moscow and St Petersburg were the main sources of inspiration.

At Pavlovsk, Maria Feodorovna dedicated a pavilion to the
numerous poets and artists who came to stay for some time, to take
delight in the garden scenes and to work. An album filled with
signatures and comments tangibly testifies to this. In the Rose
Pavilion (Andrei Nikiforovich Voronikhin, 1807-12; enlarged by Rossi
and Gonzaga, 1814) there were plates with the names of some of the
country's most distinguished poets, including among others, Karamzin, Zhukovsky, Derzhavin and Krylov. Vasily Andreevich Zhukovsky's life and work in particular was closely tied to Pavlovsk.[4] Some
of his finest elegies and romances are dedicated to this Parnassus, to
the landscape scenery and to Maria Feodorovna. The sketches he
made in the garden came to illustrate the first guide to Pavlovsk,—
Storkh's *Putevoditel po sadu i gorodu Pavlovsku* (Guide to the Garden
and Town of Pavlovsk, 1843).

Like another *son of Nature*, a gentleman of the Russian province
portrayed himself and his countryside leisure in a letter to
Zhukovsky.

If I were a skilled draughtsman, I would depict myself as a young man,
looking exactly like Vasily Andreevich, lying on the unfinished foundation
of the house; he would let one hand rest on the lyre, rub his eyes with the
other, while looking at a postal card, and with a yawn he would exclaim:
I shall attain to it. This would be the inscription on the drawing. At his feet
there would be some drafts for future writings, a sketch for a flowerbed and
an hourglass with a rose festoon twisted round it.[5]

The comparison with Zhukovsky alone clearly reflects the esteem some poets enjoyed at the time. They counted among the most appreciated and frequent guests at the Russian country houses around 1800. The comparison moreover holds some important attributes such as the lyre and the hourglass, flowers such as roses and the art of drawing, which are key notions in the garden and landscape poetry of the period.

Time and Twilight

The lyre is an allusion to the classical tradition. Apollo, the Greek patron of the arts, was often shown with this musical instrument. Greek as well as Roman literature of antiquity inspired idylls and pastorales dedicated to nature's elements and to mythological patrons of nature.

The first generation of Russian nature poets considered themselves part of this tradition. Not only did they read, study and translate the classical poets, but a certain familiarity with contemporary Western trends based on this heritage was also at hand, and German as well as English poets were taken as models. More than once, however, the Russian poets rewriting foreign poems in their mother-tongue did not explicitly acknowledge their model. As in the visual arts of the time, it was understood that sources could be used without restraint.

"Poets of the heart" was the label Karamzin accorded upon the classical interpreters of the pastorale in his poem "Poezia" (Poetry, 1787).

> They praised the pleasures of the country scenery,
> and their listeners were fascinated by the beauty of nature,
> without art by the delights of the countryside. When Homer sings,
> every soldier, every hero, respecting Theocritus,
> throws down his arms — now the shepherd is the hero.[6]

Karamzin himself very much enjoyed the serene life in the Russian countryside, for which his close relations to the Imperial Court as well as to several noble families proved convenient. Periodically he stayed at Pavlovsk and in the Chinese Village at Tsarskoe Selo, and later he was invited to Sukhanovo near Moscow to live, to compose and to work on his voluminous *Istoriya gosudarstva Rossyskogo* (History of the Russian State, 1818-29).

"Poezia" was Karamzin's tale of the genesis of poetry itself. He considered the art of writing to be intimately connected with the idea of the world as a marvellous, godly creation. In a rich metaphorical

84. Bogoroditske. Walking and viewing, reading and painting were Bolotov's own favourite pastimes when outdoors.

language Karamzin asserted that the roses in Paradise gave humanity the impetus to praise God's work, with words as well as with the tones of the lyre, and a universal desire to celebrate other elements of nature arose. Karamzin dwells with the idyllic tradition of antiquity, and from there he goes on to Ossian, Shakespeare, Milton and Thomson, and finally to Klopstock, one of the foremost German idyllists.

In Russia, Thomson won much fame for his poem devoted to the seasons. His emphasis on the elusive character of things very often induced the reader with a melancholic mood. Karamzin aimed at investing his poems with a similar sentimental atmosphere, and he consequently often wrapped his landscape impressions in twilight or in the darkness of late evening hours, with a preference for autumn over the other seasons. The poem entitled "Osen" (Autumn, 1789) epitomizes this aesthetic.

> The dry leaves are falling;
> The cold breeze above
> Has stript of its glories
> The sorrowing grove.

The hills are all weeping,
The field is a waste,
The songs of the forest
Are silent and past.[7]

The portrayal of the fading landscape is accompanied by an aged traveller's sighs when confronted with this spectacle and his final giving in to time:

But man's chilling winter
Is darksome and dim;
For no second spring-tide
E'er dawns upon him.[8]

The poets indeed succeeded in turning the cult of elusiveness into a popular motif.

The garden theorists also focused on letting the hours of the day and the seasons come to the fore in the general layout of the country houses and their adjoining pleasure grounds. Bolotov gave much reflection to this question and, following Hirschfeld, devoted several pages to recommending plants that would allow the garden visitor to indulge in different moods. Similar concerns occupied Nicolai Aleksandrovich Lvov (1751-1803), who designed country seats and gardens in the Moscow and Torchok regions in addition to realizing a series of building projects in St Petersburg. Lvov, who was also a poet, wrote a treatise based on his work on the Bezborodko garden in Moscow, and described his decision to propose three different promenades in this landscape garden: One for the morning, another for day, and a third one for the evening.

The area destined for evening promenades is more spacious than the others, it is situated across the lower part of the garden. Big trees border the wide shady roads...which either lead into the woods or to the water...[9]

No garden writer, of course, could rival the poets' language when portraying the atmosphere in such gardens. Lvov's own poems bear testimony to this, as do Zhukovsky's.

Starting his stroll in the bright morning light, Zhukovsky in "Slavyanka. Elegiya" (The Slavyanka. An Elegy, 1815) ingeniously lets the quiet flow of the river define his route in time and space. The season chosen for this promenade in the Slavyanka Valley in the Pavlovsk garden is, of course, autumn, and the tone and the colours of the scenery are all being perceived as indicators of the final hours of the day. The poem begins:

Gentle river Slavyanka, how pleasant is your current,
When on a day in autumn,
Attired by the last and fading beauty of Nature,
The hills are looking down at your waters.[10]

And continues,

The day fades away...the wood in the shade bends down to the waters;
The trees are dressed in evening mirk,
And only a crimson band of evening glow
Touches its quiet tops.

The eastern bank is brightly lit in a glow,
The splendid home of tsars on the golden slope
Radiates, like a giant who looks into the mirror of waters,
In his secluded greatness.[11]

Nothing ever remains the same in nature, and the lonely and roman-tic traveller, alias the poet, was keen to become immersed in the my-stery behind this process.

As opposed to Bolotov or any other garden professional or ama-teur, the poet was seldom concerned with any practical horticultural doings. He remained a spectator, watching, describing and celebra-ting the way in which, for example, the movement from day to night brings about a new enigmatic atmosphere. Purposefully, water is the very first element Zhukovsky celebrates in "Slavyanka" as well as in "Vecher. Elegiya" (Evening. An Elegy, 1806), another famous poem inspired by the Pavlovsk garden. Thus, the initial words of "Evening" are:

The brook, winding over the white sand,
How pleasant your quiet harmony is.
How sparkling is your flow into the river!
Come to me, o heavenly Muse,

With a wreath of young roses and with a golden flute;
Bend thoughtfully over the foaming waters
And, with animated sounds, sing and glorify the hazy evening
Wrapped in dozing Nature.[12]

Water represents a change, a process by itself, which befitted the gar-den poet's combined urge to use a specific route around the land-scape and to create an illusion of movement, and ultimately of elusiveness, in his work.

A promenade in the Tsarskoe Selo garden placed the Big Pond at

85. *Pavlovsk. The Slavyanka river winding itself through the landscape. This scenery inspired some of Russia's great poets.*

the centre of attention, in order to better view the many new and fashionable scenes placed near its irregular banks or slightly off the path leading around the pond. In Derzhavin's "Progulka v Tsarskom Sele" (A Promenade at Tsarskoe Selo, 1797), the couple is actually enjoying the varied scenery from a boat.

> ...between the pillars and edifices of Themis,
> Which she [Catherine the Great] erected to the glory of Russian heroes,...
> I spent some pleasurable moments with young Plenira
> While sailing on the little lake,
> Far away from everybody...[13]

The element of water here clearly serves as the poet's medium for getting to know the garden and its monuments, but in other poems, the water itself is the main subject, catalysing *rêveries* and melancholic thoughts.

It is a shepherd who introduces the poet to the language of the two streams in Nikolai Lvov's "Rucheiki" (The Brooks, 1787). With Derzhavin, on the other hand, the scenery is not only akin to that of a pastoral, but the waning of time, and thus the presence of death, is

86. *Pavlovsk. The Rose Pavilion served as a place of rest to Maria Feodorovna's visiting poets and artists.*

the focal point in several of his poems. The following extract is from his "Vodopad" (The Waterfall, 1791-94):

> He sits, and muses on the rapid stream,
> While deep thoughts struggling from his bosom rise:
> 'Emblem of man!' here brightly pictured seem
> The world's gay scenery and its pageantries,
> Which, as delusive as thy shining wave,
> Glow for the proud, the coward and the slave.
>
> So is our little stream of life poured out,
> In the wild turbulence of passion: so,
> Midst glory's glance and victory's thunder-shout,
> The joys of life in hurried exile go —
> Till hope's fair smile and beauty's ray of light
> Are shrouded in the griefs and storms of night.
>
> Day after day prepares the funeral shroud;
> The world is grey with age: — the striking hour
> Is but an echo of death's summons loud —
> The jarrings of the dark grave's prison door:
> Into its deep abyss — devouring all —
> Kings and the friends of kings alike must fall.[14]

87. *Tsaritsyno. The pavilion entitled Beautiful View was thought of as one of the finishing points of the morning promenade.*

Time and Death

When meditating upon the garden landscapes, the poets alternately used natural and architectural motifs as their point of departure. Karamzin, who, together with Lvov, must be considered a pioneer in the new genre, was familiar with Delille's poem *Les Jardins, ou l'Art d'Embellir les Paysages*, and he dedicated one of his most descriptive poems on the effects nature had on the sensible mind to the French painter-poet: "Melankholiya. Podrazhenie Delilyu" (Melancholy. Imitation of Delille, 1800).

> O Melancholy! The most delicate play
> From grief and distress to pleasure and delight!
> There is still no gaiety, though no torment,
> Despair has gone...Yet, with tears having dried
> You dare not glance around the world
> And you look like your mother, Grief.
> You escape from splendour and from people,
> And twilight is dearer to you than bright days.
> You are fond of silence, you listen to the sombre
> Murmur of leaves and mountain rivers,

Roaring winds and sea waves.
You like the woods and you admire deserts;
In solitude you are closer to yourself;
Gloomy Nature attracts your tender glance:
As if it grieved with you.
And when daylight is disappearing from the sky,
In deep thought you gaze at it,
To you, nor the loud fuss of courteous spring,
Nor summer with its luxurious, lustre and
Ripening fruits are dear, no, you prefer
the feeble autumn, when it withers
And tears off its garlands with a languid hand,
And is waiting for death.[15]

Yet the reading of Delille did not inspire Karamzin to celebrate garden monuments in memory of late family members and friends. The elements of nature remained his prime subject. Delille dealt with the question of tomb stones and graves in the following way:

Here, far from madding crowds, your vigils keep,
With you the woods, the flowers, the streams shall weep.
Each object to the wretched seems a friend.
To clasp the tomb o'er which your tears descend (...)
In these sad monuments parade offends;
Ill pomp with landscape, art with sorrow blends.[16]

Other Russian poets however, followed the Western trend of celebrating funerary monuments:

Come, a white tombstone can be seen
In the shadow of the old pine trees;
Under it your unfortunate friend lies:
Honour his remains and cry!
Let your sad soul feel
How under the cover of the night
The wind wails over the silent grave...[17]

Though the tradition of burying or setting monuments to one's friends was never as strong in the Russian sentimental gardens as in France or Germany, these poets certainly portrayed a typical trend.

No other garden in Russia was as rich in family memorials as Pavlovsk. The entire garden was dedicated to the past, to Maria Feodorovna's childhood memories, to the impressions she gathered during her Grand Tour, and to her German and Russian families. The Family Grove represented a light atmosphere, whereas the Memorial to the Parents and the Mausoleum to Pavel struck an opposite chord.

88. *Tsaritsyno. The landscape scenery as seen from one of the windows of the pavilion entitled Beautiful View.*

The idea of these impressive *tableaux* was to awaken melancholy and the deepest feelings of sorrow.

The mourning daughter, sister and wife were, of course, particularly drawn to these allusive temples, as was Zhukovsky. In 1802 he had made a Russian version of Thomas Gray's "Elegy in a Country Churchyard", which proved to be as important for his own creative work as the discovery of Thomson had been for Karamzin. Some years later, in "The Slavyanka. Elegy" Zhukovsky was to express the sentimentality and dream visions which the funerary monuments at Pavlovsk had awoken in him.

And suddenly a deserted temple emerges in wilderness before me;
An overgrown path; grey bushes all around;
Amongst the crimson linden a dense oak seems black
And death-like fir trees slumber.

Sad memory lives here;
And bending its pensive head down to the urn,
It talks with the ever faithful Dream
About what exists no more.

Here everything spontaneously invites to meditation;
Everything inspires us with languid depression;
As if it listened to the voice of bygone times
That comes from the grave.
This temple, this dark dome, this quiet mausoleum,
This torch that grows dim and is turned down,
All this reminds us that the happiness and grandeur of today
Are only twinkling moments, no more.[18]

In fact, inspired by Pavlovsk, Zhukovsky was to compose some of the best poems ever written on a garden.

To increase the effect of surprise and grandeur, and to guarantee the utmost quietness around it, the Mausoleum to Pavel had been placed slightly off one of the main paths. Moreover this corner was one of the most densely planted in the entire garden, with the trees carefully selected so as to signalize the prevailing mood.

Sometimes the mausoleum is mirrored in the waters;
Or the hill overgrown with grass and crowned by trees;
Sometimes the weeping willow is bending its supple branches
Down to the intertwined roots,
And it plunges its head into the streams;[19]

Zhukovsky was so fascinated by this "plenitelnaya kartina", or "enchanted image", that the whole scenery turned into a sacred place to him. Here the poetic mind encountered the unknown.

Zhukovsky heard voices, he talked to them, and the melancholic visions temporarily gave way to an image of a different nature. A rebirth was being announced to the genius of the poet:

I stare...and I think that all that is gone forever
Revives in this lovely vision;
And all that is promised by life and even all that does not exist in life,
My heart hopefully accepts.[20]

But it was a dream, as in the poet's imaginary meeting with his youth in "Evening. An Elegy". Even the poet was incapable of transgressing the universal laws of time and space. Thus, Zhukovsky's interpretation of one of the great leitmotifs of Romantic poetry had to end in the garden microcosmos, the nature and the art of which had awakened such imaginative forces. In his "Evening. An Elegy", Zhukovsky ultimately envisages the mourning to take place at night at his own tomb.

In "Tsarskoselsky lebed" (The Swan of Tsarskoe Selo, 1851), Zhukovsky was inspired by yet another of Russia's famed Imperial gardens. He died the following year. In the garden at Poreche a monument was erected in Zhukovsky's honour, which became to many Russians a pilgrimage site. Its significance rivalled that of Rousseau's tombstone on the Isle of Rousseau at Ermenonville. Yet only the latter was to set an aesthetical pattern to be copied extensively and slavishly, though never in Russia. Here the garden patrons only honoured the national writers.

Few other poets are as closely associated with Russian garden history as Pushkin (1799-1837). During his younger years at Tsarskoe Selo, Catherine's garden served as inspiration to some of his most famous poems. The key scene in the short story entitled "Kapitanskaya dochka" (The Captain's Daughter, 1836) is placed in this very "abode of tranquility". As a guest, Pushkin also visited many gardens around St Petersburg as well as Moscow, praising some of them in his works.

Little more than twenty years after Karamzin in "The Countryside" had furnished a hedonistic portrayal of the delights of the Russian landscape, Pushkin wrote a poem with the same title (1819). Yet Pushkin did not have the sole aim of celebrating life in the countryside. He also wanted to criticize and condemn the moral values of the ruling classes, and to stress the huge gap between them and the peasants or serfs.

> But an awful thought darkens my mind:
> Amongst the blossoming fields and hills
> The friend of humanity notices with sorrow
> The terrible disgrace of ignorance everywhere.[21]

Over the years this criticism became stronger, culminating after the Rebellion of the Decembrists in 1825.

Pushkin's strong nationalism and growing social consciousness made him particularly popular with the ideologists of the Soviet period. Big festivities were arranged in 1937, on the centenary of his death in a duel; Tsarskoe Selo was renamed Pushkin, Moscow's leading museum of foreign art was called the Pushkin Museum, and dozens of Pushkin monuments were erected on city squares and in public parks. The quay in Moscow's Central Park of Culture and Rest, formerly known as Gorki Park (named after one of the most celebrated Soviet writers), was also named after the poet. All this helps to explain why, in the traditional Soviet understanding, Pushkin's landscape and garden poetry has been considered far above Zhukovsky's odes and elegies.

The Garden and its Texts

Apart from inspiring the poets, the garden in itself forms an interesting body of text. Inscriptions occur on a variety of monuments and other structures, the large majority of which is confined to war monuments, as the following from the Kagul Obelisk in Catherine's garden at Tsarskoe Selo:

In commemoration of the victory at the Kagul River in Moldavia on the 21st of July 1770, where the Russian Army, numbering seventeen thousand, under the command of General Count Peter Rumyantsev, turned Galilbei, the Turkish Grand Vizier, with a force of one and a half thousand, to flight to the Danube River.

Like the Chesma Column in the Big Pond and the Morea Column, which was placed near the little waterfall, the Kagul monument commemorated one of Russia's victories during the First Turkish War.

Another important group of inscriptions concerns the obelisks and columns erected to commemorate special events, such as a visit by Catherine to the country residence of one of her higher officials. This pattern repeated itself under Pavel and later. As for Count Sheremetev's Kuskovo, it was decided to link the reference to Catherine's visit to this palace in 1775, to her visit to Moscow that very year to celebrate the victory over the Turks:

Catherine the Great, who astounded the whole world with her glorious victories over the Ottomans and who let her loyal subjects celebrate the useful peace, was pleased to visit the host of this house, Count Peter Borisovich Sheremetev on March 22 and on August 23, 1775, and her Majesty granted marble and set up a monument as a token of gratitude and in commemoration of victory.

So reads the inscribed plaque on the tall obelisk in Kuskovo's parterre garden. The context set by the pleasure garden did not diminish the rather official tone of such inscriptions. Instead it equalled that employed on monuments erected in the Russian towns before, under and after Catherine's reign.

In a shorter form, inscriptions on some of the temples, arches, columns and grottoes in the Imperial gardens, as well as in the gardens of the Russian nobility and gentry, informs one about the addressee or about a specific philosophical or moral concept. Examples include "To my beneficent husband", "The end of the world", "Rose without thorns" and "His name is eternal". These dedications follow the convention of the contemporary Western gardens, but the Russian texts are generally shorter.

The same holds true for the inscriptions on tombstones and other funerary structures. However the inscription dedicated to Zemira, Catherine's favourite dog, in the Tsarskoe Selo garden is an exception:

Here lies the body of Zemira, and the sorrowful Graces should throw flowers on to her grave. Like Tom [Sir Tom Anderson, another beloved dog of Catherine's], her ancestor, and like Lady, her mother, she was faithful, ran beautifully, and had only one defect, she was a little bit short-tempered, but her heart was kind. When you love somebody, you become very apprehensive of everything, and Zemira was so much in love with all that the world, as such, loves. Was it possible to remain calm facing the rivalry of so many people? The Gods who witnessed her tenderness, should have awarded her with immortality for her faithfulness, in order that she could be with her sovereign forever.

Despite the resemblance above, there are hardly any parallels on Russian ground to the numerous examples of poems, whether ancient or contemporary, whether idylls or elegies, found on selected stones and benches in the English, French or German landscape gardens.

More than any other, the English garden artist and poet William Shenstone defined this pattern in his famous Leasowes garden as in his writing. In his highly normative *Unconnected Thoughts on Gardening* (1764), Shenstone recommended the application of moral sentences and poems to "please, or to instruct the mind / And pass each tedious hour."[22] Partly imitating, partly expanding this pattern, Watelet, Girardin and other garden theorists discussed and exemplified the importance of such poetic texts in the garden setting. Besides, Watelet was something of a poet himself as demonstrated in his garden at the Moulin-Joli.

Hirschfeld, on the other hand, had little interest in poetry, and Bolotov was not the type to compensate for this when propagating the landscape garden and Hirschfeld's doctrines in *Ekonomichesky Magazin*. So, although Russia as early as from the last quarter of the

89. *Pavlovsk. The World's End Column is one of the most evocative motifs of the garden area named the New Silvia.*

18th century on possessed a certain tradition of national nature and garden lyrics, and although many of the classical and contemporary European idyllists were known, poetry by and large remained a medium to be enjoyed through reading books, or listening to others reading aloud. Poetry was not permitted to adorn the gardens of the time.

There is another literary aspect of 18th and early 19th century European garden culture which was not particularly welcomed in Russia either. It is the guidebooks or detailed, versified descriptions dedicated to specific garden landscapes. The writings of Watelet, Girardin, Delille, among others, seem for very long to have been fully sufficient for the Russian garden enthusiasts. These foreign works may actually have not only served as sources of inspiration for the layout of gardens, but also as interpretative studies.

Bolotov's descriptions of his redoing of the gardens of his native Dvoryaninovo and of Bogoroditske, and Lvov's essay on his work at Bezborodko are basically the only detailed writings of the Catherine age dealing with garden design. None of them were actually given a form with any literary pretensions, nor were their primary readers the potential visitors to Bogoroditske or Bezborodko. In fact, it was

90. *Pavlovsk. The Peel Tower. This pastoral building with a thatched roof has a room painted after French rococo themes.*

not until the publication of Storkh's guide to Pavlovsk in 1843, that the Russian garden enthusiasts were given a guidebook to one of their own gardens. Here they were finally allowed to read about the meaning of the garden *tableaux* and about the people who had created the palace and garden ensemble.

Painters and Perceptions

All the main rooms were decorated with panels, while the walls and ceilings were covered with linen and painted with sticky paints. A hunting scene was depicted on the walls of the hall, there were landscapes in the reception room as well as in his mother's study, while the walls in the bedroom...were painted with groves. (Blagovo, 1790s)

While landscape gardens were being laid out in most of Europe, British and Continental garden writers were discussing the advantages of using sketches executed by professional landscape painters, in practical design work. By the middle of the 18th century, one French architectural theorist stated: "It is essential that a landscape

91. Sketch by the Italian theatrical painter Gonzaga who, at Pavlovsk, created a series of grandiose landscapes.

artist is also an excellent painter..."[1] The case of William Kent was widely known and much esteemed. Having begun his career as a landscape painter, he finished as one of Britain's great garden designers.

In France, it was Hubert Robert (1733-1808) who came to embody this idea of a fusion between painting and landscape design.[2] In 1778 he was named garden designer to Louis XVI and contributed to projects at Versailles, Trianon and Rambouillet. In addition to the King, René Louis de Girardin, the owner of Ermenonville and the author of *De la Composition des Paysages, ou des moyens d'embellir la Nature autour des Habitations, en joignant l'agréable à l'utile* (1777), was an important garden patron to Robert. Moreover, Robert's correspondence with Jean-Joseph Delaborde, the owner of Méréville, and his work in this garden give useful insights into his working methods as a painter of prospective garden views.

Robert's contributions to Ermenonville (1778-79) responded, in practice, to what Girardin had asserted in his theoretical work:

When I discuss the visual effect of your design, you are well aware that the landscaped tableau can be invented, sketched, drawn, coloured, retouched by no other artist than the painter of landscapes.[3]

The landscape painter was able to produce drawings or painted sketches for the patron to imagine:

...the effect of the perspective, the relationship between the different planes, the right proportions of the objects, the degradation of the colours, the type and the form you will have to accord to your buildings.[4]

Such preparatory works could help avoid subsequent changes of an otherwise almost completed garden project. That is, the idea was not to use famous landscape paintings as sources for the layout of the garden, as has sometimes been ascertained on the basis of English garden theories of the first half of the 18th century. Instead, the design work departed from a painter's study of the given grounds and his subsequent redefinition of it on the picture plan.

No Russian garden theorist or garden artist appears to have adopted this idea,[5] but at Pavlovsk a theatrical painter was to create a series of landscapes wherein he used his talents as a painter to the fullest. It was Prince Yusupov who, as newly appointed head of St Petersburg's musical and theatrical life, brought Pietro di Gonzaga (1751-1831) from northern Italy to St Petersburg. Trained in the Venetian *veduta*-tradition and in the Milanese Gallardi brothers' manner of intricate theatrical perspectives, Gonzaga created sets for the Hermitage Theatre and other prominent scenes which were as different from the local tradition as the compositions and ideas of Piranesi, Pannini, Mengs, Robert and Winckelmann had been to the first generation of Russian artists from the St Petersburg Academy of Arts studying in Rome.

Gonzaga, however, soon benefitted from the advanced Westernization of the Russian élite. In 1792 Nicolai Petrovich Sheremetev wrote to one of the actors who advised him on the construction of his Ostankino theatre: "...I can tell that no one in Europe is better than he is".[6] With this in mind, Sheremetev understandably hired Gonzaga to design the stage sets on the grand occasion of Pavel's coronation in 1797. At Arkhangelskoe, Prince Yusupov had Gonzaga design the theatre building and a great number of sets.

Catherine's disinterest in Gonzaga's work has generally been accounted for by the fact that Gonzaga was a freemason, but equally relevant may be the Empress' generally less active role as a patron of the arts during her last years on the throne. Pavel and Maria Feodorovna, on the other hand, greatly appreciated Gonzaga's talents and passed along many important commissions to him.[7] They also provided him a home at Pavlovsk, where he and his family spent their summers, from 1798 or 1799 up until the death of Maria Feodorovna in 1828. Over the years, the spectrum of his artistic endeavours grew.

92. *Pavlovsk owes many of its charms to the interplay between the waters, the foliage and the softly sloping grounds.*

At Pavlovsk and Gatchina, he designed and masterminded a large number of specially organized celebrations and theatrical performances, for which he often used motifs from the Imperial gardens.

A genre in which Gonzaga excelled was monumental fresco painting. Various sources of the early 19th century reveal how Gonzaga decorated the surfaces of many a garden pavilion at Pavlovsk. Some also speak of the extensive palace gallery visible from the Slavyanka Valley, and of the palace rooms, the open-air theatre, the library and so on.[8] One of the few, relatively well-preserved examples of Gonzaga's frescoes can be seen on the Peel Tower. Classical colonnades and ornaments were as much a part of Gonzaga's trompe l'oeil repertoire as garden *treillages* and Russian villages. What struke the contemporary beholder about these works was not so much the pastorale atmosphere as Gonzaga's illusionism, which gave rise to legends similar to those known from antiquity.

Inspired by his preparatory work on the Arkhangelskoe Theatre, Gonzaga in 1817 published *Remarques sur la construction des théatres, par un artiste*. Ten years later, at the age of seventy-six, he was officially appointed Architect of the Imperial Theatres.[9] In practice, it was his son Paolo who specialized in construction work, whereas

Pietro di Gonzaga continued designing stage sets and, at Pavlovsk, seized the opportunity of using nature's own materials as his brush and paints. His idea was to mold the natural landscape according to his aesthetic ideals.

Gonzaga's first monograph on aesthetics, *La musique des yeux*, came out in 1800.[10] One of his basic principles was to propagate the same aesthetics to various artistic genres. As the title of Gonzaga's book says, the key notion is the creation of music for the eyes. Rhythm of space and modulations of colours are considered the basic ingredients in whatever medium the artist chooses. "Our musique spreads to the fields and to the groves and transforms them into gardens."[11] Constantly changing vistas are necessary for the stimulation of the human mind. Consequently, the art of landscaping such grounds consists in:

...knowing how to discern the character of visual objects that Nature has scattered around, and to subject them to an order which will enhance the very design and make the effect more noticeable.[12]

Further along it continues:

In drawing up his plan the wise landscape artist will thus aim at a suite of different scenes, carefully arranged in dependence on the quality of the project and the configuration of the ground. In one corner only gaiety should reign, in another one gloom, further on tranquility, gentleness, cheerfulness; remarkable, morbid, horrifying places; here and there some caprice, some bizarre thing, and even some small extravagances if the project is big enough and there is need of much variety. Moving sensibly from one tone to another, either by gradations or by surprises, as the case may be, and challenging and flattering us as much as possible.[13]

Clearly enough, a certain echo of Chambers, Girardin and other garden writers is detectable in the latter paragraph.

The quest for variety inevitably leads Gonzaga to some critical remarks on formal gardens, as exemplified by "the gardens of Versailles, Schönbrunn, Sans-Souci and Peterhof", although he does not totally object to this tradition.[14] Instead, he recommends "a careful blend" of the old landscape manner and the new, summing up his theoretical lesson in the following question: "Why did Delille so regularly write with end rhymes on the irregularity that he recommends?"[15] At Pavlovsk, Gonzaga set about to create large-scale *tableaux* that were in close harmony with his theoretical doctrines. This project occupied him, more or less intensively, for about two decades.

Every aspect of Gonzaga's design proposals was discussed with, and had to be approved by, the ever attentive Maria Feodorovna. One of Gonzaga's main objectives was to clear the undergrowth in order to create a varied suite of open and enclosed spaces, of groves alternating with meadows and water. Another important concern was the foliage. Next to the visual effect brought about by their form and colour, the trees were thought to connote specific feelings. Gonzaga used, as his main themes, birches and pines. As distinctive marks of the Russian nature, they fitted in perfectly with the national significance that Pavlovsk came to have under Alexander I (1801-25), a significance which was nourished by the grandiose celebrations Maria Feodorovna repeatedly staged on the occasion of Russia's military victories. Light birches were particularly favoured because of their colours, their elegance and their graphic effect. To soften the contrast between the dark evergreen pines and the slender white birch trunks with their light blazing foliage, other sorts of trees such as oaks and lindens were used.

Gonzaga called himself a surgeon and a tree pruner, and amidst the thick forest and undergrowth north of the palace, the self-proclaimed doctor laid out the Valley of Ponds. The valley, which stretches down to the Lower Slavyanka and to Cameron's ensemble of ruins, include such highly allusive motifs as the Venus Pond and the Isle of Love. Yet, it is the interplay between the waters, the foliage and the softly sloping grounds that, foremost, lends this corner its charms.

Still Gonzaga's true masterpiece in landscape art is the orchestration of the vast area called the White Birches. No Russian gardener was ever to attain the grandeur and the subtle play of forms and colours which he attained in this easternmost part of the Pavlovsk landscape. On a plan, the radial pattern formed by the eight roads which lead up to a big cirle of birch trees, looks very much like that of a city's main traffic point. The scale for that matter also justifies this comparison. However, the visual and spatial experience on site is entirely of another order. In the days of Maria Feodorovna, the visitor would usually come to this remote corner by horse-drawn carriage, and not by foot as today's visitor to Pavlovsk. In either case, though, the vista and the dimensions are absolutely overwhelming.

The geometrical layout of the area becomes subordinate to the horizons which are formed, on one hand, by the softly undulating row of trees on the periphery of the White Birches, and on the other hand, by a perfect circle made up of slender samples of the trees for which the entire scenery was named. Between the two vertically oriented belts lies a gap where the visitor is continually moving

93. *Pavlovsk. The White Birches. The ring of birch trees forming the very centre of this unique outdoor setpiece.*

towards one horizon or the other. Not only are the visitors agents in this spatial play, but they are beholders of this visually captivating spectacle before them.

As opposed to the Valley of Ponds, which is a direct outcome of the landscape garden aesthetics, the birch scenery contains in itself the essence of two different worlds forming the two basically contradictory ways of perception marking the formal and the informal garden. The White Birches represents the "careful blend" which Gonzaga spoke of in *La musique des yeux*. His idea was not to experiment with two perceptive modes in two separate parts of the same garden (as was so often the case from the Catherine age right up to the Soviet city parks). Gonzaga's aim was to create an entity out of them. His application of aesthetical refinement and originality to the rich nature resources of Russia resulted in one of the most grandiose and stunning garden sceneries that has ever been seen.

Paintings in Gardens

The Dutch House (1749) was one of the motifs to offer a mental journey to the garden visitors of Kuskovo. Not only had the canal

94. *Kuskovo. All details of the Dutch House, its garden and setting, were created so as to match popular prototypes.*

setting, the building itself and the small garden been patterned so as to imitate a corner of a Dutch town; the interior was equally convincing, thanks to the blue and white Dutch tiles and the collection of Dutch paintings. The whole setting may have been created in memory of Boris Petrovich Sheremetev, who was Field Marshal under Peter the Great and therefore directly exposed to the Emperor's fascination with the Dutch mentality, technology and taste. Yet there was one more element in the Dutch House to look at and admire: A figure with the illusion of a real person.

Trompe l'oeil paintings of life-size figures, executed on large wooden boards that could be moved around for various purposes, were popular in Europe from the second half of the 17th century. Generally, the Dutch are considered the founders of this tradition. Samples were brought to Russia under Peter, later inspiring some Russian painters to experiment with this genre. The Sheremetev family actually set out to build up a collection of illusionistic figures.[16] Several Dutch-inspired trompe l'oeil paintings of books and manuscripts also formed part of their collections at Kuskovo.

Like wax figures, the painted illusionistic figures were basically created to entertain guests. The whole point lay in the figures' ability

95. *Kuskovo's Dutch House is one of the motifs most frequently sought out by today's Russian Sunday painters.*

to play on the beholder's perception, to make him believe that he had something real before his eyes and to maintain this illusion for as long as possible. It was a sort of surprise game. Primarily the figures were used in some of the interiors at Kuskovo, but on especially festive occasions the figures were placed in the bosquets. Some of them wore costumes rivalling those of the garden visitors, while others depicted shepherds and gardeners among others. The figures may also have appeared between the green settings of Kuskovo's green theatre.

In contrast to such figures, illusionistic garden or landscape views on large-scale screens for outdoor use do not seem to have been much favoured in 18th century Russian settings. Some indeed existed, but descriptions or literary references to such works are very rare. Hirschfeld once more appears to be useful as a source. These are thus his remarks on Yaroplets, a country house some ninety kilometres from Moscow belonging to Count Chernishev:

This master, who thanks to his originality, taste and tireless energy knows how to improve and embellish territories of a considerable size, has arranged the first entry to the courtyard of his country house with the help of eight perspective views, so that they present to one's eyes the entire

96. Kuskovo. As the pendant of the Dutch House, the Italian House once held Count Sheremetev's painting collections.

region with its village houses and farms in the distance, and the stables at close quarters, and so that it all looks like one big, almost boundless garden with ever changing prospects.[17]

Based on Western paradigms, similar scenarios undoubtedly adorned gardens and courtyards other than this one, some ninety kilometres from Moscow.

As a horticulturist and landscape artist, Bolotov was on principle not concerned much with the visual arts, but in a few instances the art of painting appears to have caught his attention. One such case also concerns the occurrence of an illusionistic figure in a garden setting. In Bolotov's album from the garden at Bogoroditske, a rather impressive old giant is shown in some scenes from the rocky landscape near the Big Pond. The figure, known as the Chronicler, is a painted one and is placed against the rocky hill itself. The giant seems to be instructing visitors which garden motifs to turn to. His looks and his pose indicate that, contrary to the peasants or the elegant figures at Kuskovo, he is not a participant in the fashionable garden life. The eremites found in the grottoes and caves of the English landscape gardens, so carefully described by Hirschfeld and others, may have inspired Bolotov just as much as the figures he had seen with his own eyes at the Sheremetev family's palaces.

Illusionistic painting is the subject of two articles in *Ekonomichesky Magazin*.[18] During the summer of 1785 Bolotov found himself experimenting with paints, various ground materials and prospective drawing in the Bogoroditske garden. He subsequently discussed these experiments in two articles to be published later the same year. What motifs Bolotov had been working on is not clear from either of these articles. Bolotov, who otherwise owed much to Hirschfeld, merely emphasizes the independent character of his work. From other articles by Bolotov where he deals with the Bogoroditske garden, it becomes clear that he did a painting showing the remains of an old monastery, and another one of a ruinous stone tower. Unfortunately, though, neither of these works is included in the garden views which Andrei Timofeevich did with his son.

To Bolotov, such paintings represented an alternative kind of garden scene in which means other than the traditional ones were employed. The idea, he explained in *Ekonomichesky Magazin*, was to have:

...a series of scenes, either on the ground or on hill slopes or on another elevated place facing the garden or the house in a position to be clearly seen from there, either in the form of contours or as a front view...[19]

Once completed, the painting:

...was covered with fragments of bricks or planks and sometimes with different clays and sands, or even with earth that had different colours, or the like...[20]

Because of the use of such materials and because the desired visual effect depended on a certain distance of sight, the genre obviously did not fit in everywhere. Bolotov thought that only suburban gardens would form an adequate setting.

New as well as old buildings were considered apt, but Bolotov preferred ruins. He mentioned towers, triumphal arches, city walls, bridges, obelisks and temples, that is, structures which basically alluded to the building traditions of the past and which, from an iconographical viewpoint, corresponded to the real structures of the landscape garden. As for figures, Bolotov contented himself to speak of such as part of the architectural views.[21] He did not mention the giant in the Bogoroditske garden.

For those who found it difficult to get the right proportions or to paint from memory, he recommended drawing up a preparatory design.

There is a double benefit from that; first of all, the drawing should be pressed against the glass right in front of the hill, in order that one can see the contours of the drawing on the background of the slope, and ascertain whether they are too small or too big when they are transferred on to nature. Secondly, the mentioned drawing can be used as a model or a curve, and a painter can reproduce the features on the ground in correspondence with the details on the glass.[22]

Aesthetically, the painted scenes aimed at surprising the garden visitor, just as real garden pavilions, ruins or monuments did.[23] Yet paintings were much cheaper, and it need not take more than three or four days, Bolotov claimed, to do one work. He did his very best to compensate for the lack of illustrations in *Ekonomichesky Magazin*, and gave his readers detailed advice in writing on where to place the views, how to meet the ideal viewpoint, and what kind of paint to use.

Yet despite Bolotov's best intentions, there appears to have been a very small audience to this aspect of his teachings. Because the materials used in the outdoor paintings were so fragile, the Bogoroditske decorations did not survive very long. They may actually have vanished before Bolotov, both father and son, made the album with watercolours in 1786.

Gardens in Paint

At Gatchina, Pavel's favourite residence, flower ornaments adorn the garden and palace halls. The parterres of the Dutch-inspired garden beneath the towering grey palace building seem to continue on to the parquet of the White Hall. Landscape paintings or landscape panels of a certain size were also a much appreciated part of many palace and country house interiors from the last quarter of the 18th century. Great numbers of the nobility and gentry urged their artists, many of whom were serfs, to do such decorations, frequently in imitation of those found in the Imperial pleasure palaces on the outskirts of St Petersburg.

The icon painters had occasionally delighted in rendering plants and intricate floral patterns of the *hortus conclusus*. With the Western influence under Peter, landscape and garden paintings, seen as a purely secular phenomenon, became more and more popular. The painters of the first half of the 18th century used landscapes or garden views as backdrops for various literary picture genres, whereas cartographers were generally concerned with the creation of garden plans and pictures of garden architectural elements. Under Catherine, gardens lended themselves more and more to artistic portrayals.

Garden art was no longer primarily a subbranch of architecture, and painters showed an increasing interest in rendering the variety of the grounds, the lakes, the trees and the flowers. Oil paintings and watercolours gradually complemented the traditional engravings, yet a certain conservative approach also held. Some artists continued to do engraved views similar to those produced while Peter was carrying through his grand-scale garden projects.

One representative of this genre is Mikhail Ivanovich Makhaev (1716-70). Makhaev worked in suburban St Petersburg and Moscow, for the Court as well as for the nobility. He dedicated two albums to Tsarskoe Selo and Kuskovo, which are his greatest works. Both albums date from the 1760s and early 1770s, but neither was devoted to the developments which were then initiated to create modern landscape gardens. Instead, Makhaev focused on the architectural elements of the old palace and garden ensembles.

The most excellent representative of the first generation who worked with the landscape and garden in the new fashion, was Semen Feodorovich Shchedrin (1745-1804). He was among the very first students of the St Petersburg Academy of Arts to be sent abroad to study landscape painting. His nearly ten years (1767-76) of study in France and Italy assured that his working techniques and his pictures with motifs from the Imperial gardens around St Petersburg fully corresponded to contemporary Western examples of landscape and garden painting. The works of Mikhail Matveevich Ivanov (1748-1823) and Feodor Yakovlevich Alekseev (1753-1824) are also worthy of note for their giving a vivid insight into pleasurable life in the Russian countryside around 1800.

Soon after his return from Europe, Shchedrin did a series of views from Catherine's landscape garden at Tsarskoe Selo, although he was above all a favourite of Pavel's and Maria Feodorovna's. Shchedrin's very first work from the archducal summer residence dates from 1780. However, the majority of his views from Pavlovsk and Gatchina date from the 1790s. They are oil-paintings and gouaches, some of which served as patterns for engravings. This clearly explains why Shchedrin's views from Pavlovsk and Gatchina are much better known than those he did at Tsarskoe Selo in the late 1770s.

Shchedrin's views from Pavlovsk nearly form a complete visual guide to the attractions of this garden. Following the Western idyllistic landscape tradition, Shchedrin also introduced quietly pasturing cattle and sheep in his views from the Slavyanka Valley. With the exception of the rowers who take the guests down the Slavyanka, his figures all have a meditative and admirative attitude to the much varied landscape. An angler occasionally appears, but nobody is ever seen working in the garden. Shchedrin's universe indeed comes very close to the Arcadia of the antique, as interpreted by Claude Lorrain or Nicolas Berghem.

Shchedrin, who for many years taught landscape painting at the St Petersburg Academy of Arts, did not aim at topographical accuracy. What he wanted to depict was a certain hedonistic atmosphere which was closely connected with the specifics of the Pavlovsk landscape. How he viewed and portrayed a corner of this garden is clear in "View of the Pavlovsk Palace, the Centaur Bridge and the Apollo Colonnade" (c. 1792, engraved by I.V. Chesky, 1801), in which he collected a number of significant architectural motifs, each depicted from the viewpoint that seemed to suit it best. The structures were then redistributed on the picture plane in order, firstly, to attain as comprehensive and varied a picture as possible and secondly, to create a dynamic interaction between various structures such as the palace with the colonnade and the Centaur Bridge spanning the quiet Slavyanka with the tufa bridge leading over the sprawling cascade. The grove in the middle of the picture is the Family Grove. The many diagonal and winding lines which guide the visitor through the scenery, and the interplay between open and closed, light and dense areas, ultimately correspond to the compositional pattern of the landscape garden itself.

To a degree never matched by any of his pupils working with the Pavlovsk motifs, Shchedrin applied this method of composition to all of his views from the garden, meaning these are not merely architectural views, as Makhaev's works from Tsarskoe Selo and Kuskovo were. On the other hand, Shchedrin never left out the garden buildings or monuments in order to concentrate on the landscape itself. The closest he ever got to this approach was in "View of the Peel Tower" (1796, engraved by I.V. Chesky, 1801). However the Peel Tower was still the reason for Shchedrin to paint this view. With the exception of the Family Grove, which was more of a garden space than a garden *tableau*, Cameron's and Brenna's buildings, bridges or monuments remained the visual highlights in the practical layout and in the desired perception of the Pavlovsk garden.

Thanks to the recommendations and descriptions furnished by Hirschfeld, Chambers, and others, the cult of horror scenes in landscape gardens in the West also became known in Russia. Yet the Russian patrons and landscape designers never really took to this trend, perhaps because practically no Russian garden patrons had been to the Alps or seen the volcanoes in southern Europe. The natural and relatively undramatic scenery of the countryside around Moscow and St Petersburg was by and large preferred to the staging

97. The Pavlovsk Palace, the Centaur Bridge and the Apollo Colonnade in S.F. Shchedrin's interpretation.

of seemingly wild, deserted and gloomy sceneries like those found in the Méréville garden (1784-86). Some cascades and gorges were indeed thrown in relief during the garden promenade, but such motifs were never allowed to attain the size or effect of their counterparts in British, German or French landscape gardens.

The reason for this has not previously been discussed in Russian or Soviet garden studies, but may have to do with Russia neither longing for nor intellectually needing to transplant such sceneries. If one yearned for nature in its original state, it was right there. After all, the Russian gardens, as well as all other types of man-made landscape and city developments, covered such a tiny part of the immense and little explored lands of this country.

Shchedrin's vision stayed normative for the next two or three generations of Russian landscape and garden painters. Typically, there was always some neat building or bench to remind the viewer that this was a garden, and not the proper and occasionally horrifying landscape untouched by humankind.

Catherine's Favourite French Painter

In late 18th century France, the works of Hubert Robert were thought to hold the essence of what gardens and pleasurable life in the countryside should be like. Since an important number of Russian patrons, not least Catherine herself, had a particularly high esteem for French culture, philosophy and art, it was natural to take an interest in this very influential landscape and garden painter. Actually, nowhere is there as good and representative a selection of Robert's decorative landscape and garden paintings as in Russia.

The popularity of Robert's paintings has nourished the hypothesis that Robert also had an immediate impact on the development of the Russian landscape garden. Supporting this idea is the fact that he designed several gardens, some of which even belonged to Louis XVI, and others like Ermenonville and Méréville, which ranked among the finest landscape gardens in France. Yet the whole question seems to have been looked upon too simplistically. Firstly, the pattern of influences on Russian late 18th century gardening was rather complex, which the genesis of the landscape gardens at Tsarskoe Selo and Pavlovsk alone indicate, as do Bolotov's experiments and his interpretation of Hirschfeld. Secondly, the timing of Russian garden fashions also contradict conclusions as to Robert having played a normative role. Several landscape gardens had already been developed on the outskirts of St Petersburg and Moscow by the time a significant number of Robert's Italian and French garden views entered Russian collections in the mid 1780s. The purchasing of Robert paintings seems to have been more of an aftereffect to this development than any real catalyst. He may in fact have had a more direct influence on the theatrical sets and on the landscape genre of the period than on the gardens.

It was Count Alexander Sergeevich Stroganov who introduced Robert's work to Russia. Stroganov was well-known for his "très beau Cabinet", compiled during his diplomatic career in Paris and Rome.[24] According to the brochure of the Paris Salon of 1773, four of Robert's Roman city and garden views were in the Stroganov collection. In his capacity as one of Catherine's highest officials and closest advisers, Stroganov never hesitated to let the Empress know of his latest findings, including those concerning the arts. Catherine became very enthusiastic about Hubert Robert. Through Stroganov, she passed on a number of commissions, she bought his works, and twice she officially invited him to come to Russia to work for her.

Pavel, who was otherwise so much against his mother's tastes, followed Catherine in her interest for Robert. The commissioning of four paintings for Gatchina was the immediate outcome of Pavel's and Maria Feodorovna's visit to his workshop during their Grand Tour. Several more works entered the collections at Pavlovsk. In addition to the Imperial family, including the later Alexander I, a growing number of noblemen in St Petersburg and Moscow became keen buyers of works by Robert. Others contented themselves with acquiring some of the numerous engravings that were done after Robert's works. Bolotov thus hung a series of his architectural views in the entrance hall at Bogoroditske. Finally, the St Petersburg Academy of Arts took measures to honour Robert although he declined all invitations to visit Russia. The title *associé libre* was bestowed upon him in 1802.

Only in one single, though not yet fully researched case, did Robert concern himself with a Russian motif. It is thought that Stroganov, maybe on Catherine's initiative, asked him to paint something different from an Italian or French view. Robert did a view from the Empress' new garden at Tsarskoe Selo, notably the Ruin Tower. Grimm told Catherine the following about it:

The second painting is by Robert, member of the Academy. It represents a View from Tsarskoe Selo, and this name gave me a terrible palpitation while I was looking at the painting. Robert assured me that this painting had been commanded by Count Stroganov on behalf of Her Imperial Highness ...Robert, whose main gift consists of painting ruins, is presumably in his element in his own country. Wherever he goes, his speciality is being eulogized and he finds the newest and most beautiful ruins in the world.[25]

The inscription on the painting is in Russian letters, and Stroganov is likely to have told Robert how to make it: "P[isal] Yiv. Robert v. Pariye, 1783" (Painted by the painter Robert in Paris, 1783). No suggestions have been made as to Robert's source, but he was probably introduced to the imagery of the Tsarskoe Selo garden by means of a print; it may have been Busch's plan, maybe a work no longer known.

Extensive research has brought to light which of Robert's paintings entered the Russian pleasure palaces and private collections in and after the Catherine period.[26] Fantasies and views of the classical monuments of Rome and scenes from the abandoned overgrown Italian Renaissance gardens were in the majority. In fact, Robert's eleven-year long stay in Rome (1754-65), at the very peak of the first archaeological excavations, had a lasting effect on his choice of motifs. On orders from Louis XVI, Robert visited the Roman sites in Provence in 1783 and subsequently did a new series of antique views. In the Gatchina collection, for example, both aspects of

Robert's approach to the antique were represented. However Robert's views from the pleasure gardens outside Paris were also in favour with his Russian clients.

The creation of two Hubert Robert halls in the 1810s at Prince Yusupov's pleasure palace at Arkhangelskoe marks a climax in the Russian élite's taste for the French painter.[27] To evoke the proper allusions, a selection of recently excavated antique marbles were placed in the room preceding the Robert *salons*. Ruinous monuments, bridges and similar structures are seen in the four big *tableaux de place*, for which one or two of the scenes are clearly indebted to scenes in the gardens at Ermenonville and Méréville that Robert knew so well. Some smaller paintings of his were exhibited together with other European works in Prince Yusupov's picture gallery at Arkhangelskoe.

Some thirty years later, yet another remarkable Hubert Robert interior came into being on Russian soil. The Tudor-styled dining hall at Prince Vorontzov's Alupka Palace on the south coast of the Crimea was decorated with four monumental landscape and garden views. Antique-inspired motifs as well as scenes from the gardens of Ermenonville and Méréville appear once again.[28] The existence of such iconography in the decorative scheme of Alupka is in perfect tune with the spirit in which this palace and garden ensemble was created. Alupka was in itself an imaginative replica of various elements of Europe's cultural past.

Political Platforms

Great events have never displeased me, and great conquests have never tempted me. I too do not see that peace is very near. It is amusing that the Turks are being made to think that we cannot carry on the war for long. If they were not blinded by passion, how could these people have forgotten that Peter the Great waged war for thirty years, sometimes against the same Turks, sometimes against Swedes, Poles and Persians, without the Empire's being reduced to extremity? On the contrary, Russia has always emerged from each of these wars in a more flourishing state than before; and war has really been a stimulus to industry. Each of our wars has given birth to some new resource, which lent more life to trade and commerce... (Catherine the Great, 1770)

From a formal viewpoint, two of the greatest fountains of the Petrine period and the Stalin period have several features in common. The Great Cascade with the Samson Fountain and the fountain dedicated to Friendship among Peoples, are centrepieces in the two gardens for

98. *Peterhof. On special occasions visitors by the hundreds thronged the Great Cascade in tsarist days.*

which they were created, Peterhof and VSKhV (the All-Union Agricultural Exhibition, later to be renamed VDNKh, the Exhibition of the Socio-Economic Achievements of the USSR, and as of the post-Soviet period VVTs, The All-Union Exhibition Center). Both fountains are very large, and when they are turned on, ten thousand litres of water run through the complex hydraulic system.[1] Gilded figures of monumental size adorn both fountains and lend them an iconographical meaning that is closely connected to the ideological universe of the two gardens.

VSKhV was one of the most prestigious projects of the late 1930s, as far as urban planning and gardening was concerned. The classical principles of architecture were being explored anew, as demanded by the architectural theorists of the Stalin period. When summing up the politico-aesthetical program of the Stalin period, one Soviet architectural historian very aptly called his article, published in 1953, the year before Stalin died: "The Mastering of the Classical Heritage in the Architectural Practice of the National Republics of the USSR".[2] Classical quotations were emblems of practically every official

99. *Peterhof. Pomp and circumstance is very much part of the political imagery of the Great Cascade.*

building erected under Stalin. The apartment blocks lining the highways also followed this pattern, as did many a pavilion in the public parks of the time.[3]

VSKhV was supposed to serve didactic as well as recreational purposes. The idea was to create a grand-scale exhibition area and a city park with an expanse of greenery. The area chosen for the complex was situated on what was then still the outskirts of the city. In the late 18th century, this area formed part of the extensive pleasure grounds surrounding the Sheremetev family's Ostankino Theatre Palace. Just like the First All-Union Agricultural Exhibition on the bank of the Moscow river, the VSKhV was laid out according to a strict geometrical plan. Fountains comparable only to those of the Petrine period were built, and the scale of the parterres was also patterned after such landscape monuments of great politico-historical significance. An imposing array of palaces, pavilions and arches were erected, before the complex was opened in 1939.

Axiality and geometry determined the scheme of the Central Pavilion (A.V. Shchuko, V.G. Gelfreikh and A.P. Velikhanov, 1936), as well as the adjacent square. The enormous white colossus was overloaded with pillars, columns, attics, carnices, wall-reliefs, and

100. Moscow boasts this fountain, inaugurated in the Stalin period. Its
ideological message is Friendship among Peoples.

ornaments, all more or less distorted in comparison with the antique
norm. After all, a specific Stalin style and not just a simple replica
was the intention. As Soviet symbols were mandatory on state-
commissioned architecture, the hammer and sickle, stars and ears of
wheat intermingled with the traditional decorative elements of neoclassicism. VSKhV stood for the new stylistic and ideological
stereotypes.

As much as VSKhV was founded to exhibit the results of the
young Soviet state in the fields of agriculture and industry, it was
also very much a creation dedicated to tomorrow's achievements.
One of the central pieces of the VSKhV was the fountain dedicated
to Friendship among Peoples (K.T. Topuridze and G.D. Konstantinovsky). Clearly, the idea was to announce the prospect of a better
world, which was one of the target results of the Soviet regime. A
colossal ear of corn, a favourite emblem of prosperity in the Soviet
period, forms the centrepiece of the fountain. Fifteen female figures
surround this motif, each of them representing one of the republics
which made up the Soviet Union. The figures vary in their dress,
adornments and attributes, so as to distinguish between their
different national background. Such characteristics were officially

approved of and supported in the Stalinist ideology, as long as they were subordinated to the ideals of egality and peace between the people who had, often by force, been incorporated into the Soviet family of nations.

Contrary to the utopian dimension characterizing this fountain, as well as numerous other monuments of the Stalin years, the meaning of Peterhof's Samson Fountain points back in time. For all its allegorical apparatus, it alludes to something very concrete, a solemn and closed moment of the past. It is a celebration of a specific time in the history of the Russian Empire. On June 27, 1709, on St Sampsonius' Day, the Russians crushed Charles XII and his troops at Poltava in the Ukraine. Henceforth, the Samson metaphor for the Russian people or Peter came into general use. To mark the 25th anniversary of the Battle of Poltava, the Samson Fountain, the tallest and most powerful in the Peterhof ensemble, was placed in the centre of the pool at the very foot of the Great Cascade. It shows the legendary hero forcing open the lion's jaws from which a twenty-one metre jet of water shoots upwards. The lion is borrowed from the Swedish coat of arms.

Peter, who died in 1725, never saw this monument. But conceptually, it was close to the sculpture "Peace and Prosperity" which the Florentine Pietro Barratta had been asked to create for the Summer Garden in memory of Peter's successful conclusion of the Great Nordic War and the signing of the Peace Treaty of Nystad in 1721. Besides, it was also an Italian who created the Samson sculpture. His name was Bartolomeo Carlo Rastrelli (1675-1744), father of Elizabeth's favourite architect. The formal links between Rastrelli's sculptures and numerous Western representations of Hercules fighting a lion should be noted. However at Peterhof, Samson rather than Hercules is the key figure.

On a more general level too, the entire Peterhof ensemble reflects Peter's political success and military victories. A majestic emplacement, high above the Gulf of Finland, had been chosen for this new Imperial summer residence, where water became a key element in the extensive gardens. Memoirs by the dignitaries who visited Peterhof testify to the great impression that the sea route and the very approach to the palace made. Canals, fountains, cascades, and bassins, adorned with biblical, mythological and politico-allegorical motives, demonstrated to what extent Peter had based Russia's fame upon control of the sea. In this, the Peterhof iconography is a continuation of the motives applied to the outdoor bas-reliefs for example, and the ceiling paintings of the Summer Palace.

The Great Canal, which is nearly six hundred metres long and

101. *Peterhof. The Neptune Fountain in the Upper Garden is one of several references to Peter's success as a military victor.*

lined with fountains, forms the first segment of Peterhof's huge axial complex. The canal allowed the visitor to make a slow and solemn *entrée* and to be completely overwhelmed by the *grandeur* of the palace ensemble. The focal point was the palace building and the Great Cascade. The latter comprises of no less than seventy-five fountains and is framed by the Great Grotto, the Small Grottoes and three cascade stairways. Le Blond and the Italian architect Nicolo Michetti, who was in Russia from 1718 to 1723, were the masters of the Great Cascade, whereas Peter himself furnished a preliminary drawing for the canal. In August 1723 the fountains were started amidst great festivity.

The cascade is a synthesis of sculpture, architecture and grand-scale water jets and streams. A wealth of statues, bas-reliefs, masks,

102. *Peterhof. The Samson Fountain of the Great Cascade commemorates Peter's victory over Charles XII of Sweden.*

herms, mascarons, and corbels, all in gilded bronze, lead or marble, adorn the cascade stairways. The two lateral ones are closed off by tritons and allegorical representations of the rivers Volkhov and Neva, an old bearded man and a stout maiden respectively. Many other sculptures and bas-reliefs celebrate, in allegorical form, Peter's obsession with the sea and the Russian victories in the Baltic.

In the Upper Garden, the Great Cascade and the Samson Fountain are counterbalanced by another motive alluding to Peter's ambition to use the sea as a means of gaining power.[4] A crowned Neptune stands on a pedestal in the big, central pool. He holds his trident and is surrounded by horses spouting water. The sculpture, dated 1734, is also the work of Rastrelli, but it was based on an idea conceived by Peter in 1723. It has a certain similiarity to the great fountains in the Versailles parterres.

It was obviously this very pattern which, much later, also influenced the sculptors and hydraulic engineers who served the Soviet state. This is evident from the fountains they created for the parks of culture and rest, for the VSKhV, and the extensive gardens below the Moscow University skyscraper.

Military Commemorations

As in the Petrine age, intensive warfare was also on the agenda under Catherine. A Black Sea fleet was established, and on several occasions it came into fierce fighting against the Turks. The Empress wanted to extend the Russian borders southwards, and the ultimate goal was not only strategic in controlling the way out of the Black Sea, but to capture Constantinople. While the First Turkish War was still going on, Catherine was concerned with the development of her new and fashionable landscape garden at Tsarskoe Selo. This coincidence was to be immediately reflected in the iconography of the garden. Visitors to the Imperial summer residence would consequently, on their promenade past the many different garden scenes, be reminded of the political and military achievements of the ruling Empress.

The letter to Voltaire wherein Catherine speaks of her garden as "a game of skittles" is dated August 14, 1771, at the peak of the First Turkish War. The same letter holds the following enumeration of war memorials:

The Battle of Kagul, where seventeen thousand men fought a hundred and fifty thousand, inspired the erection of an obelisk, with an inscription, stating simply the event and the name of the General. After the naval victory at Chesme, a rostral column was erected in the middle of a very large lake. The capture of the Crimea will be immortalized by a large column; the descent in the Morea and the capture of Sparta, by another... Besides this, in a wood behind my garden, I have had the idea of building a temple of memory, to be approached through a triumphal arch. All the important events of the war will be engraved on medallions, with simple and short inscriptions in the language of the appropriate country, giving the date and the names of the participants. I have an excellent Italian architect, who is drawing up the plans for this building, which will, I hope, be a handsome one, in good taste, and will commemorate the history of this war. The scheme is giving me great pleasure.[5]

The architect Catherine refers to is Antonio Rinaldi. Yet nothing became of the memorial temple. Instead of what Catherine had envisaged, a triumphal arch dedicated to Prince Orlov (Rinaldi, 1772) was erected.

It was also Rinaldi who designed the monuments which took their names from the battles of the Morea, Kagul and Chesma. He used antique forms, primarily of Roman origin, and the monuments were made

...of the finest possible marble, which the Italians themselves admire. Some of it comes from the shores of Lake Ladoga, the rest from Yekaterinburg in Siberia... It comes in nearly every colour.[6]

The Kagul Obelisk (1771), which Pushkin was to praise in two of his most celebrated poems, "Vospominaniya v Tsarskom Sele" (Memories from Tsarskoe Selo, 1814) and "Elegiya" (An Elegy, 1819), does not comprise of any trophies or attributes of war. Only a short inscription reminds one of the historical event that inspired the erection of the monument.

In contrast, the rostrals decorating the Morea Column (1771) and the Chesma Column (1771-76) immediately point to the battles fought at sea,[7] and the reference to the role played by the Russian fleet is further emphasized by the position of the Chesma Column in the Big Pond. This and the very size of the monument makes it an unusual representation in a landscape garden setting. It is visible from anywhere along the path that winds its way along the banks, and the eagle on the very top also testifies to the unambiguously heroic language of this *tableau*.

Yet another monument in the Tsarskoe Selo garden commemorates the First Turkish War, or so it is said in practically all studies on this garden. The monument in question is Velten's Ruin Tower, which stands on an artificial hill not far from the Orlov Arch. At first sight, the red-brick tower looks very much like a folly. It seems to have been placed here to surprise the meditative garden stroller and

103. *Tsarskoe Selo. The Chesma Column commemorates one of Catherine's
victories in the war against the Turks.*

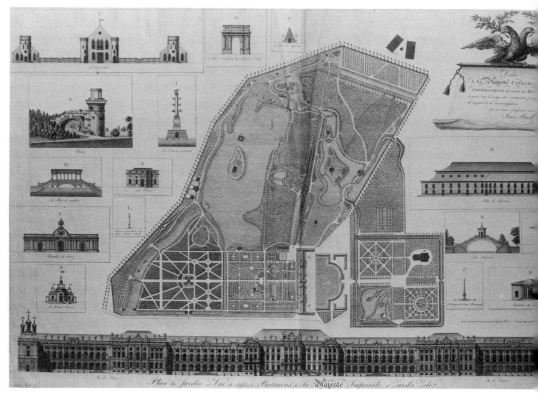

104. Plan of Tsarskoe Selo. Views of some of the most significant motifs of the garden have also been included. The Ruin Tower is on the upper left.

to help increase the stylistic and connotative richness of the garden space. It is only the inscription above the arch which turns this impressive *tableau* into a war monument. It reads: "To commemorate the war that the Turks declared on Russia, this stone was laid in 1768."

The First Turkish War started that year, but Velten however, did not design the ruin till 1771. That is, neither the genesis nor the meaning of this structure is as unambiguous as Rinaldi's war monuments. The collections of the Hermitage in fact include no less than five sketches by Velten for the Tsarskoe Selo Ruin Tower. Each represents a different architectural vocabulary, ranging from Roman antique or English gothic to a structure crowned by a Chinese-inspired pagoda.

In practice, the most striking feature was perhaps the ruinous character of the tower. This solution had not up to now, been applied to any Russian gardens, whereas from around 1750 several Continental garden owners had followed the British example in safe-guarding existing building fragments in their gardens or constructing a new garden ruin. Taking the size and the radical character of the Ruin Tower into consideration, it is surprising that Catherine does not refer to it in her correspondance. But perhaps the tower was not meant to be a war monument. If it had been, Velten would most probably have stuck to the traditional and universally understood antique vocabulary connoting fame and victory, as Rinaldi did.

Russia continued to fight the Turks long after Catherine. Some seventy years after Rinaldi had designed war monuments for Tsarskoe Selo, another war-related *tableau* was created. It was placed on the southwest bank of the Big Pond, thus literally facing the Chesma Column. The occasion was the end of the Third Turkish War (1828-29). Yet in this case a completely different aesthetical pattern than that applied to Rinaldi's works was chosen. The new structure (Ippolit Antonovich Monighetti, 1852), which was called the Turkish Bath, was given the form of a minaret. It was covered by multi-coloured tiles and garnished with abstract ornaments of typical Islamic inspiration. Yet the primary function of this garden building somehow hinders one in calling it a monument. It is perhaps the closest the Russians ever came to the folly. Over the years, many other Russian gardens were provided with genuine war memorials. Columns and obelisks commemorating the Crimean War (1853-56) and the First World War (1914-18) are obvious examples, and the tradition has been revived in the present century. After the Second World War the Soviet regime set about creating war monuments and victory parks on a scale that justifies comparison to the designs and projects carried out under Peter and Catherine.

A Nationalistic Wave

Moscow experienced a political and cultural revival after Catherine became Empress. The building of two new Imperial residences in the vicinity of the city, the Petrofsky Palace and the Tsaritsyno Palace, should be understood as one of the results of Catherine's endeavour to reestablish some of Moscow's former importance and glory. The architects Bazhenov and Kazakov looked into the history of the city's existing buildings and reused elements in their work that clearly stood for the pre-Petrine period.

Towards the end of the 18th century and in the early 19th century, nationalism permeated the spheres of Russian arts and society more and more, as it did in most other European countries of the time. The concept of the nation states played a fundamental role in the political development, and numerous intellectual projects were conceived in this spirit. At Sukhanovo outside Moscow, Karamzin was working on his voluminous study of Russia's history. Other writers and philosophers who were equally ambitious to define specifically Russian developments and values made lengthy contributions on this subject in new, enlightened magazines. Programmatic comments abounded in *Zritel* (The Spectator) and *Korifei, ili Klyuzh literatury* (The Coryphaei, or the Key to Literature). One such example is that "it is necessary to be entirely Russian. It is particularly necessary to establish one's national taste".[8]

This ambition was, not least, shared by as influential a publicist and garden writer as Andrei Timofeevich Bolotov. Thanks to his fervent propagations, other garden specialists and garden patrons also began celebrating national themes, in theory as well as in practice.

Some of the gardener's basic material, the trees and the plants, were being subordinated to this philosophy. Bolotov looked upon the birch as a typically Russian tree. It was the most common tree in the groves and forests of Dvoryaninovo and Bogoroditske and, like Hirschfeld, Bolotov was very enthusiastic about the lightness of the birch in its form and colour. It was a tree of positive and joyful connotations, and it was found particularly apt for those parts of the pleasure garden that were developed for promenades in the early morning or during the day. Nikolai Lvov applied the same philosophy when developing the Bezborodko garden, and Tsaritsyno boasted a special Morning Path, a Birch Grove and a Birch Alley. The extensive birch landscapes at Pavlovsk are the culmination of this understanding of Russian nationalism.

The characteristic white trunks were also applied in certain garden architectural *tableaux*. In the garden of the Kuzminki Palace, situated eight kilometres east of Moscow, was a Birch Cottage. Other more simple examples of birch pavilions are found in some provincial gardens. Gatchina, on the other hand, boasted a very impressive Birch Cottage. A similar structure was also created in the early 19th century in the new, so-called English Garden at Peterhof. The splendour of Gatchina and Peterhof, of course, linked up with the residences being part of the Imperial possessions.

The collections of the Museum of Architecture in Moscow hold a drawing by Lvov, which may indicate that he was the architect of the Gatchina pavilion. The drawing is from 1798. The exterior of the pavilion was made up of birch laths. The roof was flat and the structure had three segments, each of which was somewhat smaller than the preceding one, and this also contributed to the ensemble having a very special and almost geometric look. However, the interior and one facade strongly contrasted with this. A sumptuous ensemble of Ionic pilasters, mirrors, rose festoons, couches covered with pale blue silk, and a strongly ornamented wooden parquet turned the interior into a neo-classical area. In order to create a kind of truly theatrical effect, a monumental stone portal known as the Mask was added to the cottage in 1794. Yet for all this playfulness, the birch motive itself kept its national overtones.

The Napoleonic Wars (1812-15), usually referred to as the Patriotic War in Russian, gave a new and fervent impetus to nationalism in politics, philosophy and the arts. Mikhail Lermontov and Alexander Pushkin wrote some of their greatest poems under the impact of the war. At Pavlovsk, Maria Feodorovna ordered fields to be cleared, pavilions to be built, and big banners to be painted for a party to be held on the occasion of the triumphant return of her son, tsar Alexander I. Memorial columns and triumphal arches were erected in numerous gardens as well as in the cities and towns of victorious Russia. At Tsarskoe Selo, a newly built arch (V.P. Stasov, 1817) was aptly named Arch Dedicated to My Favourite Servants.

Soviet Echoes of the Tsarist Past

The extensive restoration work that was carried out a few years after the devastating German shelling of Peterhof and Tsarskoe Selo during the Second World War, indicated a strong determination of the Soviet leadership to safeguard these Imperial residences and their many emblems of political and military power. The imagery inherent in garden monuments and follies created under Peter and Catherine was studied by an audience, who was in need of creating its own war monuments and victory parks.

To use Hirschfeld's words once again, "space, air and fine views" remained fundamental demands, where and whenever public gardens were to be created.[9] Yet such gardens should also have wide open spaces, "for the people to meet and expand at specific moments of happiness or distress".[10] Hirschfeld advocated a "patriotic garden design" in order that the people should be enlightened "while enjoying their leisure time", and instead of antique sculptures, works of art inspired by patriotism and national services, for example, sculptures representing "heroes, legislators, rescuers and enlightened personalities", should adorn the public park.[11] The ideologists of the Stalin period knew where to look for patterns, and the so-called Alleys of Heroes or Alleys of Nations in the new parks of culture and rest owe their iconography, or part of it, to certain ideas of 18th century Europe.

Yet, the planned Alley of Heroes in Moscow's Central Park of Culture and Rest, to name but one much discussed example, would not possibly have fulfilled the demands of the post-war Soviet garden creators and visitors. What they wanted was new public areas which were dedicated to the nationalism and heroism the Soviet army had demonstrated during the war, and solely this. When characterizing the new type of city park, it was decided that the term *pobeda* (victory) was to be used. If *memorial* had kept its former popularity, it would have implied too much emphasis on the historic past, and so possibly to the detriment of the officially imposed vision of *homo sovieticus'* light and prosperous future. Besides, in Russian the Second World War has usually been referred to as the Great Patriotic War. *Victory park* was thus in all respects an impeccable designation.

From the late 1940s every Soviet town, from Vilnius in the West to Vladivostok in the East, was gradually being furnished with monuments commemorating the heroes of the Great Patriotic War, the battles, the victims, the tragedies and the final glory. And in most of the so-called Hero Cities, a Victory Park was created. One of the largest and most significant parks of this kind is, not surprisingly, at Volgograd, formerly Stalingrad.

A number of cities in what, till 1989-91, was commonly referred to as the countries of the Eastern bloc were also supplied with Victory parks. The park in Berlin stands out among these. But for a long time there was one main exception. Moscow did not have a Victory Park. For more than four decades this was a cause of great political and public concern.

The first idea of creating a war memorial in Moscow goes back, not to 1945, but to 1942. An official competition was later held in 1957, and close to twenty competitions have been organized since then. The latest wave of projects was presented under President Mikhail Gorbachov (1985-91), and the decisive measures to start work on the actual building site were also being taken then. Though many architects departed from the concepts found back in the guidelines of 1942, the drafts, models and ideas that the public has been invited to study and comment upon in the years of *glasnost* were extremely diversified. Designs in a neo-Russian style alternated with neo-classical and numerous other forms.

Some proposed to place a victory monument in the Alexander Garden (Osip Bove, 1821-23), right beneath the walls of the Moscow Kremlin, the Alexander Garden having been remodelled in the immediate wake of the Great Patriotic War. Here stand the imposing red-granite blocks commemorating the Hero Cities of the Soviet Union, and right below the slope leading up to the Red Square burns

105. *Moscow's Victory Park, inaugurated fifty years after the end of World War II, echoes memorials of the tsarist gardens.*

the Eternal Flame on the Tomb of the Unknown Soldier. Other parties involved in the creation of Moscow's Victory Park wanted to place it somewhere in the huge recreational zones outside the city. A very similar pattern of ideas has marked the discussions in the past years about rebuilding the church of Christ the Redeemer, which was torn down as part of Stalin's urban policy and planning.

While the authorities in the late 1980s were moving towards a final decision on where and how to create Moscow's Victory Park, the old city parks continued to be the location of the annual celebrations of Victory Day, on May 9. Moscow's Central Park of Culture and Rest was always a great centre of attraction. And over the years, thousands of veterans, Party representatives, and families have gathered on that day, on the parterres and broad alleys behind the antique-inspired entrance of the first Soviet park of culture and rest.

Most recently, Moscow's Victory Park (pre-opening 1993; official opening 1995) has become a reality. The ensemble is the work of a group of architects, headed by Anatoli Trofimovich Polyanski. In addition to the parkland, the area encompasses the enormous Museum of the Great Patriotic War, which holds a picture gallery, the veterans' halls, archives and so forth. Various kinds of armoury are exhibited outdoors, and a church has also been erected in the extensive grounds. The complex is placed just off one of Moscow's main streets. But Kutuzovsky Prospect, as the street is called, is more than a major traffic lane and the route the black Zil limousines take from the presidential *dacha* to the Kremlin. It derives its name from the marshal who stopped Napoleon, and on the vast and gently sloping field, called Poklonnaya Gora (literally the Bent Hill) where the park now unfolds in a series of stone terraces, bosquets and flower beds, the Russian and the French armies were once fiercely fighting.

As the whole subject of the Victory Park is a sore one, a broad range of critical comments have been put forward from the very day the park was officially opened. The fact that a former battlefield has been used seems to have raised the strongest criticism. When seen in the context of Russia's historical gardens and parks though, the lack of specific war monuments or emblems is particularly striking. The heroic or glorifying aspect which was so dominant in the tsarist gardens, not least at Tsarskoe Selo, and in the Victory parks that were laid out in the 1940s and 1950s, has disappeared. Firstly, this may be seen as a result of the big gap between the historical event that lies at the origin of this park creation and the practical realization of it. Secondly, it reflects a general desire in today's Russia to be extremely critical towards the Soviet past, its ideology, clichés and manners. Yet, no alternative name to Victory Park has been suggested. Future use will determine what kind of public area Moscow's Victory Park ultimately is.

FINAL REMARKS

And hundreds of thousands of steps of enemies and friends,
friends and enemies sleep a mortal sleep.
But the ending of the shadows of this procession cannot be
discerned from the granite vase to the palace door.
There my white nights whisper
of some great and secret love.
And all twinkles of mother-of-pearl and jasper,
But the source of the light is hiding on the quiet.
(Akhmatova, *The Summer Garden*, 1959)

Russia's Historical Gardens Today

In the past few years, a deep crisis has manifested itself in Russia. It has affected practically all fields and all levels of Russian life and society. Russian history being in the process of re-evaluation and rewriting, historians, restorers and artists are facing new tasks. This phenomenon is having a clear impact upon the ways in which Russia's historical gardens are being approached.

As for the active users, that is the Russian population as such, the recreational aspect of course is the chief asset. Now, as before, millions of Muscovites and other citizens living in Russia's big cities very much enjoy having green zones within easy reach. The public parks, whether they stem from the Catherine or from the Stalin period, serve as a welcome extension to the tiny living quarters that many people still tacitly have to accept. The ideological apparatus of Soviet origin has faded out, and the architectural set pieces have severely weathered. Large-scale restoration projects will indeed soon be a prerequisite to the safe-guarding of the gardens and parks of the Soviet period. As far as the use of the gardens of the 18th and 19th centuries is concerned, occasional musical and theatrical performances, public dancing and fireworks among the historical set pieces are all activities that reassure the people in their transgression of the Soviet set of values and their fervent longing to experience and demonstrate a spiritual kinship with their ancestry of tsarist times.

It goes without saying that the traditions marking life in and around the so-called *dachas* (usually a wooden cottage or house for use during leisure time) have changed, since Russia's 19th century writers dwelt on these often nearly paradisiac places. Guided by post-Soviet economics and the new patterns of life that Russia's *nouveaux-riches* enjoy, building enterprises nowadays also include large-scale summer residences. Yet, the *dacha* surrounded by its wild garden, a vegetable garden and some apple trees will probably always embody the Russian's dream of how to spend Saturdays and Sundays from April to September. As tradition has it, recreational value here merges with the utilitarian aspect of horticulture. In the vicinity of the big cities and dotted around the landscape, one today finds tens of thousands of small lots, the soil of which is being cultivated as intensively as never before in the history of Russian horticulture. On most lots, humble structures of plastic, spare wood or sheet metal serve as some kind of *dacha*. The increasing popularity of this pattern is one significant outcome of the trend towards private ownership of land.

While great amounts of fruit and vegetable are being harvested from these lots, historians and restorers are actively contributing to a horticultural revival within the Russian borders. New studies are being conducted and old ones, the scope and results of which have been held secret since the early 1930s, are being taken up again. Restoration projects concerning gardens of the tsarist past continue, the focus now considerably widened so as to encompass, not only the former Imperial gardens and the sumptuous noble estates, but also the residences and gardens formerly belonging to the Russian noblemen and gentlemen out in the province.[1]

Finally, Russian artists are beginning to take an interest in using and interpreting the natural environment, including the historical gardens. Traditional landscape and garden painting was never ruled out in the Soviet period, and this genre still has many talented representatives. But there has up till now not been any trend which might be compared with Western artists' dedication to land art, earth art, outdoor installations and ecological manifestations. The art genres which were supported in the former Soviet Union for self-evident ideological reasons meant that few Russian artists risked the plunge into such experimental work. Besides, "ecology" was for a very long time a term of abuse.

But this is changing. The point is that the historical garden should not necessarily look as it once did, or was planned to do. Some kind of intrusion is being allowed for, and in some places it is strongly furthered by the cultural élite, if not by the visitors. The gardens at Kuskovo and Tsaritsyno have, on a temporary basis, hosted a number of art works which were created specifically for these grounds. The

106. Kuskovo. Two little girls dressed up for a promenade in one of the gardens of Russia's tsarist past.

future role of Tsaritsyno as the home of Moscow's Museum of Contemporary Art will undoubtedly bring about many more activities of this kind. It may ultimately change the common idea of Tsaritsyno as an enigmatic work of art of the Catherine period.

In the West, the artists' dialogue and interference with the landscape, whether natural or man-made, has quite often struck some basic aesthetical and mental chords with the public. New questions concerning our attitude to the environment and to ecology have been raised. And some experiments have even proved crucial as far as the survival of old landscape and garden designs is concerned. If this attitude is welcomed and new artistic expressions developed on the Russian soil, it will imply a necessary new step in our perception, interpretation and use of the gardens of the tsars and of the Russian nobility. An inspiring complement to the current scientific endeavours as well as to the nostalgia which occasionally marks professionals and garden visitors alike, is likely to be the outcome. When viewed in this light, it becomes even more clear that Russia's historical gardens are indeed in the process of a many-faceted rediscovery and revival.

Appendix

Notes on Some Russian and Soviet Gardens

The idea of this appendix is to furnish a brief guide to most of the palaces, country estates and gardens dealt with in the present book. In a few cases, ensembles which were created either before or after the Catherine age will also be mentioned. The gardens are listed in alphabetical order, and cross-references to old and obsolete names are included. The present use of the gardens will also be indicated. The sign * refers to another garden mentioned in the appendix.

Alupka

After the Crimea had been captured in 1783, a series of country estates were soon to be created in the mild climate of this southernmost corner of the Russian empire.

Alupka is one of the most sumptuous palace and garden ensembles on the south coast of the Crimea. It owes Count M.S. Vorontsov its existence. English and German architects (E. Blore, W. Hunt, et al.) provided the palace building (1832-51) with Tudor, as well as Islamic, elements. The garden was also laid out by foreigners. Here Italian, French and Spanish traditions came to the fore. The ground on the southern side which extends right down to the banks of the Black Sea is very steep, and terraces, cascades and flights of stairs determine the formal schema of this lush garden.

Today the palace and garden ensemble is a museum. To approach Alupka by sea is indeed the most charming way of entering the Vorontsov estate.

Arkhangelskoe

Situated twenty-six kilometres west of the Moscow Kremlin, the Arkhangelskoe estate takes its name from the Church of the Archangel Michael (1667). The Golitsyn family acquired the estate in 1703.

The mid-18th century ensemble having fallen into disrepair, Prince N.A. Golitsyn had serf-craftsmen build a new neo-classical palace in the 1780s from drawings by the French architect C. de Guerney. Italian-born G. Trombara designed the garden, the main features of which include the existing terraces, extensive parterres, and a series of monuments and pavilions. Part of the natural woods were also added to the new garden. Comprehensive restoration work was carried out in the 1810s and 1820s under Prince N.B. Yusupov. New developments, including the construction of a theatre (P. di Gonzaga, 1818), were also realized. The art and antiques collection was considerably enlarged, and a rich sculptural program came to adorn the garden.

In the Soviet period, the Arkhangelskoe palace and garden complex was under the auspices of the Ministery of Defence. Two comprehensive building blocks were erected in the garden in the 1950s to house a military sanatorium.

The palace museum has been under restoration for several years. It is due to open in 1997.

Bogoroditske

This town is situated in the vicinity of Tula, 180 kilometres southeast of Moscow. It would hardly have ever appeared in the history of Russian gardens if it was not for A.T. Bolotov, the most influential and productive garden writer of tsarist Russia. Bolotov created dozens of gardens in the Tula region from the mid 1760s up to the 1790s, and he defined the urban plan of the city of Bogoroditske, among other places.

In 1784-86, Bolotov was commissioned to embellish the grounds next to the Bogoroditske Palace (I.Ye. Starov, 1771-76). The ensemble was destined for A.G. Bobrinsky, the son of Catherine the Great and Prince Orlov. Initially, a densely wooded area near the neo-classical palace was turned into a pleasure grove. Bolotov's subsequent development of the Bogoroditske garden earned him the reputation as the creator of the Russian landscape garden. Part of the garden was laid out with formal parterres, but landscape aesthetics soon came to the fore, inspired by Bolotov's reading of the German C.C.L. Hirschfeld's theoretical writings. The naturally sloping landscape was furnished with various architectural motifs, including an antique-inspired rotunda, garden ruins, a grotto, carved-out quarries, and so forth.

Despite its presently rather dilapidated state, the Bogoroditske garden allows for pleasant promenades. The palace opened as a museum in 1992. The museum and its exhibition program are devoted to Russian country house culture of the late 18th and 19th centuries, with special emphasis on the Bobrinsky family.

The Central Park of Culture and Rest (Gorki Park) see *The Neskuchny and Golitsyn Gardens

Gatchina

The history of this Imperial palace goes back to the time of Peter the Great. He gave the land, situated forty-five kilometres southwest of St Petersburg to his sister. Subsequently, a number of high officials owned Gatchina. In 1765 Catherine acquired it and presented it to her favourite, Count Orlov.

A palace was built (A. Rinaldi, 1766-81) and extensive gardens were laid out on both sides of the waters dividing the ground. One of the main features of the landscape garden was the archipelago with its winding waters, paths and many bridges, the Island of Love being the nucleus of this part of the layout. A series of pavilions and monuments also formed part of the program. Gardeners of British origin were employed.

When Catherine, after Orlov's death, offered Gatchina to Pavel and Maria Feodorovna, her son and daughter-in-law, the new owners set up their own court here and had the palace ensemble enlarged (V. Brenna, 1790s). Some elements of the landscape garden were sacrificed to give way to patterns more apt for the parades and martial displays that Pavel was so fascinated by. An open-air amphitheatre was also added. When Pavel came to the throne in 1796, he made Gatchina his official residence. He did his utmost to transform the ensemble into a military camp, whereas his wife Maria Feodorovna continuously nourished her passion for *Pavlovsk.

Gatchina is now a museum. A large-scale restoration project has been in progress for several years. New halls are continuously being opened and the gardens are also being worked on.

Gorki Park see *The Neskuchnoe and Golitsyn Gardens

Izmaylovo

The name of this estate, situated nine kilometres northeast of the Moscow Kremlin, stems from the Izmaylovo family. In the 16th century, Romanov acquired the estate, and after the founding of the Romanov dynasty, Izmaylovo became one of the favourite Imperial summer residences. Gardens, some of which held Italian-inspired fountains, were laid out, and the woods were used for the Royal hunt. A model farm and a collection of live exotic animals were also important features of the Izmaylovo estate. It was here that Peter the Great as a boy, planned manoeuvres with his toy regiments and became fascinated with sailing.

Izmaylovo was a popular resort under the last tsars. In 1931 it was turned into one of the new Soviet parks of culture and rest. It was renamed Stalin Park. New facilities were added for the 1980 Olympics. Today, Izmaylovo Park features one of the largest green areas near Moscow.

Kolomenskoe

Situated high above the Moscow river and with a magnificent view, Kolomenskoe became the summer residence of the tsars in the 16th century. It lies ten kilometres southeast of the Moscow Kremlin.

Two of the existing churches go back to the founding period. Tsar Aleksey was the builder of a great wooden palace (1667-71; demolished under Catherine the Great). Peter the Great spent part of his childhood at Kolomenskoe. Catherine the Great as well as Alexander I had small palaces built here.

Today, the churches and an impressive suite of 600-year-old oak trees bear testimony to the history of Kolomenskoe. The site is now a conservation area, and several religious as well as civil buildings have been moved here from other parts of Russia.

Kuskovo

This estate, situated thirteen kilometres east of the Moscow Kremlin, belonged to the Sheremetev family from 1623 right up to the Bolshevik coup. This family was one of the richest and most influential families in tsarist Russia.

In the mid 18th century Field Marshal P.B. Sheremetev created the estate, as it now appears. Serf-architects (F.S. Argunov, A.F. Mironov, et al.) and a few specialists (K. Blank, et al.) designed the ensemble. Apart from the wooden palace (1769-77) and the church, the ensemble features several garden buildings the most important of which are the Dutch House, the Italian House, the Grotto and the Hermitage. Due to the formal layout of the garden and its sumptuous motifs, including the large waters, Kuskovo was called the 'Moscow Versailles'. With work beginning in the early 1770s, a landscape garden was added to the formal garden. Russian theatrical history owes much to the open-air theatre of Kuskovo. Later the *Ostankino theatre became the Sheremetevs' favourite scene.

The palace building is now a museum, and the orangery houses the National Ceramics Museum. While the garden pavilions are being restored, the grounds however are not being paid nearly as much attention as the large St Petersburg gardens.

Lomonosov, see Oranienbaum

Marfino

Situated thirty-five kilometres north of Moscow, the palace ensemble (M.D. Bykovsky, 1830s) that can be seen today at Marfino was built for the Panini family. The structures are indebted partly to 17th century Moscow architecture and partly to English Tudor. Next to the main building, an ornate bridge is a crucial element to the layout. Extensive terraces connect the main building with the pond. The remaining part of the garden takes the form of a grove, crisscrossed by paths. The two-storeyed, antique-inspired garden pavilion is quite unique.

In the Soviet period a sanatorium for the employees of the Ministry of Defence was built next to the Marfino ensemble. The buildings and the garden structures are in very poor state.

The Neskuchny and Golitsyn Gardens

Neskuchny was considered, up till 1917, as Moscow's finest garden. It was founded by the General Prosecutor, Prince N.Yu. Trubetskoi in 1753. The garden, the name of which literaly means *pleasure garden*, was situated just two kilometres from the Kremlin on the banks of the Moscow river. The dominant feature was the carefully cut bosquets. Slightly closer to the Kremlin, and still on the river embankment, was another country estate (M.F. Kazakov, 1780s), named Golitsyn after the owners of the grounds.

In the course of the 19th century, the Neskuchny and Golitsyn gardens came to look more and more like wooded landscape gardens, with attractive ponds, paths and pavilions. When Moscow's urban plan was modified in the late 1920s and the Stalinist policy on the city's public parks was put into effect, both gardens were integrated with the development of the first so-called park of culture and rest, the Central Park of Culture and Rest (A.Vlasov; inaugurated 1928). In 1932 the park was named after the author Maxim Gorki.

In Vlasov's opinion, the historical gardens were ideal for individual promenades. This standpoint was propagated in dozens of parks of the Soviet period. However, the first part of the new Soviet park was laid out in a manner indebted to the formal tradition. It was destined for the recreation and the official politico-cultural education of the masses. Entrance to the park was from Moscow's main ring-road, the so-called Garden Ring. Sports facilities, a fairground, theatres, restaurants, and so forth, were also provided for.

The original name of the park was re-introduced in 1993. As in Soviet times, it remains Moscow's largest and most popular recreational area.

Oranienbaum

Like *Peterhof, Oranienbaum is situated on the south coast of the Bay of Finland, forty-one kilometres west of St Petersburg. In 1710 Peter the Great gave this tract of land to Field Marshal A.D. Menshikov, to build a suitable country residence.

The Great Palace (G. Schädel and M. Fontana, 1710-25) in Russian baroque style faced towards the sea. Following the example of Peterhof, a sumptuous garden in the formal manner was laid out. The ensemble was called Oranienbaum because of its pride in the hothouses with exotic fruits. In 1754 Elisabeth I, the daughter of Peter the Great, gave Oranienbaum to the future Peter III. It was he who initiated the building of a second palace (A. Rinaldi, 1758-62).

Following the successful coup against her husband Peter III, Catherine the Great took over Oranienbaum and declared it her official summer residence. Yet very soon *Tsarskoe Selo became her favourite country residence. The Chinese Palace (A. Rinaldi, 1762-68) as well as the impressive two-storeyed garden pavilion with a 532 metre switchback (1760-68) were erected by the order of Catherine. Part of the new gardens was laid out according to the British landscape tradition.

The ensemble deteriorated under successive rulers. In the Soviet period, notably in 1948, Oranienbaum was renamed Lomonosov, after one of Russia's great 18th century erudites. It was renamed Oranienbaum in 1992. Restoration has been in progress for many years. The Palace of Peter III, the Chinese Palace and the Sliding Hill are open to the public. Yet the gardens remain one of the least kept palace grounds of the St Petersburg area.

Ostankino

Situated twelve kilometres north of the Moscow Kremlin, the village of Ostankino was owned by Prince Cherkassy in the early 17th century. The Sheremetev family took over the estate in 1743, and Count N.P. Sheremetev decided to rebuild the main house, not far from the 17th century Church of the Trinity.

As earlier at *Kuskovo, another country residence near Moscow belonging to the Sheremetev family, serf-architects (F. Camporesi, P. Argunov, A.F. Mironov, et al.) were entrusted with the building and garden project. The key element of the classically styled palace (1791-98) was the Ostankino theatre. The garden had formal parterres and bosquets as well as a wooded area with ponds, natural slopes and intimate pavilions.

In the Soviet period, one part of the Ostankino garden was turned into the Dzerzhinsky Park, a public park named after the founder of the Cheka, the secret police. Another part of the garden was transformed into the Main Botanical Gardens (founded 1945). The remains were integrated with what was to become known as the Exhibition of the Socio-Economic Achievements of the USSR (VDNKh, inaugurated 1939), a huge parkland featuring gardens, squares and pavilions heavily furnished with antique-inspired motifs so as to comply with the Stalinist architectural dogmas. Today, N.P. Sheremetev's palace holds the Ostankino Museum of Serf Art. What is left of the 18th century garden in the immediate vicinity of the main building has not been restored.

Pavlovsk

Situated only three kilometres from *Tsarskoe Selo, Pavlovskoe, as the place was called till the end of the 18th century, was much favoured by the Court because of its hunting facilities. On the occasion of the birth of her first grandson in 1777, Catherine offered the site to Pavel and Maria Feodorovna.

They followed the tradition of hiring foreign architects, artists and gardeners to develop a new and fashionable summer residence. In adjunction with the existing hunting lodges, gardens were laid out. Numerous architectural elements (C. Cameron, 1778-1801), including pavilions, monuments and ruins, were integrated with the natural slopes, the waters and the plantation. The garden soon ranked among Russia's foremost landscape gardens. After some years the palace building followed (C. Cameron, 1782-86). It was heavily indebted to the Greek and Roman antique paradigms as well as to the Palladian tradition.

In the 1790s, significant alterations (V. Brenna) to the main building were carried out. Parterres, bosquets and terraces were also added. After Pavel's death in 1801, Maria Feodorovna continued the sentimental trend in her garden patronage. Her plant collection was also continuously expanded. New ingenious landscapes (P. di Gonzaga), made from nature's own elements, were created during the first quarter of the 19th century.

At the end of the 19th century, Pavlovsk ceased to be an Imperial residence. The ensemble was heavily damaged during the Second World War. The major part of the palace and garden complex has been fully restored. The palace is now a museum.

Peterhof

The genesis of Peterhof, a huge palace and garden complex situated thirty kilometres west of St Petersburg on the southern shore of the Gulf of Finland, is closely tied to the emergence of Russia as a modern Westernized state. Peter the Great became interested in this area when supervising the construction of the Kronstadt fortress. The place was referred to in 1705 by the German name of Peterhof, and building activity began in 1709.

Peter being the prime mover and an active contributor to numerous architectural projects of the first quarter of the 18th century, his idea was to make Peterhof a summer residence echoing French and Italian traditions. As had been the case at the *Summer Palace and Garden a few years earlier, foreign architects and gardeners were also called upon.

The Great Palace in baroque style goes back to the Petrine years (J.-B.-A. Le Blond, 1714-21; enlarged during the reign of Elisabeth by B.F. Rastrelli, 1747-54). A series of moderately sized buildings, including the Marly and the Monplaisir Palaces, were also erected in the 1710s. Parallel to this, extensive gardens in the formal manner (Peter and Le Blond) were being developed. Thanks to the creation of a complex hydraulic system, Peterhof was soon to boast water works that exceeded the great French models. The cascades and fountains (N. Michetti) were inaugurated in 1723.

Peterhof was an important Imperial residence during the 18th and 19th centuries. Successive rulers had new palaces built and new gardens designed, e.g. the English ensemble (G. Quarenghi, 1779-94) and the Alexandria Palace (A.A. Menelaws, 1826-29). Next to 18th century Russian baroque, neo-classical and gothic forms were favoured.

Peterhof was made a museum in the 1920s. The ensemble was severely damaged during the Second World War, but restoration has been going on ever since, the focus being on Peter's palace and garden. In 1945 the German name Peterhof was replaced by Petro-dvorets, Russian for Peter's palace, but Peterhof is now back in use. Recently the waterworks and gilded sculptures of the Great Cascade have undergone restoration.

Petrofsky

Situated eight kilometres from the Moscow Kremlin, on the road to St Petersburg, the Petrofsky Palace (M.F. Kazakov, 1775-82) was erected by order of Catherine as a travel residence. A blend of Western and Moscow building traditions is at hand here, as is also the case at Catherine's second Moscow palace, *Tsaritsyno. The wooded grounds surrounding the building site were cleaned up, and a geometric pattern of paths was laid out. The place is occupied by the Moscow School of Cadets and cannot be visited.

Pushkin see *Tsarskoe Selo

Sokolniki

Known in the 17th century as the falconers' (*sokolniki*) place, the woods, situated seven kilometres north of the Moscow Kremlin, were for a long time a favourite Imperial hunting ground. Later it became a popular recreational area for the Muscovites, and in 1931, a few years after the Socialist urban program was initiated, Sokolniki was named a park of culture and rest. It was provided with sports facilities, a theatre, pavilions and arenas for mass gatherings. Sokolniki remains one of Moscow's main parklands.

The Summer Palace and the Summer Garden

Laid out in 1704 in the heart of St Petersburg, this ensemble was one of Peter's very first building enterprises in the new Northern capital of Russia and indeed his first essay in the Western garden manner. The palace was placed on the very banks of the Neva river, opposite the SS. Peter and Paul Fortress. Canals were soon to surround the grounds on the remaining three sides. As the name indicates, the palace was to serve as the Imperial family's summer residence. The Summer Palace kept this function until *Peterhof was built.

Following Peter's taste for Western aesthetics, techniques and manners, specialists of Dutch, Italian and French origin put their mark on the palace (D. Trezzini, 1710-12) and the garden. The grounds were laid out in the formal manner (I. Matveev, J. Rosen, Peter the Great, A.J.-B. Le Blond, et al.). Fountains, ponds, pavilions and sculptures, many of which were bought in Italy, adorned the area. Under Peter the garden was much used for diplomatic receptions and public events, such as fireworks and musical performances. New extensive residences and gardens were added by Peter's widow Catherine I, and by his daughter Elizabeth, but none of these structures were upheld for more than a few generations.

The fountains of the Summer Garden and many of the pavilions were destroyed in a flood in 1777. After that the Summer Garden never attained its former glory. Its primary role now was that of a public park, and to this day it offers some of St Petersburg's most popular promenades. Peter's Summer Palace opened as a museum in 1934. Over the years various projects for the reconstruction of the mid 18th century garden have been outlined, but none of them have been started.

Tsaritsyno

This ensemble was planned to be Catherine the Great's Moscow summer residence, situated not far from *Kolomenskoe, thirteen kilometres southeast of the Kremlin.

Catherine bought the village of Chornaya Gryaz and the nearby palace from Prince Kantemir in 1775. The majestic name Tsaritsyno was accorded to the locality when the construction of an Imperial residence began. Several palace buildings, an opera house, grandiose bridges and gateways, formed part of the ambitious project (V.I. Bazhenov, 1775-85; M.F. Kazakov, 1785-92). A unique blend of classical orders, elements of Moscow baroque, and traditional Russian imagery were characteristic of the Tsaritsyno ensemble, which was however never to be completed. The terrain in front of the Great Palace was levelled to create a parterre garden, whereas the natural slopes and the waters were maintained in the designs for the landscape garden. Pavilions offering pleasant views and places for meditation were placed in various sections of the garden.

Tsaritsyno never served its initial purpose, but the exciting landscaped setting has been enjoyed by the public since the late 18th century. In the past few decades restoration work has been undertaken, as far as the architectural structures are concerned. Moscow's future Museum of Contemporary Art will be at Tsaritsyno. The grounds are maintained for the Muscovites to enjoy sunbathing, swimming, strolling, and in the winter, skiing.

Tsarskoe Selo

The land called Saari Moos (Finnish for high ground), situated twenty-five kilometres south of St Petersburg, was chosen by Peter the Great as a present for his wife, the future Catherine I. A stone palace (1717-23) was built, and a small largely Dutch-inspired garden was laid out. The locality was renamed Tsarskoe Selo, meaning Imperial Village.

Under Russia's two great 18th century rulers, Elizabeth and Catherine the Great, Tsarskoe Selo was enlarged several times. The palace was turned into the official Imperial summer residence. Named after Elisabeth's mother, Tsarskoe Selo's first inhabitant, the Catherine Palace (B.F. Rastrelli 1752-56) was built in a sumptuous Russian baroque style. The old garden was considerably widened. More canals, alleys, bosquets and architectural motifs were fitted into the formal garden. The Hermitage, which was to lend its name to the St Petersburg Hermitage, and the sumptuous Grotto are also the works of Rastrelli.

Foreign architects continued to dominate the Imperial building program under Catherine. The Scotsman C. Cameron added the Agate Rooms with a hanging garden and the Cameron Gallery (1779-86) to Rastrelli's palace. In adjunction to the formal Elizabethan garden, an extensive landscape garden (J. Busch, et al.) was laid out in the 1770s and 1780s. This garden boasted a suite of landscape motifs, ruins, monuments and pavilions which appealed to the enlightened intellect as well as to the emotions. The structures (V.I. and I.V. Neelov, C. Cameron, A. Rinaldi, Yu.M. Velten, et al.) reflected various stylistic sources of inspiration, including Greek and Roman antique, Chinese and gothic. The Alexander Palace (G. Quarenghi, 1792-96) and the Alexander Park were destined for Catherine's grandson, the future Alexander I.

Tsarskoe Selo served as an Imperial summer residence for more than one and a half centuries. After the February 1917 Revolution, Nicholas II, the last tsar, and his family were under house arrest at Tsarskoe Selo.

In 1918 the ensemble was renamed Detskoe Selo (Childrens' Village), and then in 1937, on the occasion of the poet's centenary, renamed *Pushkin. A small museum devoted to the Imperial family was opened in the early 1920s. In the Soviet period the palace ensemble also housed various scientific institutions. The buildings and gardens were in ruins following the Second World War. Restoration has been going on ever since, and the palace building (now a museum) and most of the garden structures have risen as a Phoenix from the ashes. As regards the grounds and the plantation, restoration has mainly taken place in the Elizabethan garden.

Резюме · Summary in Russian

Книга называется »Царские садово-парковые ансамбли. Эстетика, семантика и назначение русских садов XУIII века«. Цель данного исследования – дать подробный анализ о российских развлекательных садов. Наибольшее внимание уделено периоду царствования Екатерины Великой (1762-96 гг.).

Мировое искусствоведение проявило весьма скромный интерес к истории русского садово-паркового искусства. Политические потрясения, происходившие в России в течение последних лет, приблизили не только русскую историю и культуру к западному восприятию, но и воссоздали предпосылки для более углубленной научно-исследовательской работы, а также поездок в ныне распавшийся Советский Союз. Поэтому я считаю своевременым и важным расширить поле традиционных исследований в области садово-паркового искусства, включив в них и русское.

Вторая причина, побудившая меня предпринять исследования в этой области – возросший интерес к царской истории как со стороны историков, так и общественности на фоне многочисленных кризисов, охвативших Россию в последние годы. Количество публикаций о дворцово-парковых сооружениях XУIII-XIX вв. постоянно растет. К тому же некоторые сооружения, которые до недавнего времени были закрыты или находились в запущенном состоянии, в настоящее время реставрируются и стали доступными для посетителей. Большое значение имеет и тот факт, что Всероссийское Общество Изучения Русской Усадьбы, основанное в 1923 г., возобновило свою деятельность в соответствии с уставом.

Во время продолжительного пребывания в России я имела возможности работать в российских библиотеках, посещать музеи, ознакомиться с литературой о садово-парковом искусстве в период царствования Екатерины Великой, а также с неопубликоваными материалами и трудами, изданными только в России. В данном исследовании изложение материала впервые дано под углом зрения западно-европейского восприятия. Не менее важным было проанализировать садово-парковые ансамбли с точки зрения их многостороннего назначения, показать их организацию, содержание и использование, представить географическое месторасположение, а также познакомить с меценатскими группами, с участием многих русских и иностранных мастеров-садоводов в формировании садово-парковых ансамблей.

Книга содержит три основных раздела в соответствии с целью и направлениями исследования, обозначеными в названии. Первый раздел называется »Меценаты и их садовые проекты«. Второй раздел озаглавлен »Художники и семантика садов«. Третий раздел – »Сады и их посетители«. Анализу многих садов отведены целые главы, садово-парковые ансамбли изучены в совокупности, но вместе с этим в книге приводится анализ отдельных скульптур, монументальных сооружений и других архитектурных ценностей от их местонахождения. Чтобы показать взаимосвязь между тремя вышеназваными направлениями данного исследования я использую перекрекстные повторы между отдельными главами.

»Меценаты и их садовые проекты«: в первой главе представлены крупнейшие меценаты XYIII века. Дан анализ их любимых парковых сооружений, приведены сведения об их теоретико-практическом вкладе в садово-парковое искусство. Размышления об их эстетических взглядах на этот вид искусства и возникновении этих идеалов изложены с точки зрения современников изучаемого периода. В качестве примера представлены дворцово-парковые сооружения Санкт-Петербурга, Москвы и российской провинции.

Ключевую позицию занимает здесь, естественно, Екатерина Великая. Как известно, в своей деятельности, в том числе и в области садово-паркового искусства, она ориентировалась на своего предшественника – Петра Великого, который, говоря весьма условно, впервые в России начал создавать развлекательные парки по западному образцу. Первая глава посвящена поэтому меценатству Петра Великого. Рассматриваемые голандские, французские и итальянские источники заимствования анализируются с точки зрения их воплощения в Летнем Саду Петербурга и в Петергофе.

Вторая глава посвящена Царскому Селу. Екатерина Великая, последовав примеру Петра и Елизаветы, с помощью много путешествовавших русских архитекторов и иностранных художников, создавала в Царском Селе сады в традициях английских пейзажных парков, наиболее современных на западе.

В третьей главе говорится о графах Голициных, Юсуповых, рассказывается об их вкусах, эстетических взглядах на это искусство. В качестве примера приведены две усадьбы – Архангельское и Кусково. В эти ансамбли, несколько позднее, чем в императорские дворцово-парковые сооружения под Санкт-Петербургом, были внесены элементы, заимствованные из традиций всех значительных западно-европейских направлений паркового искусства.

А.Т. Болотов своим личным примером и многочисленными трудами в области сельского хозяйства, лесоводства, плодоводства и садово-паркового искусства оказал большое влияние на многие поколения российского провинциального дворянства, представители которого стали настоящими садовыми мастерами-любителями. Переводы Болотова из *Теории садово-паркового искусства* немецкого теоретика С.С.Л. Гиршфельда сыграли важную роль в ознакомлении с эстетикой английских пейзажных парков. Тема четвертой главы – труды Болотова и его участие в формировании дворцово-паркового ансамбля в Богородицке.

»Художники и семантика садов«: принимая во внимание важную роль, которая отводилась во многих развлекательных парках России конца XYIII века античному искусству, первые две главы этого раздела посвящены картинам на эту тему.

Основной обьект исследования в первой главе – парковые картины. Особое внимание уделяется сюжетам, воспроизведенным из мира античности в целом ряде дворянских усадеб, расположеных в окрестностях Москвы – Останкино, Суханово, а также деятельности Болотова. В этой главе есть цитаты из дидактического стихотворения французского теоретика Жака Делиля *Сады.* Это произведение было излюбленым чтением в дворянских кругах. Именно Делиль был толкователем символики западно-европейских пейзажных садов того периода.

Шотландский архитектор Ч.Камерон, которого привезли в Россию для возведения Царского Села для императрицы Екатерины Великой, считался наиболе авторитетным интерпретатором античного искусства. Во второй главе – в центре внимания его работы по формированию пейзажного парка в Павловске. Сюжеты этого парка, навеянные античностью, рассматриваются в сопоставлении с западно-европейскими традициями того периода, воспевавшими поэтику храмов и руин, пасторальные мотивы.

В третьей главе анализируются примеры экзотических мотивов – китайских, исламских, египетских – в российских парках. Благодаря переводам Екатерины и публикациям Болотова отрывок английского архитектора-теоретика Чеймберса нашол отклик и в России. Кроме Ораниенбаума и Царского Села, в качестве примеров описаны и некоторые небольшие провинциальные усадьбы.

При участи русских архитекторов В.И. Баженова и М.Ф. Казакова в старинной столице Москве был возведен целый ряд экспериментальных сооружений по мотивам средневековья. Это явление нашло отражение как в архитектуре, так и в орнаментальном декоре. Изучение материалов о том, каким должен был стать парково-архитектурный ансамбль Царицыно, т. е. екатерининское Царское Село под Москвой, свидетельствует о том, что это явление в те годы носило в определенной степени политический характер. В этой связи часто употребляется понятие »готика«. В четвертой главе обращается внимание на то, что понятие »готика« в России употреблялось по отношению многих исторических, но наиболее часто, средневековых мотивов. Масонские ложи, рыцарские романы и ордена, замки входящие в композицию сада – это темы, которые используются для описания того особого мира, который так страстно культивировал сын Екатерины Великой – Павел I.

»Сады и их посетители«: этот раздел о том, как на практике использовались развлекательные сады периода царствования Екатерины Великой, о том, какие широкие возможности имели эти парковые ансамбли для развлечений.

В центре внимания – садовые пейзажи и архитектурные сооружения для интеллектуального времяпрепровождения. В книге описаны также компоненты, использованные в сценографии парка, более доступные постетителям для наслаждения. Первая глава посвящена таким образом светским развлечениям, местам уединения и медитации, ботаническим занятиям, крупным театральным представлениям.

Писатели и художники – темы соответственно второй и третьей главы. Императорский двор и некоторые дворянские семьи проявляли большой интерес к пейзажным паркам, увлекаясь одновременно поэзией о природе. Источником вдохновения поэтам служили в первую очередь естественные пейзажные картины парков. Это подтверждают примеры из творчества Карамзина, Державина и других поэтов того времени. Особое значение в исследовании придается поэзии Жуковского, темой которой является парк в Павловске.

Что же касается художников, сади конца XYIII века, являлись, для них источником творческого вдохновения, так и для поэтов служили местом для философских размышлений. Так, итальянский театральный художник П. ди Гонзага создал в Павловске, в частности, свою совершенно уникальную серию пейзажей, моделью ему послужили естественные ландшафтные картины парка. В Богородицке Болотов экспериментировал с иллюзорной архитектурной живописью. Тема природы и садово-парковых ансамблей завоевала одновременно большую популярность и в творчестве молодого поколения профессиональных художников России и Запада. Описание ландшафтных картин С.Ф. Щедрина и Г. Робера использованы для освещения этой темы.

В заключении говорится о политических и военных событиях, послуживших темой для формирования многих парковых картин. Отправным моментом, как и в первом разделе, служит начало XYIII столетия, увлечение Петра Великого парковой скульптурой и памятниками, прославляющими какую-то личность или событие. Следующий узловой момент – склонность Екатерины Великой отмечать таким же образом свои военные победы. Далее идет речь о советских традициях в садово-парковом искусстве. Упоминаются так называемые парки победы с их иконографическими мотивами, заимствованными, в частности, из Петергофа и Царского Села.

Заключительная глава этой книги содержит размышления о будущем садово-парковых ансамблей, об увлечении современных художников парковым пространством и историей парков.

List of Illustrations

Notes

If not otherwise indicated, the quotations from Russian, German and French sources have been translated by the author of the present book.

For a translation of the titles of Russian books and articles, please compare with the Selected Bibliography.

Introduction

1. The very first studies appeared in the magazine entitled *Starye gody* (The Old Times, 1907-16), and much was summed by V.Ya. Kurbatov in his voluminous *Sady i parki* (Gardens and Parks, 1916), wherein Russian and Western gardens were given equal treatment. Many of the authors contributing to *Starye gody* were descendants of former country house owners, and they added fragments of family memories to their narratives on individual estates. But it was the Society for the Study of Russian Country Houses which initiated a truly systematic research on the historical gardens, based on studies on site and archival findings.

    The Society was officially founded in 1923, just after the Civil War. The members, who were practically all professionals, published numerous books and articles, the latter in particular in the magazine *Sredi kollektsionerov* (Among Collectors, 1923-29). Yet the Stalin regime was in disfavour of the Society's program. The study of 18th century architecture and gardens was thought to have a higher meaning only when it could be fitted into the mould of the newly declared socialist art. Several members of the Society were arrested in the early 1930s, and the archives were destroyed.

    German bombings during the Second World War laid the Imperial palaces outside St Petersburg to ruin, and the subsequent restoration work was a cornerstone in the post-war nationalistic program. It has been argued that several of the Soviet leaders felt a spiritual kinship with the tsars, and this circumstance may have additionally furthered the dispatch with which the old designs rose like a phoenix from its ashes. In writing too, focus was on the residences of the tsars. Gradually, though, the gardens of the nobility and the gentry also claimed attention, and the field of study moved from St Petersburg to Moscow.

    Arkhitektura podmoskovskykh usadeb (Country House Architecture in the Moscow Region, 1955) by N.Ya. Tikhomorov, was the first study to sum up this approach. A much broader analysis concerning the same region followed in *...v okrestnostyakh Moskvy. Iz istorii russkoi usadebnoi kultury XVII-XIX vekov* (...in the Surroundings of Moscow. From the History of Russian Country House Culture of the 17th-19th Centuries, 1979), edited by M.A. Anikst and V.S. Turchin. Besides, next to D.S. Likhachov's *Poeziya sadov. K semantike sadovo-parkovykh stylei* (The Poetry of Gardens. On the Semantics of Garden and Park Styles, 1982), which departs from the poets' readings of gardens, this is the only historical garden analysis to have benefitted from a certain interdisciplinarity. Moving from a specific tradition of form, *Russkie regulyarnye sady i parki* (Russian Formal Gardens and Parks, 1963) by T.B. Dubyago is a classic, but has not been followed up by other studies of this genre. Only *Russkie sady i parki* (Russian Gardens and Parks, 1988) by A.P. Vergunov and V.A. Gorokhov boasts a truly general scope. But it is basically a compilatory work, and lags behind the above mentioned studies as far as originality and the provision of new data are concerned.

In 1991 the Society for the Study of Russian Country Houses was re-established. Today, publications, conferences and study tours form the core of its program, as was the case in the 1920s, and a group of similarly enthusiastic historians make up its forum. If bad economics does not drown the many initiatives, much can be awaited from this side.

PATRONS AND PROGRAMS

Peter's Western Patterns

1. From *Specimens of the Russian Poets*, (translated by John Bowing), London, 1821, VIII.

2. For a discussion of Russia's contacts with the *Latins* and the *Germans*, see J.H. Billington, *The Icon and the Axe. An Interpretative History of Russian Culture*, New York, 1970, 78-114.

3. For details on Peter's Western acquisitions, see T.B. Dubyago, *Regulyarnye sady i parki*, Leningrad, 1964, 317, note 44, & ibid., 321. A catalogue concerning Peter's book collection was established in his lifetime, and one of the headings was 'Published Books on Garden Elements, with Engravings.'

4. As for the Dutch aspect of St Petersburg, G.H. Hamilton has asserted that it "is more apparent in the decorated gables of a few houses in the early engravings than in any monumental structures." *The Art and Architecture of Russia*, Harmondsworth, 1987, 436, note 275/18.

5. No other data on Jan Rosen has been found. His name, and nothing more, is frequently mentioned in Russian and Soviet studies.

6. From a description of St Petersburg by N.G. Georgi, 1794, quoted by D.S. Likhachov, *Poeziya sadov. K semantike sadovo-parkovykh stilei*, Leningrad, 1982, 127. Georgi did not describe Le Blond's modifications, and therefore his text can be quoted here in relation to the Dutch features contained in the early Summer Garden.

7. Some of the most elaborate examples of this manner were at Kuskovo and Pavlovsk. As for the latter, see the description by P. Storkh, *Putevoditel po sadu i gorodu Pavlovsku*, St Petersburg, 1843, 42-43.

8. From the Archives of the Imperial Court at St Petersburg, quoted by D.S. Likhachov, op.cit., 121, note 33.

9. From Bergholz' diary, written 1721-25 and published 1916, quoted by A.P. Vergunov & V.A. Gorokhov, *Russkie sady i parki*, Moscow, 1988, 52.

10. From Bergholz' diary, quoted by G.R. Bolotova, *Letny sad*, Leningrad, 1988, 12.

11. One of the first horticultural handbooks to be published in Russia was N. Osipov, *Podrobny slovar dlya selskikh i gorodskikh okhotnikov i lyubitelei Botanicheskago, uveselitelnago i khozyaistvennago sadovodstva*, 2 vols., St Petersburg, 1791-92. In this case *uvesitelny* entered the title.

12. From a German travel description, 1710-11, quoted by D.S. Likhachov, op.cit., 125.

13. T.B. Dubyago, op.cit., passim; G.R. Bolotova, op.cit., passim; A.P. Vergunov & V.A. Gorokhov, op.cit., passim.

14. From the memoirs of 1710 of Just Juel, Danish minister to Peter's Court, quoted from T.B. Dubyago, op.cit., 30-31: "It should be noted that, like the tsar, so all Russians refuse to give up any of the old Russian habits which can serve

their glorification."

15. C.C.L. Hirschfeld, *Theorie der Gartenkunst*, Leipzig, 1779-85, V, 287.

Catherine's Favourite Garden

1. An example is L. Réau & G.K. Loukomski, *Cathérine la grande, inspiratrice d'art et mécène*, Paris, 1930, passim.
2. G.H. Hamilton, *Art and Architecture in Russia*, Harmondsworth, 1987, 289.
3. Catherine quoted by G.H. Hamilton, op.cit., 337.
4. For a discussion of Pushkin's *Bronze Horseman* and Falconet's sculpture, see J.H. Billington, *The Icon and the Axe. An Interpretative History of Russian Culture*, Washington, 1970, passim. The author states that Pushkin's interpretation "struck a resonant chord in the Russian apocalyptical mentality", ibid., 332.
5. L. Réau (ed.), 'Correspondance artistique de Grimm avec Catherine II', *Archives de l'art français*, XVII, 1931-33, 61. The letter is dated August 23, 1779.
6. Ibid.
7. Catherine quoted by A.P. Vergunov & V.A. Gorokhov, *Russkye sady i parki*, Moscow, 1988, 225.
8. Girardin, and not Gérardin, is the most commonly used spelling. In the late 18th century, French garden writings on the landscape genre were also well-known in Poland and Hungary, and the first Pole to write on the aesthetics of the landscape garden, A.F. Moszyński, chose French, the then preferred language among princes and nobles. Moszyński's treatise has been republished not long ago, *Rosprawa o ogorodownictwie angielskim*, (1774), Wroslaw, Warsaw, Krakow, Gadansk, 1977.
9. See M. Headfield, *A History of British Gardening*, Harmondsworth, 1985, 79.
10. C.C.L. Hirschfeld, *Theorie der Gartenkunst*, Leipzig, 1779-85, V, 289.
11. Catherine in a letter, dated June 23, 1772, to Voltaire, quoted by G.H. Hamilton, op.cit., 334.
12. It is not quite clear what year John Busch came to Russia. One of the most authoritative studies on the gardens of the St Petersburg region states 1770, see A.N. Petrov, a.o. (eds.), *Pamyatniki arkhitektury prigorodov Leningrada*, Leningrad, 1985, 68. A.G. Cross, however, says 1774 in his introduction to Dimsdale, Baroness E.: *An English Lady at the Court of Catherine the Great. The Journal of Baroness Elizabeth Dimsdale*, Cambridge, 1989, 102, note 3. In any case, the name of Catherine's gardener should be spelt Busch, and not Bush as Cross does, following Lady Dimsdale.
13. Ibid., 70-71. According to A.G. Cross, Baroness Elizabeth Dimsdale knew Busch before he went to Russia, ibid., 50.
14. J.C. Loudon, *An Encyclopedia of Gardening*, London, 1835, 246.
15. See A.P. Vergunov & V.A. Gorokhov, op.cit., & A.N. Petrov, a.o. (eds.), op.cit., 72.
16. The Neelovs also made a number of contributions to the old Elizabethan garden, e.g. the Upper Bath.
17. Dimsdale, Baroness E., op.cit., 55.
18. L. Réau (ed.), op.cit., 195. The letter to Grimm is dated September 4, 1794.
19. Ibid., 90. The letter is dated November 7, 1780.
20. Ibid., 102. The letter is dated June 23, 1781.
21. Ibid., 61. The letter is dated August 23, 1779.

Princely Gardens

1. C.C.L. Hirschfeld, *Theorie der Gartenkunst*, Leipzig, 1779-85, V, 286-91.
2. Ibid., 289.
3. In the immediate vicinity of the former grounds of the Annenhof complex lies a no less historic building, the Lefort Palace (D. Aksamitov, 1697-99) which was presented by Peter the Great to his Swiss advisor Franz Lefort. The building now houses the Russian Military Historical Archive.

4. Ibid., 291.
5. Quoted by V.I. Novikov, *Ostafyevo. Literaturnye sudby XIX veka*, Moscow, 1991, 5. Voikov's translations of Delille, published twice in the early 19th century, confirmed the impact of the landscape garden in Russia. A new Russian translation by I.Ya. Shafarenko of Delille's poem was published in 1987.
6. Prince de Ligne quoted by I. Grabar, 'Ostankinsky dvorets', *Starye gody*, 5-6, 1910, 11.
7. Like many other architects, whether foreign or Russian, only the name of Chevalier de Guerney occurs in the current literature on Russian architecture and gardens. No further information on his life and work is given.
8. Catherine mentions the two Italians in her letter to Grimm, dated August 23, 1779. L. Réau (ed.), 'Correspondance artistique de Grimm avec Catherine II', *Archives de l'art français*, XVII, 1931-33, 61.
9. Quoted by M.P. Korzhev & M.I. Prokhorova, *Arkhitektura parkov SSSR*, Moscow, 1940, 3.
10. In the 19th century, Catherine's green belt (1775) was repeated on the outer city ring. This was then called the Sadovoe Koltso, that is the Garden Ring. Yet it did not survive Stalin's plan for Moscow. All the trees lining the 16 kilometre long Sadovoe Koltso were felled and a multi-lane motorway was created. Massive new buildings, including three of Moscow's skyscrapers, were erected on either side. The loss of the greenery of the Garden Ring was compensated for by the extensive planting of trees along the city's quays and the major streets.
11. A. Vlasov, 'Tsentrelny park kultury i otdikha im. Gorkogo', *Arkhitektura SSSR*, 7, 1934, 47.
12. Up till the 1980 Olympic Games, Lushniki remained Moscow's largest sports arena.
13. For more details on the different parts of the park, see op.cit., 48-49.
14. Ibid., 44.
15. A. Vlasov, 'Tsentralny park stolitsi', *Arkhitektura SSSR*, 10-11, 1935, 49. In the Soviet period, Tsarskoe Selo was renamed *Detskoe Selo*, meaning the Children's Village, and then *Krasnoe Selo*, the Beautiful, or Red Village.
16. M.P. Korzhev & M.I. Prokhorova, op.cit., 6.
17. Ibid., 3.
18. In 1933 an official workshop was set up to make proposals for a renewal of the city's profile. "In order to renovate, radical measures are necessary. We need a surgeon", the urban developer Vladimir Semyonov wrote. His and the architect Sergei Shchnernychev's *General Plan* for the Renewal of Moscow was accepted two years later by the Central Committee.
19. Quoted by O.S. Yevangulova, 'Gorod i usadba vtoroi poloviny XVIIIv. v soznanie sovremennikov', *Russky gorod. Issledovaniya i materialy*, VII, Moscow, 1984, 181.

The Garden and the Gentry

In the following, *Ekonomichesky Magazin* is referred to in abbreviated form, EM. The author quoted in connection with articles published in this magazine is Andrei Timofeevich Bolotov, if no other name is otherwise mentioned.

Like many other garden writers of the late 18th century, Bolotov devoted the larger part of his attention to utilitarian gardening, forestry and questions of botany. In the first ten issues of the magazine, Bolotov did not strive to create any homogeneity or suite of arguments regarding content. What Bolotov did, was to draw up summaries of the impressions he gained from books and illustrations and from visits to various gardens. His main articles published in EM on gardening as an aesthetical discipline are, by year of appearance:

'About Fountains', EM, V, 1781, 113-22. Yet, this very article may stem from another hand than Bolotov's, but it remains the first in EM dealing exclusively with non-utilitarian garden elements.
'About Groves and Small Woods Situated Near Settlements', EM, V, 1781, 129-44.
'About the Adornments of Pleasure Groves', EM, V, 1781, 289-301.
'On Old Gardens', EM, XI, 1781, 81-93.
'Continuation on the Redoing of Old Gardens', EM, XI, 1781, 113-26, 179-91, 226-38, 257-68, 289-302, 321-34, 352-67.
'On Redoing Old Gardens', EM, XII, 1782, 81-91, 113-25, 145-57, 177-88, 209-20.
'Something about Gardens of the Modern Taste', EM, XIX, 1784, 305-13.
'Some Practical Remarks about Gardens of the Newest Taste', EM, XX, 1784, 17-31.
'Practical Remarks about the Transformation of Common Natural Groves into Pleasure Groves', EM, XX, 1784, 33-48.
'Some Practical Remarks about Grottoes', EM, XXI, 1785, 129-42.
'On Some New Kind of Life and Light, but Nice Garden Elements Anyway', EM, XXIII, 1785, 129-43.
'Continuation on Illusionistic Garden Elements', EM, XXIII, 1785, 145-58.
'Some More about Water Elements in English Gardens', EM, XXIII, 1785, 225-38, 241-55.
'Some More about Gardens and Their Origin', EM, XXV, 1786, 49-58, 65-389.

Using Hirschfeld and Chambers as his main sources, Bolotov takes his readers from Babylon to Rome, from Italian Renaissance gardens over French formal gardens to English landscape gardens, from the Nether-

lands to Sweden, etc.

Then, based on Hirschfeld, follow five articles on the general principles of landscape gardening, see EM, XXVI, 1786, 65-78, 81-94, 97-107, 321-31, 337-52.

The subsequent issues of EM hold articles by Hirschfeld on specific garden elements. Some articles, though, include Bolotov's personal remarks. They are:

'Some Practical Remarks about Garden Buildings', EM, XXIX, 1787, 33-42.
'General Remarks about Grottoes and Caves', EM, XXIX, 1787, 97-108, 113-25.
'Continued Remarks about the New Sort of Gardens', EM, XXX, 1787, 113-20.

Once extracts from Hirschfeld's *Theorie der Gartenkunst* dominated EM (XXV, XXVI, XXVII, XXX, XXXI, and XXXII, issues covering the years 1785-87), Bolotov by and large gave up writing on garden aesthetics himself. His work in this phase was mainly editorial. One major exception, though, is the article entitled 'Some Remarks about Gardens in Russia', EM, XXVI, 1786, 49-63. Few articles by Bolotov are as programmatic as this one; see the chapter entitled "A National Appeal" in Part One in this study.

By 1788 Bolotov again appeared as the author of the majority of articles in EM. But his way of writing had undergone some changes since he started his massive publishing of Hirschfeld. This is evident from the following articles:

'Some More Practical Remarks about the New Sort of Gardens, or so-called English Gardens', EM, XXXIX, 1789, 17-30.
'Continued Practical Remarks about English or New Natural Pleasure Gardens', EM, XXXIX, 1789, 33-47.

'Continuation of Various Practical Remarks on New Gardens', EM, XXXIX, 1789, 49-62.

These three articles held summaries of Bolotov's and Hirschfeld's ideas.

Bolotov was no longer concerned with teaching something new and revolutionary to his readers. The following three reasons may account for this. Firstly, contemporary garden aesthetics had already been discussed in EM from various viewpoints, and landscape gardens had significantly won popularity in the 1780s. Secondly, practical design work was not nearly as absorbing to Bolotov as it had been when he was laying out the Bogoroditske garden. Thirdly, Bolotov was much involved with experimenting with fruit trees at that time. Some years later his voluminous study on apples and pears would appear. In fact, fruit trees and fruit bushes were Bolotov's main concern in the very last issue of EM, XL, 1789. And so the horticulturist, who had had a tremendous impact on Russian garden aesthetics of the first two decades of the Catherine period, ended up discussing his old speciality.

Given Bolotov's role in the history of Russian gardening, a good deal of this material certainly ought to be published. I have done some preliminary work, including translating some of Bolotov's articles and notes, in view of this, and hope to go into detail with it at some later point.

1. Quoted by O.S. Yevangulova, 'Gorod i usadba vtoroi poloviny XVIIIv. v soznanii sovremennikov', *Russky gorod Issledovaniya i materialy*, Moscow, 1984, 175.

2. There are numerous instances of Bolotov referring to the economics of gardening. Thus, in the article entitled 'On Old Gardens', EM, XI, 1782, 92: "I should say that my recommendations will be useful only for those who wish to improve their old gardens without unnecessary and expensive ventures, but who wish, in spite of this, to achieve noticeable results." Interestingly enough, one of the copies of EM now belonging to the Russian State Library, Muzei Knigi (The Department of Rare Books), originally belonged to Peter Borisovich Sheremetev who was one of the great garden patrons of the Catherine age.

3. 'On Redoing Old Gardens', EM, XII, 1782, 81.

4. He wrote this work at Dvoryaninovo, 1797-1801.

5. This argument has been strongly nourished by Bolotov's essay 'Some Remarks about Gardens in Russia', EM, XXVI, 1786, 49-63.

6. 'On Redoing Old Gardens', EM, XII, 1782, 125.

7. Ibid., 86.

8. For Bolotov's discussions of parterres and their emplacement, see ibid., passim, and 'Some Practical Remarks about Gardens of the Newest Taste', EM, XX, 1784, passim.

9. L. Kovshova, 'Bogoroditsky ansambl. Usadba i gorod', unpublished dissertation, St Petersburg, 1992, 50.

10. EM, XX, 1784, 33-48.

11. Ibid., 42.

12. 'On Redoing Old Gardens', EM, XII, 1782, 87 & 113.

13. 'Some Practical Remarks about Gardens of the Modern Taste', EM, XX, 1784, 17. Here came the moment when Bolotov felt prepared to inform his readers about the new European aesthetics. In the very same article he said: "In the spring of this year, 1784, I was busy with gardens of this kind, as I was given the task of improving and putting into order an area at a certain famous house that was so uncomely and in some places almost so ugly, that it did not correspond to

the beauty of the house; the redoing of the grounds was carried out on my own responsibility, owing to which I had the opportunity to get some practice in this field and, first of all, in the creation of the so-called English or, to be more correct, of beautiful and natural gardens; I had the opportunity to transform most uncomely environments into such beautiful and pleasant places that, to my surprise, not only specialists in gardening and persons with subtle taste highly appreciated the results achieved, but this was appreciated by the simple people who seemed to be unable to perceive the natural beauty and enjoy the contact with Nature." (EM, XX, 17)

14. 'Something about Gardens of the Modern Taste', EM, XIX, 1784, 305. Earlier in the article 'About the Adornments of Pleasure Groves', EM, V, 1781, 289, Bolotov had said, by way of introduction: "With regard to English gardens that are very fashionable nowadays and have become common all over Europe, it can be said that they are worth talking about."

15. EM, XXV, 1786, passim & EM, XXVI, 1786, passim. Hirschfeld's *Theorie der Gartenkunst*, 5 vols., Leipzig, 1779-85, was published simultaneously in French, as *Théorie de l'art des jardins*. But there is no reason to believe that Bolotov worked on this edition. Firstly, nothing indicates that he knew French. Secondly, whenever extracts from other foreign books on gardening were published in EM, Bolotov chose German examples.

16. 'Some More about Water Elements in English Gardens', EM, XXIII, 1785, 227.

17. Ibid., 225-38, 241-55.

18. 'On Some New Kind of Life and Light, but Nice Garden Elements Anyway', EM, XXIII, 1785, 129-43 & 'Continuation on Illusionistic Garden Elements', EM, XXIII, 1785, 145-58.

19. 'Some Practical Remarks about Grot-

toes', EM, XXI, 1785, 129-42.

20. Up until 1917, the album was supposedly kept with other archival materials in the bell tower, which was burned down that year.

21. The drawings are referred to in V. Makarov, 'Andrei Bolotov i sadovoe iskusstvo v Rossii XVIII veka', *Sredi kollektsionerov*, 5-6, 1924, 26-32.

22. The Picture Department, Museum of History, Moscow. A copy also painted in watercolours, but in a bigger format than the original, has been commissioned by the Bogoroditske Palace Museum. This album is on permanent display.

23. 'Continued Practical Remarks about English or New Natural Pleasure Gardens', EM, XXXIX, 1789, 35.

24. Bolotov's desire to create something different from the English and Continental garden tradition also made him claim that sheep were not welcome in the Russsian gardens, see 'About the Art of Making Lawns in English Gardens', EM, XXII, 1785, 8-11.

25. 'Continuation of Various Practical Remarks about New Gardens', EM, XXXIX, 1789, 54.

26. See Bolotov's guide with the relevant plant names in Latin and Russian, written on the basis of some German colleagues' expertise and experience, 'Something for Those Who Adore English Gardens', EM, XXI, 1785, 161-66.

27. 'Continuation of Various Practical Remarks about New Gardens', EM, XXXIX, 1789, passim.

28. 'Some Remarks about Gardens in Russia', op.cit.

29. Ibid., 49. Bolotov refers to Hirschfeld's lengthy descriptions of European and Oriental gardens, but regrets that his idol never mentioned Russian gardens. In fact, this is not so. See C.C.L. Hirschfeld, op.cit., Vol. 5, Leipzig, 1785, 286-91. Apparently, Bolotov never bought or read this final volume.

30. 'Some Remarks about Gardens in Russia', op.cit., 60-61.

STYLES AND SEMANTICS

From Paradise to Mount Parnassus

1. For a discussion of the Russian medieval poets' gardens, see D.S. Likhachov, 'Sad i kultura Rossii', *Dekorativnoe Iskusstvo*, 12, 1982, 38-45.
2. Prince I.M. Dolgoruky quoted by O.S. Yevangulova, 'Gorod i usadba vtoroi poloviny XVIIIv. v soznanii sovremennikov', *Russky gorod. Issledovaniya i materialy*, Moscow, 1984, 183.
3. Popular myths about the noblemen or gentlemen arose, and the people misunderstood as well as mocked the names of the elegant garden pavilions. Examples of this are listed in M.A. Anikst & V.S. Turchin (eds.), *...v okrestnostyakh Moskvy. Iz istorii russkoi usadebnoi kultury XVII-XIX vekov*, Moscow, 1979, 184.
4. Prince Peter Mikhailovsky Volkonsky quoted by V.I. Pilyavsky, *Sukhanovo*, Leningrad, 1986, 44.
5. J. Delille, *Selskoi zhitel, ili georgike frantsuzkie*, Moscow, 1804. A translation of Delille's *L'homme des champs*.
6. J. Delille, *The Gardens, A Poem*, London, 1798, 2.
7. Ibid., 22.
8. Ibid., 4-5.
9. Ibid., 90. On English and French examples.
10. Ibid., 76. On Moulin-Joli.
11. Ascribed to Matvey Feodorovich Kazakov, c. 1790; modifications by Vasily Petrovich Stasov.
12. Ibid., 39.
13. Ibid., 40.
14. Ibid., 67.
15. Ibid., 89.
16. Ibid., 98.
17. Ibid., 94-95.
18. Ibid., 8. Also on Poussin.
19. For a critical attitude to this taste, see A. Delaborde, *Description des nouveaux jardins de la France et de ses anciens châteaux, mêlée d'observations sur la vie de la campagne et la composition des jardins*, Paris, 1808, 109: "...these fashionable parade tombs that are being multiplied in the gardens out of a childish affectation for emotion and melancholy."
20. See V. I. Pilyavsky, op.cit., 131.
21. J. Delille, *Épître sur les Voyages*, Paris, 1765, 28.
22. Quoted by I. Grabar, 'Ostankinsky dvorets', *Starye gody*, 5-6, 1910, 12.
23. Nikolai Petrovich Sheremetev quoted by P. Weiner, 'Zhizn i iskusstvo v Ostankino', *Starye gody*, 5-6, 1910, 38.
24. For a discussion of the serf artists' role in the building of late 18th century palaces and country houses, see ibid., 42, & S.V. Bessonov, 'Krepostnye arkhitektory v Arkhangelskom', *Arkhitektura SSSR*, 9, 1934, 67-69, and M.A. Anikst & V.S. Turchin (eds.), op.cit., passim.
25. Ostankino's Italian Hall matches the Italian House (1770s) in the Kuskovo garden with regard to function and name.
26. Quoted by B. Mikhailov, 'Nauchnaya spravka po chertazham Uveselitelnogo Sada s vyyasneniem voprosa ob avtora osnovnogo proekta', unpublished study of Ostankino, Moscow, 1977, 4.
27. "...one could make small hills, sliding hills, as they used to do in Russia, or like those you find when you pass the Alps", A.F. Moszyński, 'Essay sur le jardinage anglois' (1774), *Rosprawa o ogrodownictwie angielskim*, (A. Morawinska, ed.), Wroslaw, Warsaw, Krakow, Gdansk, 1977, 141-42.
28. A.T. Bolotov, 'Some Practical Remarks about Garden Buildings', *Ekonomichesky Magazin*, XXIX, 1787, 34.
29. Ibid., 35.

Classical Quotations

1. V. Paperny, *Kultura "dva"*, Ann Arbor, 1979, holds a particularly interesting analysis of Stalinist architecture. See also A. Sarbarov, 'Stalinsky stil. Postscriptum', *Arkhitektura SSSR*, 3, 1989, 31-33, and M. Rzyanin, 'Voprosy osvoeniya klassicheskogo naslediya v arkhitekturnoi praktike natsionalnykh respublik SSSR', *Arkhitektura SSSR*, 4, 1953, 17-19.

2. V. Taleporovsky, 'Traktat Charlza Kamerona "Rimskie Termy"', *Arkhitektura SSSR*, 9, 1935, 62.

3. V.N. Taleporovsky, *Charlz Kameron*, Moscow, 1939. In the introduction it says: "particularly now, that is in our time, we have to deal with the big and serious task of learning and reworking the classical heritage", ibid., X. The only other major publication on Cameron prior to Taleporovsky's book is E. Hollerbach & N. Lansere (eds.), *Charles Cameron. Sbornik statei*, Moscow, Petrograd, 1924.

4. For a detailed discussion of Cameron's introduction to Catherine, see I. Rae, *Charles Cameron. Architect to the Court in Russia*, London, 1971, 37.

5. "That Monsieur Huber promised me several through a third party; but apparently he only produces one a year. So far I only have two. However, the subjects he has chosen are so interesting that I would very much like to have a complete set...", Catherine in a letter, dated March 31, 1770, to Voltaire. A. Lentin (ed.), *Voltaire and Catherine the Great. Selected Correspondence*, Cambridge, 1974, 78.

6. The interruption in Cameron's work at Pavlovsk seems to have been due to Pavel's unwillingness after Catherine's death to continue any project which had been initiated during his mother's reign. Secondly, Pavel may have preferred a more severe expression than Cameron's; his preference for the Italian architect Vincenzo Brenna points to this. Besides, in the late 1780s Cameron made some interesting designs commissioned by Catherine for the Crimea, Russia's latest conquest.

7. See A.N. Petrov, a.o. (eds.), *Pamyatniki arkhitektury prigorodov Leningrada*, Leningrad, 1985, 214 & A.P. Vergunov & V.A. Gorokhov, *Russkie sady i parki*, Moscow, 1988, 244.

8. For this attribution, see the lengthy quotation from Loudon by I. Rae, op.cit., 70.

9. P. Storkh, *Putevoditel po sadu i gorodu Pavlovsku*, St Petersburg, 1843, 45.

10. See e.g. G.H. Hamilton, *The Art and Architecture of Russia*, Harmondsworth, 1987, 307.

11. Curiously enough, Catherine and Maria Feodorovna were both born in the Prussian town of Stettin, in 1729 and 1759 respectively. S. Massie, *Pavlovsk. The Life of a Russian Palace*, Boston, Toronto, London, 1990, holds a wealth of interesting quotations from Maria Feodorovna's correspondence.

12. J.C. Loudon, *An Encyclopedia of Gardening*, London, 1835, 247. For a similar characterization see A. von Buttlar, *Der Landschaftsgarten. Gartenkunst des Klassizismus und der Romantik*, Cologne, 1989, 236.

13. C.C.L. Hirschfeld, *Theorie der Gartenkunst*, Leipzig, 1779-85, V, 290.

14. Sablukov, quoted pg 71.

Scenes of Exotica

1. Carmontelle quoted by C. Thacker, *Histoire des jardins*, Paris, 1981, 219. Carmontelle had borrowed these words from Jean-Jacques Rousseau's *Nouvelle Héloïse*.

2. W. Chambers, *Designs of Chinese Buildings, Furniture, Dresses, Machines, and Utensils. To which is annexed, A Description of their Temples, Houses, Gardens, &c.*, (1757), London, 1969, Preface, s.p.

3. Russia's contacts with the world of the Middle Kingdom go back to the 16th

and 17th centuries. Connections then were diplomatic and scientific.

4. An enlarged English version of Chambers' *Dissertation on Oriental Gardening* was published in 1773.
5. W. Chambers, *Designs of Chinese Buildings*, 15.
6. Ibid., 17-18.
7. Ibid., 15.
8. Ibid., 17.
9. Ibid., 16.
10. Ibid., Preface, s.p.
11. Ibid., 15.
12. See A.T. Bolotov, *Ekonomichesky Magazin*, XXV, 1786, 65-389.
13. A.T. Bolotov, 'Some Remarks About Gardens in Turkish Regions', ibid., 371.
14. Ibid., 369.
15. A.T. Bolotov, 'Some Remarks on Gardens in China', ibid., 321.
16. Ibid., 322.
17. W. Chambers, op.cit., 19.

Masonry and the Middle Ages
1. Kiev was often characterized as the mother of Russia, whereas St Petersburg was called her head.
2. One of Catherine's favourite architects, Quarenghi, did a series of drawings from Kolomenskoe and the Kremlin of architectural ensembles which were both considered among the best examples of medieval Russian buildings. Ironically enough though, the Kremlin was largely the work of imported Italian architects, who had visited Suzdal and Vladimir, more than two hundred kilometres east of Moscow, to get to know the prototypes.
3. In one of his projects for the Kremlin, Bazhenov thus proposed to keep only the red brick wall.
4. One Englishman wrote that, if ever accomplished, Bazhenov's building "would by its grandeur have surpassed Solomon's Temple, ...Hadrian's villa and Trajan's Forum", quoted by V. Snegirev, 'Arkhitekturnoe nasledie

V. I. Bazhenova', *Arkhitektura SSSR*, 2, 1937, 22.
5. Catherine thought the Tsaritsyno Palace was "too gloomy", according to N.A. Yanchuk, *Znamenity zodchy XVIII veka Vasily Ivanovich Bazhenov i ego otnoshenie k masontsvu*, Petrograd, 1916, 203.
6. It was the poet and historian Nikolai Karamzin, a contemporary of Bazhenov, who compared him to Moore as well as to Plato, see ibid., 187. At a later point, he was also compared to Mikhail Vasileevich Lomonosov (1711-65), founder of Moscow's university, see D. Arkin, 'Bazhenov', *Arkhitektura SSSR*, 2, 1937, 2.
7. Catherine in a letter to Grimm, quoted by K.I. Mineeva, *Tsaritsyno. Dvortsovo-parkovy ansambl*, Moscow, 1988, 29.
8. Catherine quoted ibid., 28-29.
9. Though the object of a series of studies, far from all of the buildings of the Tsaritsyno ensemble have been precisely dated.
10. See V. Bogolyubov, *N.I. Novikov i ego vremya*, Moscow, 1916, 183.
11. This characterization of Bazhenov's works occurs in Mikhailov's book on the architect from 1951, referred to by Yu. Gerchuk, 'Vasily Bazhenov. K 250-letyu so dnya rozhdeniya', *Arkhitektura SSSR*, 5, 1988, 90. Besides, Gerchuk establishes Bazhenov's year of birth as 1738, and not 1737.
12. See V. Bogolyubov, op.cit., 400.
13. Future studies on this may be expected. In today's Russia, the freemasonic lodges of the 18th century are looked upon as some of the most interesting pre-revolutionary institutions, and they are gradually becoming the subject of scholarly works.
14. Here Pavel, more and more marked by delusions of persecutions, committed suicide in 1801.
15. Bazhenov quoted by S. Bezsonov, 'Zhizn i deyatelnost V.I. Bazhenova', *Arkhitektura SSSR*, 2, 1937, 7.

16. E.g. J.-F. Neufforge, *Récueil élementaire d'architecture*, 8 vols., Paris, 1757-1777.
17. A.V. Pozdnukhov, 'Ob avtorstve rannikh psedogoticheskikh sooruzhenii', *Istoriya i teoriya arkhitektury i gradostroitelstva*, (V.I. Pilyavsky, ed.), Leningrad, 1980, 163.

USES AND USERS
1. A.B. Kurakin quoted from O.S. Yevangulova, 'Gorod i usadba vtoroi poloviny XVIIIv. v soznanii sovremennikov', *Russky gorod. Issledovaniya i materialy*, Moscow, 1984, 175.

Parties and Other Pursuits
1. Contrary to the Western custom of integrating the church with the main building, the church was nearly always a separate building at Russian palace ensembles and estates. Stylistic experiments such as those typical of some of the structures in the new landscape gardens were generally not applied to the church building. Here classicism prevailed. Bazhenov, though, also referred to 17th century Moscow architecture in his churches, as he did in his other designs.
2. William Coxe, 1784, quoted from *The Oxford Companion to Gardens*, Oxford, New York, 1987, article by Peter Hayden on Oranienbaum.
3. For Alexander Lvov's description, see P. Weiner, 'Marfino', *Starye gody*, 7-9, 1910, 118. Such parties seem to have also been used to literally exhibit the social gap between the master and his serfs.
4. One contemporary source quoted by M.A. Anikst & V.S. Turchin (eds.), *...v okrestnostyakh Moskvy. Iz istorii russkoi usadebnoi kultury XVII-XIX vekov*, Moscow, 1979, 192.
5. Quoted by P. Weiner, op.cit.
6. R. Lyall, *The Character of the Russians, and A Detailed History of Moscow*, London, 1823, 64.
7. Ibid.
8. Quoted by S. Massie, *Pavlovsk. The Life of a Russian Palace*, Boston, Toronto, London, 1990, 32. This book holds a wealth of interesting quotations from Maria Feodorovna's correspondence.
9. Quoted ibid., 80.
10. Quoted ibid., 79. The letter is dated October 19, 1786.
11. Quoted ibid., 31. The letter is from February 20, 1782, Pavel and Maria Feodorovna then on their Grand Tour.
12. This work was obviously much inspired by some Western source, perhaps a translation. I have not yet found the actual source in either case.
13. P.S. Pallas quoted by L.P. Aleksandrov & V.L. Nekrasov, *Neskuchny sad i ego rasstitelnost*, Moscow, 1923, XVII-XVIII.
14. Ibid., XX.
15. Ibid., XV-XVI.
16. *Kuskovo i ego okrestnosti*, Moscow, 1850, 40.
17. Ibid., 40-41.
18. For a report on this visit, see S. Lyubesky, *Selo Ostankino s okrestnostyami svoimi*, Moscow, 1868, 23.
19. See I. Kvarchinskaya, 'Vossozdat luchshie teatry XVIIIv.', *Arkhitektura SSSR*, 10, 1979, 51.
20. For the question of attribution, see O. Pankova, 'Zelyony teatr v Kuskovo', *Arkhitektura SSSR*, 5, 1953, 23.
21. Quoted by O. Pankova, *Usadba Kuskovo*, Moscow, 1940, 91.
22. Quoted by O.S. Yevangulova, 'Gorod i usadba vtoroi poloviny XVIIIv. v soznanii sovremennikov', *Russky gorod. Issledovaniya i materialy*, Moscow, 1984, 177.
23. Quoted by S. Massie, op.cit., 38.
24. Ibid.
25. A. Delaborde, *Description des nouveaux jardins de la France et des ses anciens châteaux, mêlée d'observations sur la vie de la campagne et la composition des jardin*, Richmond 1971, 3.
26. A.T. Bolotov quoted by D.S.

Likhachov, *Poeziya sadov. K semantike sadovo-parkovykh stilei*, Leningrad, 1982, 293.

27. Ibid.
28. Ibid.
29. Ibid., 293-94.
30. Quoted by O.S. Yevangulova, op.cit., 188. The poet is not mentioned by name.
31. Ibid., 187.
32. J. Delille, *The Gardens, A Poem*, London, 1798, 93-94.

Poets and Promenades

1. Quoted by D.S. Likhachov, *Poeziya sadov. K semantike sadovo-parkovykh stilei*, Leningrad, 1982, 274.
2. Ibid.
3. Ibid., 278.
4. Zhukovsky was a very erudite poet. He translated Homer, Dante, Milton, Tasso, Schiller, Goethe, a.o., and he studied French, English and German aesthetics.
5. Quoted by O.S. Yevangulova, 'Gorod i usadba vtoroi poloviny XVIIIv. v soznanii sovremennikov', *Russky gorod. Issledovaniya i materialy*, Moscow, 1984, 185.
6. N.M. Karamzin, *Izbrannye sochineniya*, Moscow, Leningrad, 1964, vol. 1, 9-10.
7. *Specimens of the Russian Poets*, (translated by J. Bowing), London, 1821, 111.
8. Ibid., 112.
9. Quoted by D.S. Likhachov, op.cit., 264, note 106.
10. V. Zhukovsky, *Stikhotvoreniya*, Moscow, 1974, 138.
11. Ibid., 141.
12. Ibid., 12.
13. G. R. Derzhavin, *Stikhotvoreniya. Proza*, Voronezh, 1980, 145.
14. *Specimens of the Russian Poets*, (translated by J. Bowing), London, 1821, 18-19.
15. N.M. Karamzin, op.cit., 74-75.
16. J. Delille, *The Gardens, A Poem*, London, 1798, 95.

17. G.P. Kamenev quoted by D.S. Likhachov, op.cit., 231.
18. V.Zhukovsky, op.cit., 138-39.
19. Ibid., 141.
20. Ibid., 142.
21. A.S. Pushkin, *Zvezda plenitelnogo schastya: Stikhotvoreniya*, Moscow, 1989, 91.
22. Quoted by J.D. Hunt, *The Figure in the Landscape: Poetry, Painting and Gardening during the Eighteenth Century*, Baltimore, London, 1976, 220.

Painters and Perceptions

1. M.-A. Laugier, *Essai sur l'Architecture*, Génève, 1972, 247.
2. For a discussion of the links between Robert's landscape and garden paintings and his garden projects, see my thesis, M. Pedersen, *Hubert Robert som skaber af den franske landskabshave. En undersøgelse af samspillet mellem Hubert Roberts landskabs- og havemalerier og hans haveprojekter*, University of Aarhus, 1983, and, by the same author, M. Floryan, 'Hortus musealis: en retrospektiv visit i den franske landskabshave', *Landskabsopfattelse og naturæstetik* (L. Bek, ed.), Aarhus, 1989, 9-20. Jean de Cailleux and Günter Herzog have discussed Robert's *oeuvre* from a similar viewpoint.
3. R.-L. de Girardin, *De la composition des paysages, suivi de promenade ou itinéraire des jardins d'Ermenonville*, Paris, 1979, 26.
4. Ibid., 28.
5. There may be little reason to assume, as L. Kashuk did in 'Peizazh Semena Shchedrina i Pavlovsky Park', *Iskusstovo*, 6, 1989, 64, that the landscape painter Semen Feodorovich Shchedrin assisted Cameron or Brenna in the designing of the Pavlovsk garden.
6. Quoted by F.Y. Syrkina, *Pietro di Gottardo Gonzaga. 1751-1831. Zhizn i tvorchestvo. Sochineniya*, Moscow, 1974, 50.
7. All Gonzaga's projects for the Imperial

Court were connected with Pavel I, Alexander I and Nicolas I. In all three cases, and with Yusupov as main supervisor, Gonzaga, among other things, designed the coronation ceremonies and the funerals.

8. Practically nothing from this library remains.

9. A temporary lack of commissions, the burning down of St Petersburg's Big Stone Theatre and other misfortunes nourished Gonzaga's dreams of designing buildings other than theatres. At one point he even characterized his theatrical work as a "light and low profession", quoted by F.Y. Syrkina, op.cit., 217.

10. It was anonymous, but the second edition of 1807 had the author's name on it.

11. P.G. Gonzague, *La musique des yeux et l'optique théatral, opuscules tirés d'un plus grand ouvrage anglais, sur le sens commun*, St Petersburg, 1807, 44.

12. Ibid., 44-45.

13. Ibid., 45.

14. Ibid., 47.

15. Ibid.

16. Today, the Kuskovo Palace Museum holds twelve such illusionistic figures. Another important collection is at Oranienbaum.

17. C.C.L. Hirschfeld, *Theorie der Gartenkunst*, Leipzig, 1779-1785, V, 291.

18. A.T. Bolotov, 'On Some New Kind if Life and Light, but Nice Garden Elements Anyway' & 'Continuation on Illusionistic Garden Elements', EM, XXIII, 1785, 129-43 respectively 145-58.

19. A.T. Bolotov, 'On Some New Kind of Life and Light, but Nice Garden Elements Anyway', ibid., 131.

20. Ibid., 131-32.

21. Ibid., 137.

22. Ibid., 140.

23. Architectural views and other illusionistic backdrops, though in slightly different techniques, also occurred in the garden theatres of the Catherine period. However, Bolotov never worked on such. For this, he remained too much of a horticulturist and a designer of real landscapes.

24. Quoted by L. Réau, 'L'Oeuvre d'Hubert Robert en Russie', *Gazette des Beaux-Arts*, 3, 1914, 175.

25. L. Réau (ed.), 'Correspondance artistique de Grimm avec Catherine II', *Archives de l'Art Français*, XVII, 1932, 185. The letter is dated May 11, 1791.

26. Yekatarina Vadimovna Deryabina, Curator of French Paintings at the Hermitage, St Petersburg, has made up a new and revised inventory of Robert paintings in Russia. The study is unpublished.

27. For details on the twelve works by Robert at Arkhangelskoe, see I.T. Unanyants, *Frantsuzskaya zhivopis v Arkhangelskom*, Moscow, 1970.

28. For details on the Robert paintings at Alupka, see A.A. Galichenko & A.P. Tsarin, *Alupka. Dvorets i park*, Kiev, 1992.

Political Platforms

1. In the 18th century, the Great Cascade was only turned on on festive days. The most recent restoration having been completed in June 1995, the Great Cascade will function in the tourist season. The big fountains at VVTs work during the summer on Sundays and on official holidays, such as May 1 and May 9, the latter being the day when the end of the Second World War is celebrated.

2. M. Rzyanin, 'Voprosy osvoeniya klassicheskogo naslediya v arkhitekturnoi praktike natsionalnykh respublik SSSR', *Arkhitektura SSSR*, 4, 1953, 17-19.

3. Following the approval of the *General Plan for the Renewal of Moscow* in 1935, Stalin had his architects change the city-scape. Extreme solutions such as those found in some of the early Soviet projects were absent. The old city was

neither closed off and turned into a museum zone, nor was it destroyed to allow the Soviet architects to start from scratch. Instead, it was decided to use the old radial city plan as the basic skeleton, and the metro system was eventually planned according to this very functional pattern. The major streets that spread out from the Kremlin, not unlike spokes, were widened, and extended to the new suburbs. And following one of the proposals already contained in the project entitled *A New Moscow*, thousands of trees were planted along these streets, or prospects as they were usually called, and along the quays, bordering the Moscow and Yauza rivers.

4. Originally, this part of the garden was laid out as a vegetable garden and orchard.
5. Letter by Catherine to Voltaire. A. Lentin (ed.), *Voltaire and Catherine the Great. Selected Correspondence*, Cambridge, 1974, 117.
6. Ibid.
7. And the inscriptions furnish the necessary information on where and when the battles took place.
8. Article in *Korifei, ili Klyuzh literatury* quoted by A. P. Valitskaya, *Russkaya estetika XVIII veka*, Moscow, 1983, 211.
9. C.C.L. Hirschfeld, *Theorie der Gartenkunst*, Leipzig, 1779-85, V, 69. Hirschfeld devoted a special chapter to the discussion of the public garden, ibid., 68-74.
10. Ibid., 68.
11. Ibid., 70.

new developments in the spheres of agriculture and forestry are now also being experimented with at Yasnaya Polyana, Tolstoi's country estate. Many places formerly belonging to Russia's writers and visual artists remain largely unknown to an audience outside Russia, but certainly ought to be brought to attention, especially now that cultural exchange is not only a slogan in agreement between East and West, but indeed a living reality.

FINAL REMARKS

1. Next to the former Imperial gardens, artists' rural residences and city dwellings counted among the landmarks that traditionally entered the Soviet restorers' scope. Aleksei Tolstoi's mansions are one such point in case, and

Selected Bibliography

Russian and Scandinavian titles of articles and books have been translated whenever they first appear. The same applies to Russian magazines. Square brackets mark the translation.

Names of Western authors of articles and books, which have been translated into Russian, have not been transcribed. The usual English spelling is used. Yet whereever the names occur as part of any title, they have been transscribed.

A number of topographical names occur in square brackets to indicate the present usage of names.

Abesinova, N. 1989. 'Istoricheskie parki Kryma', [Historical Parks of the Crimea], *Arkhitektura SSSR*, 1, 69-71.

Abolina, R. 1962. 'Simvol i allegoriya v skulpture', [Symbol and Allegory in Sculpture], *Iskusstvo*, [Art], 12, 12-22.

Adams, W.H. 1979. *The French Garden 1500-1800*, New York.

Aleksandrov, L.P. & Nekrasova, V.L. 1923. *Neskuchny sad i ego rasstitelnost*, [The Neskuchny Garden and Its Plantation], Moscow.

Anikst, M.A. & Turchin, V.S. (eds.), 1979. *...v okrestnostyakh Moskvy. Iz istorii russkoi usadebnoi kultury XVII-XIX vekov*, [... in the Surroundings of Moscow. From the History of Russian Country House Culture of the 17th-19th Centuries], Moscow.

Anisimov, A.V., Lebedev, A.V., Pavlova, T.N., a.o., 1989. *Dosug v Moskve*, [Leisure Time in Moscow], Moscow.

Aranovich, D. 1935. 'Planirovka i arkhitektura parka kultury i otdykha', [The Design and Architecture of Parks of Culture and Rest], *Arkhitektura SSSR*, 5, 30-37.

Arkhangelskaya, N.Ye. 1936. *Pavlovsk*, Leningrad.

Arkhitektura SSSR, [Architecture of the USSR], 1934, 5. Special issue on parks of culture and rest.

Arkhitektura SSSR, 1937, 2. Special issue on V.I. Bazhenov.

Arkhitektura SSSR, 1938, 10. Special issue on M.F. Kazakov.

Arkhitektura SSSR, 1939, 9. Special issue on the Exhibition Dedicated to the Economic Achievements of the USSR, VDNKh.

Artamonov, V.A. 1974. *Gorod i monument*, [Town and Monument], Moscow.

Aspesæter, O. 1970. 'Fransk barokk på russisk jord', [French Baroque on Russian Soil], *Landskap*, 2, 33-39.

Åman, A. 1987. *Arkitektur och ideologi i Stalintidens Östeuropa. Ur det kalla krigets historia*, [Architecture and Ideology in Eastern Europe of the Stalin Period. From the History of the Cold War], Malmoe.

Baltrusaitis, J. 1976. 'Jardins et pays d'illusions', *Traverses*, 5-6, 94-112.

Baranova, O. 1983. *Kuskovo. 18th Century Russian Estate and the Museum of Ceramics*, Leningrad.

Bardovskaya, L.V. 1982. 'Anglyskie gravyury v kollektsii Yekatarinenskogo dvortsa-muzeya i ikh vliyanie na formirovanie Yekatarinenskogo parka v 70-e gody XVIII veka', [English Engravings in the Collection of the Yekatarine Palace-Museum and Their Influence upon the Design of the Garden in the 1770s], *Russkaya khudozhestvennaya kultura xviii veka i inostrannye mastera*, conference papers, The Tretyakov Gallery, Moscow, 43-45.

Beauty, Horror and Immensity. Picturesque Landscape in Britain, 1750-1850, 1981, exhibition catalogue, Fitzwilliam Museum, Cambridge.

Bek, L. 1983. *Arkitektur og livsmønster*, [Architecture and the Way of Living], Copenhagen.

Bek, L. 1988. *Virkeligheden i kunstens spejl*, [Reality in the Mirror of Art], Aarhus.

Belanina, V. 1987. *Pavlovsk. A Guide*, Moscow.

Bessonov, S.V. 1934. 'Krepostnye arkhitektory v Arkhangelskom', [Serf Architects at Arkhangelskoe], *Arkhitektura SSSR*, 9, 67-69.

Bessonov, S.V. 1935. 'Arkhitekturno-khudozhestvenny oblik Arkhangelskogo', [The Art and Architecture of Arkhangelskoe], *Arkhitektura SSSR*, 8, 44-53.

Bessonov, S.V. 1936. 'Sukhanovo. Istoricheskaya spravka', [Sukhanovo. A Historical Study], *Arkhitektura SSSR*, 4, 58-61.

Billington, J.H. 1970. *The Icon and the Axe. An Interpretative History of Russian Culture*, New York.

Bogolyubov, V. 1916. *N. I. Novikov i ego vremya*, [N. I. Novikov and His Time], Moscow.

Bolotov, A.T. 1780-89. Articles and notes published in *Ekonomichesky Magazin*, [The Economic Magazine], 40 vols.

Bolotov, A.T. 1952. *Izbrannye sochineniya po agronomii, plodovodstvu, lesovodstvu, botanike*, [Selected Writings on Agronomy, Fruit Cultivation, Forestry, and Botanics], Moscow.

Bolotov, A.T. 1986. *Zhizn i priklyucheniya Andreya Bolotova, opisannye samim im dlya svoikh potomkov*, [The Life and Adventures of Andrei Bolotov, Described by Himself for His Descendants], Moscow.

Bolotova, G.R. 1988. *Letny sad*, [The Summer Garden], Leningrad.

Bondarenko, I. March, 1911. 'Podmoskovnye dvortsy XVIII veka', [18th Century Palaces in the Surroundings of Moscow], *Starye gody*, [The Old Times].

Boroblevsky, V.G. 1787. *Description de Kouskova, maison de plaisance appartenant à son excellence monsieur le comte Pierre Borissowitch de Cheremettoff*, Moscow.

Boroblevsky, V.G. 1787. *Kratkoe opisanie sela Spaskavo Kuskovo prinadlezhashchago Ego Syatelstvu grafu Petru Borisovichu Sheremetevu*, Russian edition of *Description de Kouskova*, Moscow.

Boye, G. 1972. *Havekunsten i kulturhistorisk belysning*, [Landscape Design from a Cultural Historical Angle], 2 vols., Copenhagen.

Brookes, J. 1987. *Gardens of Paradise. The History and Design of the Great Islamic Gardens*, London.

Bryson, N. 1987. *Word and Image. French Painting of the Ancient Régime*, Cambridge.

Budylina, M.V., Braitseva, O.I. & Kharlamova, A.M. 1961. *Arkhitektor N.A. Lvov*, [The Architect N.A. Lvov], Moscow.

Bulabina, L., Rapaport, V. & Unanyants, N. 1971. *Arkhangelskoe*, Moscow.

Bulabina, L., Rozantseva, S.A. & Yakimchuk, N.A. 1983. *Arkhangelskoe*, Moscow.

Buttlar, A. von, 1989. *Der Landschaftsgarten. Gartenkunst des Klassizismus und der Romantik*, Cologne.

Cameron, Ch. 1772. *The Baths of the Romans, Explained and Illustrated, with the Restorations of Palladio Corrected and Improved*, London.

Cameron, Ch. 1939. *Termy Rimlyan. Ikh opisanie i izobrazhenie vmeste s izpravleniyami i dopolnenymi restavratsiyami Palladio*, Russian edition of *The Baths of the Romans*, Moscow.

Carter, H.B. 1974. *Sir Joseph Banks and the Plant Collection from Kew sent to the Empress Catherine II of Russia 1795*, London.

Cauquelin, A. 1989. *L'invention du paysage*, Paris.

Chadwick, G.F. 1966. *The Park and the Town. Public Landscape in the 19th and 20th Centuries*, London.

Chambers, W. 1771. *O kitaiskikh sadakh. Perevod iz knigi, sochinennoi g. Chambersom, soderzhashchei v sebe opisanie kitayskikh stroeny, domashnikh ikh uborov, odeyany, makhin i instrumentov*, Russian edition of *Traité des édifices*, St Petersburg.

Chambers, W. 1772. *A Dissertation on Oriental Gardening*, London.

Chambers, W. 1776. *Traité des édifices, meubles, habits, machines et ustensiles des chinois. Compris une description de leur temples, maisons, jardins, &c.*, (1757), Paris.

Chambers, W. 1969. *Designs of Chinese Buildings, Furniture, Dresses, Machines, and Utensils. To which is annexed, A Description of their Temples, Houses, Gardens, &c.*, (1757), London.

Charles Cameron, c. 1740-1812, 1967-68, exhibition catalogue, Edinburgh, Glasgow, London.

Clifford, D. 1962. *A History of Garden Design,*, London.

Cook, O. 1984. *The English Country House. An Art and a Way of Life*, London.

Curl, J.S. 1991. *The Art and Architecture of Freemasonry. An Introductory Study*, London.

Delaborde, A. 1971. *Description des nouveaux jardins de la France et de ses anciens châteaux, mêlée d'observations sur la vie de la campagne et la composition des jardins*, (1808), Richmond.

Delille, J. 1765. *Épître sur les Voyages*, Paris.

Delille, J. 1782. *Les Jardins, ou l'Art d'Embellir les Paysages. Poème*, Paris.

Delille, J. 1798. *The Gardens, a Poem.* London.

Delille, J. 1800. *L'homme des champs, ou les Géorgiques Françoises*, Strasbourg.

Delille, J. 1804. *Selskoi zhitel, ili georgiki frantsuzkie*, Russian edition of *L'homme des champs*, Moscow.

Delille, J. 1816. *Sady ili iskusstvo ukrashat selskie vidy. Sochinenie Delillya*, Russian edition of *Les Jardins*, St Petersburg.

Dennerlein, I. 1972. *Die Gartenkunst der Régence und des Rokoko in Frankreich*, Bamberg.

Derzhavin, G.R. 1980. *Stikhotvoreniya. Proza*, [Poems. Prose], Voronezh.

Dimsdale, Baroness E. 1989. *An English Lady at the Court of Catherine the Great. The Journal of Baroness Elizabeth Dimsdale*, (1781), ed. by A.G. Cross, Cambridge.

Dokuchaeva, O.V. 1982. 'Zhivopisnye figurnye obmanki Kuskova', [Painted Illusionistic Figures at Kuskovo], *Russkaya khudozhestvennaya kultura XVIII veka i inostrannye mastera*, conference papers, The Tretyakov Gallery, Moscow, 43-45.

Dokuchaeva, O.V. 1987. 'Peizazhny park v Rossii vtoroi poloviny XVIII veka v predstavlenie sovremennikov', [The Russian Landscape Garden of the Second Half of the 18th Century in the Contemporary Mind], *Iz istorii kultury i obshchestvennoi mysli narodov SSSR*, ed. by S.S. Dmytriev, Moscow, 64-85.

Dokuchaeva, O.V. 1989. 'Peizazhny park v Rossii vtoroi poloviny XVIII veka v soznanii sovremennikov', [The Conception of the Russian Landscape Garden in the Second Half of the 18th Century], summary of unpublished dissertation, Moscow.

Dolganov, V.I. 1935. 'Zelen v Moskve', [Greenery in Moscow], *Arkhitektura SSSR*, 10-11, 45-47.

Dubyago, T.B. 1951. *Letny sad*, [The Summer Garden], Moscow, Leningrad.

Dubyago, T.B. 1963. *Russkie regulyarnye sady i parki*, [Russian Formal Gardens and Parks], Leningrad.

Dyachenko, L.I. 1988. *Tavrichesky dvorets*, [The Tauride Palace], Leningrad.

Dyagkovskaya, T. 1939. 'Neizvestnye portrety Charlza Kamerona', [Unknown Portraits of Ch. Cameron], *Arkhitektura SSSR*, 2, 78-79.

Efros, A.M. 1979. *Mastera raznykh epokh*, [Masters of Different Periods], Moscow. Chapter about P.G. Gonzaga, 69-109.

Egura, V. 1924. 'Kuskovsky regulyarny sad', [The Formal Garden at Kuskovo], *Sredi kollektsionerov*, [Among Collectors], 7-8, 4-19.

Ekonomichesky Magazin, [The Economic Magazine], 1780-89. ed. by A.T. Bolotov, 40 vols.

Elling, C. 1942. *Den romantiske Have*, [The Romantic Garden], Copenhagen.

Emblemy i simvoly izbrannye na Rossysky, Latinsky, Frantsuzsky, Nemetsky i Aglitsky yaziki, 1788. [Selected Emblems and Symbols in Russian, Latin, French, German and English], St Petersburg.

Erdberg, E. von, 1936. *Chinese Influence on European Garden Structures*, Cambridge, Mass.

Erp-Houtepen, A. von, 1986. 'The etymological origin of the garden', *Journal of Garden History*, 3, 227-31.

Fedorov, S.I. 1960. *Usadba Marfino*, [The Marfino Estate], Moscow.

Filatov, Ye. 1990. 'Skorbnoe beschustvye', [A Painful Lack of Feelings], *Khudozhnik*, [The Artist], 5, 59-64.

Floryan, M. 1989. 'Hortus musealis. En retrospektiv visit i den franske landskabshave', [Hortus musealis. A Retrospective Visit to the French Landscape Garden], *Landskabsopfattelse og naturæstetik*, ed. by L. Bek, Århus, 9-20.

Floryan, M. 1990. 'Alle tiders have. Billeder og betydning i Katharina den 2.s Tsaritsyno', [Emblems of Time. Catherine II's Palace and Garden at Tsaritsyno], *De lyse Sale. Festskrift til Bente Skovgaard*, ed. by H. Jönsson, K. Strømstad & H. Westergaard, Copenhagen, 32-47. (English summary).

Floryan, M. 1991. 'Den politiske have. Russisk nationalisme i det grønne', [Politics and Gardens in Russia. An Iconographical Study], *Landskab. Tidsskrift for planlægning af have og landskab*, 2, 29-34. (English summary).

Floryan, M. 1994. 'Russisk nostalgi', [Russian Nostalgia], *Landskab. Tidsskrift for planlægning af have og landskab*, 4, 73-79. (English summary).

Galichenko, A.A. & Palchikova, A.P. 1989. *Alupkinsky Dvorets-Muzei*, [The Alupka Palace Museum], Simferopol.

Galichenko, A.A. & Tsarin, A.P. 1992. *Alupka. Dvorets i park*, [Alupka. Palace and Park], Kiev.

Ganay, E. de, 1913. *L'Art des jardins en France du XVIe siècle à la fin du XVIIIe*, Paris.

Ganay, E. de, 1949. *Les jardins de France et leur décor*, Paris.

Gérardin, R.L. 1777. *De la Composition des Paysages, ou des moyens d'embellir la Nature autour des Habitations, en joignant l'agréable à l'utile*, Genève, Paris.

Gerchuk, Yu. 1988. 'Vasily Ivanovich Bazhenov. K 250-letyu so dnya rozhdeniya', [V.I. Bazhenov. For His 250 Year Anniversary], *Arkhitektura SSSR*, 5, 90-99.

Gerngros, V. 1912. 'Khansky dvorets v Bakhchisarai', [The Khan Palace at Bakhchisarai], *Starye gody*, 4, 3-32.

Girardin, R.-L. 1804. *O sostavlenii landshaftov*, Russian edition of *De la Composition des Paysages*, St Petersburg.

Girardin, R.-L. de, 1979. *De la composition des paysages (1777), suivi de promenade ou itinéraire des jardins d'Ermenonville*, ed. by M. Conan, Paris.

Girouard, M. 1978. *Life in the English Country House*, New Haven, London.

Glazichev, V. 1984. 'Ot "goroda-sada" k "ekopolisu"', [From the Garden City to the Ecopolis], *Arkhitektura SSSR*, 4, 47-49.

Glozman, I. 1958. *Kuskovo*, Moscow.

Glozman, I.M. (ed.), 1976. *Kuskovo, Ostankino, Arkhangelskoe*, Moscow.

Glumov, A. 1980. *N. A. Lvov*, Moscow.

Gogolitsyn, Yu.M. & Gogolitsyna, T.M. 1987. *Pamyatniki arkhitektury Leningradskoi oblasti* [Architectural Monuments in the Leningrad Region], Leningrad.

Golovanova, T. 1968. *Pavlovsky park*, [The Pavlovsk Park], Leningrad.

Gonzague, P.G. 1807. *La musique des yeux et*

l'optique théatral, opuscules tirés d'un plus grand ouvrage anglais, sur le sens commun, St Petersburg.

Gostev, V.F. & Yuskevich, N.N. 1991. *Proektirovanie sadov i parkov,* [Designing Gardens and Parks], Moscow.

Gote, Yu.V. & Bailanova, N.B. (eds.), 1926. *Iz epokhi krepostnogo khozyaistva XVIII i XIXvv.,* [From the Age of Serf Art in the 18th and 19th Centuries], exhibition catalogue, Museum of History, Moscow.

Grabar, I. 1910. 'Ostankinsky dvorets', [The Ostankino Palace], *Starye gody,* 5-6, 5-37.

Grabar, I. 1912. 'Ranny aleksandrovsky klassitsizm i ego frantsuzkie istochniki' [Early Alexandrine Classicism and Its French Sources], *Starye gody,* 7-9, 68-96.

Grabar, I.E., Lazarev, V.N. & Kemenov, V.S. (eds.), 1953-68. *Istoriya russkogo iskusstvo,* [History of Russian Art], 13 vols., Moscow.

Grimal, P. 1974. *L'art des jardins,* Paris.

Grohmann, J.G. (ed.), 1796. *Ideenmagazin für Liebhaber von Gärten, Englischen Anlagen und für Besitzer von Landgütern,* 2 vols., Leipzig.

Grohmann, J.G. (ed.) 1799: *Sobranie novykh myslei dlya ukrasheniya sadov i dach, vo vkuse Anglinskom, Gotticheskom, Kitaiskom; dlya upotrebleniya lyubitelei Anglinskikh sadov i pomeshchikov, zhelayushchikh ukrashat svoi dachi,* Russian edition of *Ideenmagazin für Liebhaber,* Moscow.

Gurevich, I. 1980. *The Fountains of Petrodvorets near Leningrad,* Moscow.

Gurevich, I.M. 1982. *Petrodvorets,* Leningrad.

Hadfield, M. 1985. *A History of British Gardening,* Harmondsworth.

Hallbaum, F. 1927. *Der Landschaftsgarten,* Munich.

Hallmann, G. 1986. *Sommerresidenzen russischer Zaren,* Leipzig.

Hamilton, G.H. 1987. *The Art and Architecture of Russia,* Harmondsworth.

Hansmann, W. 1983. *Gartenkunst der Renaissance und des Barock,* Cologne.

Harris, J. 1979. *The Artists and the Country House. A History of Country Houses and Garden View Painting in Britain 1540-1870,* London.

Hartmann, G. 1981. *Die Ruine im Landschaftsgarten,* Worms.

Hayden, P. 1985. 'British Seats on Imperial Russian Tables', *Garden History,* 1, 17-32.

Hennebo, D. (ed.), 1985. *Gartendenkmalpflege: Grundlagen der Erhaltung historischer Gärten und Grünanlagen,* Stuttgart.

Hennebo, D. 1985. 'Tendencies in Mid-Eighteenth-Century German Gardening', *Journal of Garden History,* 5, 350-70.

Herzog, H. 1989. *Hubert Robert und das Bild im Garten,* Worms.

Hirschfeld, C.C.L. 1779-85. *Theorie der Gartenkunst,* 5 vols., Leipzig.

Hollerbach, E. & Lansere, N., (eds.), 1924. *Charlz Kameron. Sbornik statei,* [Ch. Cameron. Selected Essays], Moscow, Petrograd.

Hunt, J.D. 1976. *The Figure in the Landscape: Poetry, Painting and Gardening during the Eighteenth Century,* Baltimore, London.

Hunt, J.D. 1986. *Garden and Grove. The Italian Renaissance Garden in the English Imagination: 1600-1750,* London, Melbourne.

Hunt, J.D. & Willis, P. (eds.), 1975. *The Genius of the Place. The English Landscape Garden 1620-1820,* London.

Hussey, C. 1927. *The Picturesque. Studies in a Point of View,* London, Edinburgh.

Hussey, C. 1967. *English Gardens and Landscapes 1700-1750,* London.

L'iconologie expliquée par les figures, ou Traité complet des allégories, emblêmes & s. Ikonologiya, obyasnnaya litsami; ili polnoe sobranie allegorii, emblem, i pr., 1803. Moscow.

Ignatenko, M.M., Gavrilov, G.M. & Karpov, L.N. 1980. *Lesoparki Leningrada,* [The Forest Parks of Leningrad], Leningrad.

Ikonnikov, A. 1931: *Kitaisky teatr i "kitaishchina",* [The Chinese Theatre and "The Little Chinese"], Moscow, Leningrad.

Ikonnikov, A. 1990. *L'architecture russe de*

la période soviétique, Moscow.

Ilin, M. 1974. *Podmoskovye*, [Moscow Surroundings], Moscow.

Ilin, M. & Moiseeva, T. 1979. *Moskva i Podmoskovye. Pamyatniki iskusstva Sovetskogo Soyuza*, [Moscow and Surroundings. Artistic Monuments of the Soviet Union], Moscow.

Ivanov, V. 1984. 'Zelyonye zony Moskvy', [Moscow's Green Zones], *Arkhitektura SSSR*, 4, 22-27.

Ivanov, V.P. (ed.), 1981. *Sady i parki Leningrada*, [Gardens and Parks of Leningrad], Leningrad.

Ivanova, L.P. & Rumyantseva, N.A. 1986. *Lomonosov. Dvortsogo-parkovy muzei-zapovednik* [Lomonosov. Palace and Garden Complex], Leningrad.

Ivashchenko, V. 1895. *Istorichesky ocherk k 100 letiyu Tsaritsyna sada (Sofievki)*, [Historical Study on the Occasion of the 100 Year Anniversary of the Tsaritsyno Garden (Sofievka)], Kiev.

Ivask, U.G. 1915. *Selo Sukhanovo, podmoskovnaya svetleyshikh knyazey Volkonskikh*, [Sukhanovo, the Volkonski Princes' Country House near Moscow], Moscow.

Jacques, D. 1983. *Georgian Gardens. The Reign of Nature*, London.

Kaigorodtseva, O. 1981. 'Vozrozhdenie arkhitekturnogo ansamblya XVIII veka', [The Renaissance of 18th Century Architectural Ensembles], *Arkhitektura SSSR*, 7, 48-52.

Kalyazina, N.V. (ed.), 1986. *Dvorets Menshikova* [The Menshikov Palace], Leningrad.

Karamzin, N.M. 1964. *Izbrannye sochineniya*, [Selected Writings], 2 vols., Moscow, Leningrad.

Karra, A.Y. 1935. 'Planirovka Sokolnicheskogo parka', [The Design of the Sokoloniki Park], *Arkhitektura SSSR*, 10-11, 54-57.

Karra, A.Y. 1940. 'Planirovka Sokolnicheskogo parka', [The Design of the Sokoloniki park], *Arkhitektura SSSR*, 12, 24-26.

Kashuk, L. 1989. 'Peizazh Semena Shchedrina i Pavlovsky Park', [Semen Shchedrin's Landscape Painting and the Pavlovsk Park], *Iskusstvo*, 6, 62-68.

Kazantsev, V. 1929. *Tsaritsyno*, Moscow.

Keldysh, Yu.V. 1965. *Russkaya muzyka XVIII veka*, [Russian 18th Century Music], Moscow.

Keller, B.A. 1940. 'Ozelenenie Moskvy', [Making Moscow Green], *Arkhitektura SSSR*, 8, 4-6.

Kelly, A. 1980. 'Wedgwood's Catherine Services', *Burlington Magazine*, CXXII, 554-61.

Kennett, A. 1973. *The Palaces of Leningrad*, London.

Khudozhnik, [The Artist], 1992, 4-5. Special issue on Russian country houses.

Klyuchariants, D.A. 1985. *Khudozhestvennye pamyatniki goroda Lomonosova*, [Monuments of the Town of Lomonosov], Leningrad.

Klyuchariants, D.A. & Raskin, A.G. 1990. *Gatchina. Khudozhestvennye pamyatniki*, [Gatchina. Monuments], Leningrad.

Kokhno, B.I. 1986. *Parki-pamyatniki istorii sovetskogo gosudarstva*, [Historical Parks of the Soviet Society], Leningrad.

Kopylova, R. 1988. 'O restavratsii dvortsovo-parkovogo ansamblya v Tsaritsyne', [On the Restoration of the Tsaritsyno Palace and Garden], *Arkhitektura SSSR*, 5, 108-11.

Korshunova, M.F. 1988. *Yury Velten*, Leningrad.

Korsun, Ye.A. (ed.), 1994. *Gatchina. Imperatorsky dvorets. Trete stoletie istorii*, [Gatchina. Imperial Palace. 300 Years of History], St Petersburg.

Korzhev, M.P. 1938. 'Voprosy ozeleneniya gorodov', [Questions on the Green Zones of the Cities], *Arkhitektura SSSR*, 4, 38-43.

Korzhev, M.P. & Prokhorova, M.I. 1935. 'Park im. Stalina v Izmaylove', [The Stalin Park at Izmaylovo], *Arkhitektura SSSR*, 10-11 50-53.

Korzhev, M.P. & Prokhorova, M.I. 1940. *Arkhitektura parkov SSSR*, [The Architecture of Soviet Parks], Moscow.

Korzhukov, V.F. 1988. *Voronovo. Istoriche-skaya usadba XVIII-XXvv. Dom otdykha*, [Voronovo. A Historical Estate of the 18th-20th Centuries. A Resort Place], Moscow.

Kosarevsky, I.A. 1977. *Iskusstvo parkovogo peizazha*, [The Art of Landscape Design], Moscow.

Koshin, N.A. 1927. *Osnovi russkoi psevdo-gotiki XVIIIv*. [Sources of Russian 18th Century Pseudo-Gothic], Leningrad.

Kovalenskaya, N. 1938. 'Arkhitektura rus-skogo klassitsizma', [The Architecture of Russian Classicism], *Arkhitektura SSSR*, 9, 74-81.

Kovalevskaya, N.N. 1940. *Istoriya russkogo iskusstva XVIII veka* [History of Russian 18th Century Art], Moscow, Leningrad.

Kovshova, L.A. 1992. *Bogoroditsky dvorets-muzei*, [The Bogoroditse Palace Museum], Tula.

Kovaleva, T., *"Biblioteka Sheremetevykh" v sobranii redkikh knig Gosudarstvennogo muzeia keramiki i "Usadba Kuskovo XVIII veka"*, [The Sheremetev Library in the Collection of Rare Books of the State Museum of Ceramics and the 18th Century Kuskovo Estate], exhibition catalogue, Kuskovo, n.d.

Krafft, J.Ch. 1809. *Plans des plus beaux jardins pittoresques de France, d'Angleterre et d'Allemagne, et des édifices, monumens, fabriques, etc. qui concourent à leur embellissement, dans tous les genres d'architecture, tels que chinois, égyptien, anglois, arabe, moresque, etc. Dédiés aux Architectes et aux Amateurs*, Paris.

Krasheninnikov, A. 1991. 'Pavlovsky park', [The Pavlovsk Park], *Khudozhnik*, 9, 46-53.

Kuchumov, A.M. 1980. *Pavlovsk. Putevoditel*, [Pavlovsk. A Guide], Leningrad.

Kuchumov, A.M. & Velichko, M.A. 1976. *Pavlovsk. Dvorets i park*, [Pavlovsk. Palace and Park], Leningrad.

Kulagin, E.N. (ed.), 1990. *Vozrozhdenie iz pepla. Petrodvorets, Pushkin, Pavlovsk*, [A Rebirth. Petrodvorets, Pushkin, Pavlovsk], Leningrad.

Kurbatov, V.Ya. 1916. *Sady i parki. Istoriya i teoriya sadovogo iskusstva*, [Gardens and Parks. The History and Theory of Gardening], Petrograd.

Kurlat, F.L. 1980. *Moskva ot tsentra do okrain. Putevoditel*, [Moscow from Centre to Periphery. A Guidebook], Moscow.

Kurlov, V. 1982. 'Pamyatnik landshaftnoi arkhitektury Sukhanovo', [The Landscape Architecture of Sukhanovo], *Arkhitektura SSSR*, 5, 38-41.

Kuskovo i ego okrestnosti, [Kuskovo and Surroundings], 1850, Moscow.

Kuznetsova, O.N. & Borzin, B.F. 1988. *Letny Sad i Letny Dvorets Petra I*, [Peter I's Summer Garden and Summer Palace], Leningrad.

Kvarchinskaya, I. 1979. 'Vossozdat luchshie teatry XVIIIv.', [The Restoration of the Best 18th Century Theatres], *Arkhitektura SSSR*, 10, 51.

Kvyatkovskaya, N.K. 1985. *Marfino*, Moscow.

Kvyatkovskaya, N.K. 1990. *Ostafyevo*, Moscow.

Kyuchariants, D.A. 1994. *Antonio Rinaldi*, St Petersburg.

Laugier, M.A. 1972. *Essai sur l'architecture*, (1755), Paris.

Lavrov, V. 1937. 'Arkhitekturnaya kompo-zitsiya genplana Vsesoyuznoi selskokho-zyaistvennoi vystavki', [The Architecture of the All-Union Agricultural Exhibition], *Arkhitektura SSSR*, 2, 32-37.

Le Rouge, G.-L. 1776-87. *Détails des nou-veaux Jardins à la Mode; Jardins anglo-chinois à la Mode*, Paris.

Lebedev, G.I. & Nagibina, M.P. 1934. *Za zelyonuyu Moskvu, za zelyonye zhakty*, [For a Green Moscow, for Green Corridors], Moscow.

Lem, I. 1792-94. *Teoreticheskiya i prakti-chechiya predlozheniya o grazhdanskoi arkhi-tekture, s obyasneniem pravil Vitruviya, Palladiya, Serliya, Vinyuly i drugykh,*

[Theoretical and Practical Ideas about Civil Architecture, with an Explanation of the Rules of Vitruvius, Palladio, Serlio, Vignola and others], 3 vols., St Petersburg.

Lemus, V. (ed.), 1980. *Muzei i parki Pushkina*, [Museums and Parks of Pushkin], Leningrad.

Lemus, V. 1984. *Pushkin. Palaces and Parks*, Leningrad.

Lentin, A. (ed.), 1974. *Voltaire and Catherine the Great. Selected Correspondence*, Cambridge.

Levshin, V. (ed.), 1805-08. *Sadovodstvo polnoe, sobrannoe c opytov i iz luchikh pisatelei o sem predmete s prilozhenyem risunkov*, [A Complete Book on Gardening, Selected from the Best Authors Writing about this Subject and with Illustrations], 3 vols., Moscow.

Ligne, Prince C.J. de, 1785. *Coup-d'oeil sur Beloeil et sur une grande Partie des Jardins de l'Europe*, 2 vols., s.l.

Likhachov, D.S. 1982. *Poeziya sadov. K semantike sadovo-parkovykh stilei*, [The Poetry of Gardens. On the Semantics of Garden and Park Styles], Leningrad.

Likhachov, D.S. 1982. 'Sad i kultura Evropy', [The Garden and European Culture], *Dekorativnoe Iskusstvo*, [Decorative Arts], 3, 38-45.

Likhachov, D.S. 1982. 'Sad i kultura Rossii', [The Garden and Russian Culture], *Dekorativnoe Iskusstvo*, 12, 38-45.

Lochhead, J.J. 1982. *The Spectator and the Landscape in the Art Criticism of Diderot and His Contemporaries*, Ann Arbor, Mich.

Loudon, J.C. 1835. *An Encyclopedia of Gardening*, London.

Lukomsky, G.K. 1918. *Dvortsy-Muzei Tsarskago Sela. Kratky katalog muzeia bolshogo Yekatarinenskago dvortsa*, [The Tsarskoe Selo Palace Museums. A Short Guide to the Museum of the Big Yekatarine Palace], Petrograd.

Lunts, L. 1937. 'Obespecheno pravo na otdykh', [The Right to Leisure], *Arkhitektura SSSR*, 10, 43-55.

Lunts, L. 1940. 'Tsentralny park kultury i otdykha v Moskve', [The Central Park of Culture and Rest in Moscow], *Arkhitektura SSSR*, 6, 20-27.

Lyall, R. 1823. *The Character of the Russians, and A Detailed History of Moscow*, London.

Lyubchenko, O.N. 1984. 'Risunki uchyonogo', [Drawings of an Erudite [about Bolotov]], *Pamyatniki Otechestva*, [Monuments of the Fatherland], 1, 93-103.

Lyubchenko, O.N. 1984. *Yest v Bogoroditske park*, [There is a Park at Bogoroditske], Tula.

Lyubesky, S. 1868. *Selo Ostankino s okrestnostyami svoimi*, [The Ostankino Village and Surroundings], Moscow.

Lyulina, R.D., Raskin, A.G. & Tubli, M.N. 1981. *Dekorativnaya skulptura sadov i parkov Leningrada i prigorodov XVIII-XIX vekov*, [Decorative Sculpture in the Gardens and Parks of Leningrad and Surroundings in the 18th and 19th Centuries], Leningrad.

Maccubbin, R.P. & Martin, P. 1986. *British and American Gardens in the Eighteenth Century*, Williamsburg, Virg.

Madariaga, I. de, 1981. *Russia in the Age of Catherine the Great*, London.

Maisaik, P. 1981. *Arkadien. Genese und Typologie einer idyllischen Wunschwelt*, Frankfurt am Main, Bern.

Maisle, Yu. 1985. 'Usadebnaya arkhitektura Estonii', [Estonian Country House Architecture], *Arkhitektura SSSR*, 1, 96-99.

Makarov, V. 1924. 'Andrei Bolotov i sadovoe iskusstvo v Rossii XVIII veka', [Andrei Bolotov and the Art of Gardening in 18th Century Russia], *Sredi kollektsionerov*, 5-6, 26-32.

Mansa, L.C. 1798. *Plany Raspolozheniya i Razvedeniya Aglinskikh Sadov. Plans zu Anlagen englisher Gärten*, Moscow.

Markov, V.I. 1962. *Parki pobedy*, [Victory Parks], Leningrad.

Massie, S. 1982. *Land of the Firebird. The Beauty of Old Russia*, New York.

Massie, S. 1990. *Pavlovsk. The Life of a Russian Palace*, Boston, Toronto, London.

Materialy dlya opisaniya khudozhestvennikh sokrovits Pavlovska, [Documents Describing the Art Treasures at Pavlovsk], 1903, St Petersburg. [Includes Maria Feodorovna's description of Pavlovsk].

Matsulevich, Zh.A. 1993. 'Dekorativnaya skulptura v Gatchine', [Decorative Sculpture at Gatchina], *Stranitsy istorii zapadnoevropeiskoi skulptury. Sbornik naychnykh statei. Pamyati Zh. A. Matsulevich*, ed. by S.O. Androsov, St Petersburg, 29-42.

Meshkova, V.I. 1979. 'Prostranstvennaya organizatsiya parka sanatornogo kompleksa na osnove landshaftnogo stsenariya v usloviyakh Yuzhnogo Berega Kryma', [The Landscape as Basis for the Spatial Organization of Parks Adjacent to Resort Places on the South Coast of the Crimea], summary of unpublished dissertation, Moscow.

Micoulina, E.M. 1985. 'Questions d'actualité concernant la restauration des jardins en URSS', *Cahiers de la Section Française de l'ICOMOS: Régenérer les jardins classiques*, conference papers, Versailles.

Mikhailov, B. 1977. 'Nauchnaya spravka po chertazham Uveselitelnogo Sada s vyyasneniem voprosa ob avtora osnovnogo proekta', [A Study of the Plans of the Pleasure Garden and a Discussion of the Authorship of the Project], unpublished study on Ostankino.

Mikhailov, B. 1990. 'Sadovnik Francis Rid v Tsaritsyne i Ostankine', [The Architect Francis Reid at Tsaritsyno and Ostankino], *Arkhitektura SSSR*, 4, 104-09.

Mineeva, K.I. 1988. *Tsaritsyno. Dvortsogoparkovy ansambl*, [Tsaritsyno. Palace and Park], Moscow.

Molok, D.Yu. (ed.), 1989. *Vek prosveshcheniya. Rossiya i Frantsiya. Le siècle des lumières. Russie. France*, conference papers, Pushkin Museum of Fine Arts, Moscow.

Morel, J.-M. 1776. *Théorie des jardins*, Paris.

Morozov, G.V. 1958. *Moskva. Planirovka i zastroika goroda 1945-1957. Moscou. Aménagement et implantation de la ville*, Moscow.

Mosser, M. & Teyssot, G. (eds.), 1991. *The Architecture of Western Gardens: A Design History from the Renaissance to the Present Day*, Cambridge, Mass.

Moszyński, A.F. 1977. 'Essay sur le jardinage anglois', (1774), *Rosprawa o ogrodownictwie angielskim*, ed. by A. Morawinska, Wroclaw, Warsaw, Krakow, Gdansk.

Mudrov, Yu.V. 1992. *Pavlovsk. Watercolours, Paintings and Engravings from the XVIIIth and XIXth Centuries*, Paris.

Müllenbrock, H.-J. 1988. 'The "Englishness" of the English landscape garden and the genetic role of literature: a reassessment', *Journal of Garden History*, 4, 97-103.

Nehring, D. 1979. *Stadtparkanlagen in der ersten Hälfte des 19.Jahrhunderts. Ein Beitrag zur Kunstgeschichte des Landschaftsgartens*, Hannover, Berlin.

Neufforge, J.-F. Le, 1757-77. *Récueil élementaire d'architecture*, 8 vols., Paris.

Neverov, O.Ya. 1993. 'Skulpturnye tsikly v dekore letnogo sada', [Sculptural Cycles in the Summer Garden], *Stranitsy istorii zapadnoevropeiskoi skulptury. Sbornik nauchnykh statei. Pamyati Zh. A. Matsulevich*, ed. by S.O. Androsov, St Petersburg, 136-63.

Nikolaev, I. 1987. 'Arkhitekturnoe obrazovanie v Moskve v XVIII-XIX vekakh', [The Education of Architects in Moscow during the 18th and 19th Centuries], *Arkhitektura SSSR*, 5, 78-84.

Nikolaevskaya, E.A. 1955. 'Vodoemi v parkakh landshaftnogo tipa', [Waters in Landscape Gardens], summary of unpublished dissertation, Moscow.

Novikov, V.I. 1991. *Ostafyevo. Literaturnye sudby XIX veka* [Ostafyevo. Literary Personalities of the 19th Century], Moscow.

O poleznykh iskusstvakh i khudozhestvakh dlya sadov, [On Practical and Artful Gardening], 1779, St Petersburg.

Olausson, M. 1993. *Den Engelska parken i Sverige under gustaviansk tid*, [The English Landscape Garden in Sweden during the Gustavian Era], Stockholm. (English summary).

Oltarzhevsky, V. 1937. 'Generalny plan Vsesoyuznoi selskokhozyaistvennoi vystavki', [The General Plan of the All-Union Agricultural Exhibition], *Arkhitektura SSSR*, 2, 29-31.

Opyt o raspolozhenii sadov, [Experience from Designing Gardens], 1778, St Petersburg.

Osipov, N. 1791. *Karmannaya kniga selskago i domashnyago khozyaistva*, [A Handbook on Household and Garden], St Petersburg.

Osipov, N. 1791-92. *Podrobny slovar dlya selskikh i gorodskikh okhotnikov i lyubitelei Botanicheskago, uveselitelnago i khozyaistvennago sadovodstva*, [A Detailed Dictionary for Urban and Suburban Amateurs of Botanical, Pleasure and Vegetable Gardens], 2 vols., St Petersburg.

Osipov, N. 1793. *Novoi i sovershennoi russkoi sadovnik*, [A New and Entirely Russian Guide to Gardening], 2 vols., St Petersburg.

The Oxford Companion to Gardens, 1987. Oxford, New York.

Ozhegov, S.S. 1993. *Istoriya landshaftnoi arkhitektury*, [History of Landscape Design], Moscow.

Pankova, O. 1940. *Usadba Kuskovo. Ocherk-putevoditel*, [The Kuskovo Estate. A Guide], Moscow, Leningrad.

Pankova, O. 1953. 'Zelyony teatr v Kuskove', [The Open-Air Theatre at Kuskovo], *Arkhitektura SSSR*, 5, 22-24.

Paperny, V. 1985. *Kultura "dva"*, [Culture "Two"], Ann Arbor, Mich.

Parreaux, A. & Plaisant, M. 1977. *Jardins et paysages: le style anglais*, Lille.

Paulson, R. 1975. *Emblem and Expression.* *Meaning in English Art of the Eighteenth Century*, London.

Pechersky, M.D. 1988. *Ostafyevo*, Moscow.

Petoyan, E.M. (ed.), 1989. *Park i otdikh. Sovremenny park v sisteme organizatsii dosuga naseleniya*, [Park and Recreation. The Modern Park in the Systematic Organization of People's Leisure Time], Moscow.

Petrov, A.N., a.o. (eds.), 1977. *Pamyatriki arkhitektury Leningrada*, [Architectural Monuments of Leningrad], Leningrad.

Petrov, A.N., a.o. (eds.), 1985. *Pamyatniki arkhitektury prigorodov Leningrada*, [Architectural Monuments in the Leningrad Suburbs], Leningrad.

Pevsner, N. (ed.), 1974. *The Picturesque Garden and Its Influence outside the British Isles*, conference papers, Dumbarton Oaks, Washington D.C.

Pietro Gonzaga. Eskizi, dekoratsii, i rospisei, [Pietro Gonzaga. Sketches, Decorations, and Wall-Paintings], 1980, exhibition catalogue, The State Hermitage, Leningrad.

Pilyaev, M.I. 1889. *Stary Peterburg*, [Old St Petersburg], St Petersburg.

Pilyavsky, V.I. 1986. *Sukhanovo*, Leningrad.

Podmoskovnye sady i parki XVIII-XIXvv., [Gardens and Parks in the Surroundings of Moscow in the 18th and 19th Centuries], 1927, exhibition catalogue, Kuskovo.

Podyapolsky, S.S. (ed.), 1989. *Kompleksnaya okhrana i restavratsiya ansamblei i istoriko-kulturnykh zapovednikov*, [Complete Conservation and Restoration of Ensembles and Cultural-Historical Complexes], Moscow.

Posokhin, M.V. 1989. *Arkhitektura okruzhayushchei sredy*, [Landscape Architecture], Moscow.

Poznansky, V.V. 1966. *Arkhangelskoe*, Moscow.

Poznukhov, A.V. 1980. 'Ob avtorstve rannikh psedogoticheskikh sooruzhenii', [On the Authorship of Early Pseudo-Gothic Structures], *Istoriya i teoriya ar-*

khitektury i gradostroitelstva, ed. by V.I. Pilyavsky, Leningrad, 160-68.

Presnova, N., *Khudozhniki Argunovy v "Kuskove"*, [The Argunovs, Artists at Kuskovo], exhibition catalogue, s.l.n.d.

Presnova, N. 1992. 'Kuskovo, mily ugolok', [Kuskovo, a Delightful Corner], *Khudozhnik*, 1-2, 46-57.

Price, M. 1965. 'The Picturesque Moment', *From Sensibility to Romanticism. Essays presented to Frederick A. Pottle*, ed. by F.W. Hilles & H. Bloom, New York, 259-92.

Pushkin, A. 1984. *Collected Narrative and Lyrical Poetry*, (translated in the prosodic forms of the original by W. Arendt), Ann Arbor.

Pushkin, A.S. 1989. *Zvezda plenitelnogo schastya: Stikhotvoreniya*, [Highlights of Enchanted Happiness. Poems], Moscow.

Rae, I. 1971. *Charles Cameron. Architect to the Court of Russia*, London.

Romanenko, E.V. 1990. *Monument v gorode*, [The Monument in the City], Moscow.

Rapoport, V. 1971. *Park v Arkhangelskom*, [The Park at Arkhangelskoe], Moscow.

Rapoport, V. 1982. *Arkhangelskoe*, Moscow.

Raskin, A.G. 1978. *Petrodworets (Peterhof). Schlösser und Pavillons, Gärten und Parks, Fontänen und Kaskaden, Skulpturen*, Leningrad.

Raskin, A.G. 1984. *Petrodvorets. Dvortsy-muzei, parki, fontany*, [Petrodvorets. Palace–Museums, Parks, Fountains], Leningrad.

Réau, L. 1913. 'Catalogue de l'oeuvre d'Hubert Robert en Russie', *Bulletin de la Société de l'Histoire de l'Art Français*, 295-308.

Réau, L. 1914. 'L'Oeuvre d'Hubert Robert en Russie', *Gazette des Beaux-Arts*, 3, 173-88.

Réau, L. (ed.), 1932. 'Correspondance artistique de Grimm avec Catherine II', *Archives de l'Art Français*, XVII, 1-206.

Réau, L. & Loukomski, G.K. 1930. *Cathérine la grande, inspiratrice d'art et mécène*, Paris.

Rorschach, K. 1983. *The Early Georgian Landscape Garden*, New Haven.

Rostovtseva, G.A. 1958. *Kuskovo. Regulyarny park muzeya-usadby XVIIIv.*, [Kuskovo. The Formal Park of the 18th Century Country Home Museum], Moscow.

Rostovtseva, G.A. 1958. *Zelyony teatr v Kuskove*, [The Open-Air Theatre at Kuskovo], Perevo.

Ryldin, V. 1988. *VDNKh SSSR*, [The VDNKh-Park of the USSR], Moscow.

Rzyanin, M. 1953. 'Voprosy osvoeniya klassicheskogo naslediya v arkhitekturnoi praktike natsionalnykh respublik SSSR', [Questions on the Liberation from the Classical Heritage in the Architecture of the National Republics of the USSR], *Arkhitektura SSSR*, 4, 17-19.

Saisselin, R.G. 1985. 'The French Garden in the eighteenth century: from Belle Nature to the landscape of time', *Journal of Garden History*, 5, 284-97.

Sarbarov, A. 1989. 'Stalinsky stil. Postscriptum', [The Stalin Style. Postscriptum], *Arkhitektura SSSR*, 3, 31-33.

Sautov, I.P. 1992. *Tsarskoe Selo. Watercolours, Paintings and Engravings from the XVIIIth and XIXth Centuries*, Paris.

Semennikova, N. 1985. *Pushkin, dvortsi i parki*, [Pushkin Palaces and Parks], Moscow.

Sheremetev, S.D. 1897. *Ostankino*, St Petersburg.

Sheremetev, S.D. 1898. *Kuskovo*, Moscow.

Sheremetev, S.D. 1899. *Kuskovo do 1812 goda*, [Kuskovo until 1812], Moscow.

Shiryaev, S.D. 1927. *Alupka. Dvorets i parki*, [Alupka. Palace and Parks], Simferopol.

Schmidt, A.J. 1989. *The Architecture and Planning of Classical Moscow: A Cultural History*, Philadelphia.

Shchukina, E.P. 1952. 'Podmoskovnye usadebnye sady i parki vtoroi poloviny XVIII veka', [Landscape Gardens and Parks in the Surroundings of Moscow during the Second Half of the 18th Century], summary of unpublished dissertation, Moscow.

Shvarts, V. 1980. *Pavlovsk. Dvortsovo-parkovoi ansambl XVIII-XIX vekov*, [Pavlovsk. 18th and 19th Century Palace and Park], Leningrad.

Simvoly i emblemata. Symbola et emblemata, 1705, Amsterdam.

Sotsialisticheskaya rekonstruktsiya Yushnogo Berega Kryma, [Socialist Reconstruction of the South Coast of the Crimea], 1935, Simferopol.

Specimens of the Russian Poets, 1821, (translated by J. Bowing), London.

St. Petersburg um 1800. Ein goldenes Zeitalter des russischen Zarenreichs, 1990, exhibition catalogue, Kulturstiftung Ruhr, Villa Hügel, Essen.

Stanyukovich, V.K. 1926. 'Materialy po staromu Kuskovu', [Documents on Old Kuskovo], unpublished study, Moscow.

Stolpyansky, P.N. 1923. *Petergofskaya pershpektiva*, [The Peterhof Perspective], St Petersburg.

Storkh, P. 1843. *Putevoditel po sadu i gorodu Pavlovsku*, [Guide to the Garden and Town of Pavlovsk], St Petersburg.

Syrkina, F.Y. 1974. *Pietro di Gottardo Gonzaga. 1751-1831. Zhizn i tvorchestvo. Sochineniya*, [Pietro di Gottardo Gonzaga. 1751-1831. Life and Work. Writings], Moscow.

Taleporovsky, V. 1923. *Pavlovsky park*, [The Pavlovsk Park], St Peterburg.

Taleporovsky, V. 1935. 'Traktat Charlza Kamerona "Rimskie termy"', (Ch. Cameron's Treatise "The Baths of the Romans"], *Arkhitektura SSSR*, 9, 60-62.

Taleporovsky, V.N. 1939. *Charlz Kameron*, [Ch. Cameron], Moscow.

Thacker, C. 1978. 'The Temple of the Sibyl', *Park und Garten im 18. Jahrhundert. Colloquium der Arbeitsstelle 18. Jahrhundert Gesamthochschule Wuppertal*, conference papers, Heidelberg, 29-35.

Thacker, C. 1981. *Histoire des jardins*, Paris.

Tikhomorov, N.Ya. 1955. *Arkhitektura podmoskovnykh usadeb*, [Country House

Architecture in the Moscow region], Moscow.

Timofeev, L.N. 1980. 'K voprosu o genezise kompozitsii Vorontsovskogo dvortsa v Alupke', [On the Origin of the Vorontsov Palace in Alupka], *Istoriya i teoriya arkhitektury i gradostroitelstva*, ed. by V.I. Pylyavsky, Leningrad.

Toropov, S.A. 1927. *Arkhangelskoe*, Moscow.

Toropov, S.A. 1947. *Podmoskovnye usadby*, [Country Houses in the Surroundings of Moscow], Moscow.

Tsarin, A.P. & Galichenko, A.A. 1992. *Alupka. Dvorets i park*, [Alupka. Palace and Park], Kiev.

Unanyants, I.T. 1970. *Frantsuzkaya zhivopis v Arkhangelskom*, [French Painting at Arkhangelskoe], Moscow.

V.I. Bazhenov. 1738-1799, 1988, exhibition catalogue, Museum of Architecture, Moscow.

Valitskaya, A.P. 1983. *Russkaya estetika XVIII veka*, [Russian Aesthetics of the 18th Century], Moscow.

Vbovin, G. 1988. *Ostankino*, Moscow.

VDNKh SSSR. Soyuz iskusstva i truda, [The VDNHk-Park of the USSR. An Entity of Art and Work], 1989, Moscow.

Vedenin, Yu.A. & Fitseva, S.V. (eds.), 1992. *II mezhdunarodnoi konferentsii po sokhraneniyu i razbitiyu unikalnykh istoricheskikh territorii. Tezisy dokladov*, [2. International Congress on the Conservation and Future of Unique Historical Territories], conference papers, Moscow.

Veis, Z. & Veis, N. 1967. *V Pavlovskom parke*, [In the Pavlovsk Park], Leningrad, Moscow.

Vergunov, A.P. (ed.), 1980. *Arkhitekturnaya kompozitsija sadov i parkov*, [The Architectural Design of Gardens and Parks], Moscow.

Vergunov, A.P. (ed.), 1990. *Okhrana i ispolzovanie pamyatnikov sadovo-parkovogo iskusstva*, [Conservation and Use of Garden and Park Monuments], Moscow.

Vergunov, A.P. & Gorokhov, V.A. 1988. *Russkie sady i parki*, [Russian Gardens and Parks], Moscow.

Vidler, A. 1976. 'The Architecture of the Lodges; Ritual Form and Associational Life in the Late Enlightenment', *Oppositions*, 2, 75-97.

Vidler, A. 1992. *The Writing of the Walls. Architectural Theory in the Late Enlightenment*, London, Boston, Singapore, Sydney.

Vinogradov, K. 1929. *Ostankino. Krestyane i rabochie pri postroike ostankinskogo "uveselitelnogo doma" (teatra-dvortsa). Istorichesky ocherk*, [Ostankino. Peasants and Workers Working on the Palace and Theatre of Ostankino. A Historical Study], Moscow.

Vitruvius, M. 1785. *Marka Vitruviya Polliona ob arkhitekture, kniga pervaya i vtoraya*, Russian edition of *De Architectura Libri Decem*, First and Second Book, 2 vols., St Petersburg.

Vitruvius, M. 1790-97. *Marka Vitruviya Polliona ob arkhitekture*, 10 vols., St Petersburg.

Vittchkovsky, S. 1912. *Tsarskoe Selo*, Berlin.

Vlasov, A. 1934. 'Tsentralny park kultury i otdykha im. Gorkogo', [The Central Park of Culture and Rest, Named after Gorki], *Arkhitektura SSSR*, 7, 44-49.

Vlasov, A. 1935. 'Tsentralny park stolitsi', [The Central Park of the Capital], *Arkhitektura SSSR*, 10-11, 48-49.

Voinov, T.V. 1930. *Parkovaya rastitelnost Kryma*, [Park Plantation on the Crimea], Yalta.

Voronov, M.G. & Khodasevich, G.D. 1990. *Arkhitekturny ansambl Kamerona v Pushkine*, [Cameron's Buildings at Pushkin], Leningrad.

Watelet, C.-H. 1774. *Essai sur les Jardins*, Paris.

Watkin, D. 1982. *The English Vision. The Picturesque in Architecture, Landscape & Garden Design*, London.

Weiner, P. 1910. 'Marfino', *Starye gody*, 7-9, 115-30.

Weiner, P. 1910. 'Zhizn i iskusstvo v Ostankino', [Life and Art at Ostankino], *Starye gody*, 5-6, 38-72.

Wengel, T. 1987. *The Art of Gardening through the Ages*, Leipzig.

Wiebenson, D. 1978. *The Picturesque Garden in France*, Princeton.

Williams, R. 1987. 'Rural Economy and the Antique in the English Landscape Garden', *Journal of Garden History*, 7, 73-96.

Wimmer, C.A. (ed.), 1989. *Geschichte der Gartentheorie*, Darmstadt.

Woodbridge, K. 1986. *Princely Gardens. The origins and development of the French formal style*, London.

Wrangel, Baron N. 1910. 'Pomeshchichya Rossii', [The Gentlemen of Russia], *Starye gody*, 7-9, 5-79.

Yanchuk, N.A. 1916. *Znamenity zodchy XVIII veka Vasily Ivanovich Bazhenov i ego otnoshenie k masonstvu*, [The Outstanding 18th Century Architect Vasily Ivanovich Bazhenov and his Relationship to Freemasonry], Petrograd.

Yanpolsky, N. & Oleinik, F. 1938. 'Vosstanovlenie fresok Gonzaga', [The Restoration of Gonzaga's Wall-Paintings], *Arkhitektura SSSR*, 12, 73-76.

Yarovoy, I.Yu. 1987. 'Peizazhnye sady russkoi provintsii', [Landscape Gardens of the Russian Province], summary of unpublished dissertation, Moscow.

Yegorov, Yu.A. 1969. *The Architectural Planning of St. Petersburg*, Athens, Ohio.

Yegorova, K.M. 1975. *Leningrad. House of Peter I. Summer Gardens. Palace of Peter I*, Leningrad.

Yekaterina Velikaya. Russkaya kultura vtoroi poloviny XVIII veka [Catherine the Great. Russian Culture of the Second Half of the 18th Century], 1993, exhibition catalogue, The State Hermitage, St Petersburg.

Yelizarova, N.A. 1955. *Ostankinsky Dvorets-Muzei. Tvorchestva Krepostnykh XVIII veka*, [The Ostankino Palace and Museum. The Work of 18th Century Serfs], Moscow.

Yelizarova, N.A. 1966. *Ostankino*, Moscow.

Yelkina, A.S. 1977. *Pavlovsk*, Leningrad.

Yelkina, A.S. & Tretyakov, N.S. 1992. *Gatchinsky dvorets. The Gatchina Palace*, St Petersburg.

Yeremyna, N.S. 1976. *Letny sad*, [The Summer Garden], Leningrad.

Yevangulova, O.S. 1984. 'Gorod i usadba vtoroi poloviny XVIIIvv soznanii sovremennikov', [The City and the Country House in the Second Half of the 18th Century in the Contemporary Mind], *Russky gorod. Issledovaniya i materialy*, Moscow, 172-88.

Zabelyn, I. 1905. *Istoriya goroda Moskvy*, [The History of the City of Moscow], Moscow.

Zelenova, A.I. 1958. *Pavlovsky park*, [The Pavlovsk Park], Leningrad.

Zelenova, A.I. 1986. *Dvorets v Pavlovske*, [The Palace at Pavlovsk], Leningrad.

Zemtsov, S. 1982. 'Andrea Palladio i russkaya arkhitektura XVIII veka', [A. Palladio and Russian 18th Century Architecture], *Arkhitektura SSSR*, 9, 42-45.

Zhirnov, A.D. 1977. *Iskusstvo parkostroeniya*, [Park Design], Lvov.

Zhukovsky, V. 1974. *Stikhotvoreniya*, [Poems], Moscow.

Zrelitse prirody i khudozhestv, [A Look at Nature and the Arts], 1784, 2 vols., St Petersburg.

Index of Persons

Fox, C.J. 43
Frederik IV 19
Gallardi brothers 175
Gelfreikh, V.G. 192
George III 105, 142
Gerhard, J. 108
Girardin, R.L. de 33, 171-72, 174, 177
Golitsyn, N.A. 49-50, 82, 210
Gonzaga, Paolo di 176
Gonzaga, Pietro di 93, 129-30, 137, 152,
   158, 174*, 175-79, 211, 216
Gorbachov, M. 204
Gould 92
Gray, T. 135, 167
Grimm, F. 29, 42-43, 49, 127, 189
Grohmann, J.G. 70
Guerney, C. de 49, 210
Gustav III 33
Hadrian 102-3
Hamilton, G.H. 26
Hamilton, W. 90
Hirschfeld, C.C.L. 9-10, 15, 23, 26, 34,
   44-46, 52, 56, 64, 66-70, 98, 107, 116-18,
   161, 171, 181-83, 186, 188, 202-3, 211
Homer 78, 159
Hunt, W. 135, 210
Ilin, T. 38
Ivan III 126
Ivan IV 17,
Ivanov, M.M. 185
Kantemir 115, 125
Karamzin, N.M. 76, 158-61, 165-67, 169,
   202
Kazakov, M.F. 120-21, 125, 133, 201, 214,
   217, 219
Kent, W. 76, 137, 174
Klopstock, F.G. 160
Konstantinovsky, G.D. 193
Kozlovsky, O.A. 115
Kratsev, E. 20
Krylov, I.A. 158
Kuchelbecker 143-44
Kurakin, A.B. 136
Lafermier 154
Le Blond, J.-B.-A. 20, 24-25, 195, 217-18
Le Nôtre 24, 45
Le Rouge 97
Lem, I. 86, 88

Lenin, V.I. 52
Lermontov, M. 203
Levshin, V.A. 59, 145-46
Linné, C. von 144, 146
Lomonosov, M.V. 121, 215
Lorrain, C. 94, 186
Loudon, J.C. 37, 92, 96
Louis XIV 24-25, 56
Louis XVI 130, 174, 188-89
Lvov, A. 139, 141
Lvov, N.A. 130, 146, 161, 163, 165, 172,
   202
Lyall, R. 142
Makhaev, M.I. 185-86
Mansa, L.C. 70
Maria Feodorovna (Empress) 39, 51, 71,
   73, 80, 82, 87-88, 90-91, 93-95*, 96*,
   96-98*, 98-100*, 100-1*, 130, 142-45*,
   146, 148*, 153-54, 158, 164*, 166, 175,
   178, 185, 189, 203, 212, 216
Marie-Antoinette (Queen) 98, 152
Martos, I.P. 100
Matveev, I. 17, 19, 218
Melgunov, A.P. 77, 79
Melgunova, Ye.A. 80
Menelaws, A.A. 116, 135, 217
Mengs, A.R. 175
Menshıkov, A.D. 31, 215
Michetti, N. 195, 217
Michurin, I.F. 121
Milton, J. 160
Mironov, A. 82, 84, 213, 215
Monighetti, I.A. 201
Montesquieu, C. de S. 43
More, T. 121
Moszyński, A.F. 85
Neelov, I.V. 37, 39, 134, 220
Neelov, P.V. 37, 134
Neelov, V.I. 36-37, 39, 108, 110, 134, 220
Nicholas II 220
Norberg, F.E. 50
Novikov, N.I. 57, 127-28
Orlov, G.G. 40, 61, 198
Osipov, N.P. 59, 86, 145-46
Ossian 160
Ovsyaninkov, D. 20
Palladio, A. 40, 88, 91*, 91, 104, 113, 120
Pallas, P.S. 146

Index of Places

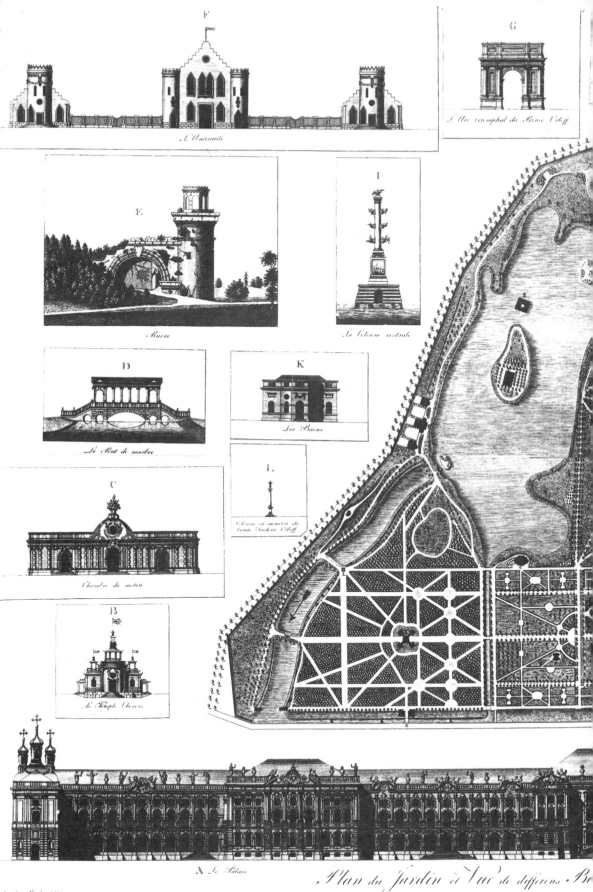

F.

G.

L'Arc triomphal du Prince Orloff

E.

I.

Ruine

La Colonne rostrale

D.

K.

Le Pont de marbre

Les Bains

L.

C.

Colonne en memoire du
Comte Frederic Orloff

Chambre du matin

B.

Le Temple Chinois

A. Le Palais

Plan du Jardin et Vue de differens Bâtimens